STUDIES IN COMICS AND CARTOONS

LUCY SHELTON CASWELL and **JARED GARDNER,** series editors

DRAWING THE LINE

COMICS STUDIES AND *INKS*, 1994–1997

edited by **LUCY SHELTON CASWELL** and **JARED GARDNER**

THE OHIO STATE UNIVERSITY PRESS · COLUMBUS

Library of Congress Cataloging-in-Publication Data
Names: Caswell, Lucy Shelton, editor. | Gardner, Jared, editor.
Title: Drawing the line : comics studies and INKS, 1994–1997 / edited by Lucy Shelton
    Caswell and Jared Gardner.
Other titles: Inks (Columbus, Ohio) | Studies in comics and cartoons.
Description: Columbus : The Ohio State University Press, [2017] | Series: Studies in comics
    and cartoons | Includes bibliographical references and index.
Identifiers: LCCN 2016049607 | ISBN 9780814254004 (pbk. ; alk. paper) | ISBN 0814254004
    (pbk. ; alk. paper)
Subjects: LCSH: Comic books, strips, etc.—History and criticism. | Inks (Columbus, Ohio)
Classification: LCC PN6710 .D67 2017 | DDC 741.5/9—dc23
LC record available at https://lccn.loc.gov/2016049607

Cover design by James A. Baumann
Text design by Juliet Williams
Type set in Minion, Myriad, and Hominis

9 8 7 6 5 4 3 2 1

to the contributors no longer with us

DAVID BERONÄ
MARK J. COHEN
WILL EISNER
ROGER A. FISCHER
ALAN FRIED
OLIVER HARRINGTON
HE YOUZHI
ETTA HULME
CHARLES SCHULZ
MARK WINCHESTER

CONTENTS

ILLUSTRATIONS

Figures

Cover Gallery

Cover images follow page xxi.

PREFACE

PROMPTED BY A CONVERSATION with like-minded people in early 1992, Richard Samuel West suggested to me that scholars of cartoon art needed a journal and that the logical home for such a publication was what was then known as the Cartoon, Graphic, and Photographic Arts Library at The Ohio State University. Various administrative approvals were forthcoming, with the understanding that it would be necessary to secure funds to support the publication costs of The Ohio State University Press to cover the journal's launch. Because the library focused on printed cartoon art, it was decided that the journal would focus on the genres of printed cartoons and the effort to enlist associate editors began. Rich volunteered to cover political cartoons and we were joined by Shelly Armitage, Associate Editor for Magazine Cartoons; Robert C. Harvey, Associate Editor for Comic Strips; and M. Thomas Inge, Associate Editor for Comic Books.

Once the editorial board was formed, discussion began about a title for the journal. Rich came forward with the suggestion that its title be *INKS: Cartoon and Comic Art Studies*. We wanted a title that would indicate both the content and the aspirations of the journal.

In the fall of 1993 an ambitious prospectus was released, which stated,

The purpose of *INKS* is to advance knowledge about print cartooning though the publication of scholarly works. . . . Submissions are welcomed from art historians, journalism historians, literary critics, and cartoonists, and it is hoped that sociologists, economists, business historians, political scientists and educators will also provide their insights. . . .

INKS strives to be the premier journal in its field as well as a forum for new concepts and debate.

There was a strong commitment to publishing interesting, lively work, not dense "Who cares?" scholarship with limited appeal and impact. The appearance of the journal was also critical. Ours is a visual field, so its journal needed to be well-designed and attractive, and to this end, a leading professional design company was hired. Thanks to a generous three-year funding grant provided by Jean and Charles Schulz, the first issue was published in February 1994. Other financial supporters joined them to augment subscription income.

The initial guidelines for authors were quite specific about submission requirements and noted that articles would be refereed by at least two reviewers in addition to the editor and the appropriate associate editor. Several regular features such as articles about cartoon-related research facilities, book and exhibition reviews, and bibliographies were published. "Emanata" was an occasional feature "intended to provide an opportunity for commentary, anecdotes of interest and historical sketches." The whimsical title was suggested by Mort Walker's *Lexicon of Comicana* in which the term "emanata" describes the graphic devices used by cartoonists to describe "what is going on inside" their characters. A cadre of outstanding cartoonists donated delightful cover art.

In late 1996 The Ohio State University Press committed itself to publish the fourth year of *INKS* in the hope that the journal could achieve financial viability, which did not occur. My last editorial in late 1997 for the final issue noted the fact that the value and quality of the journal had been affirmed by its inclusion in three prestigious scholarly indexes and that it had won a national design prize. The service and commitment of its editors and the editorial board members was outstanding.

I am grateful to the Comics Studies Society and, most especially, to my colleague Jared Gardner for launching a second series of *INKS* as their scholarly publication. I also appreciate the acknowledgement and celebration of the achievements of the journal's initial run with the publication of *Drawing the Line*.

Lucy Shelton Caswell
Founding Editor, *INKS: Cartoon and Comic Art Studies*

ACKNOWLEDGMENTS

THIS VOLUME would not be possible without the support of many individuals, twenty years ago and today. *INKS: Cartoon and Comic Art Studies* was made possible thanks to the donations of Jean and Charles Schulz and to the Ohio Joint Program in the Arts and Humanities, and, of course, to the members of the editorial board of the journal: Bruce Barber, Kenneth Barker, Will Eisner, Roger A. Fischer, Draper Hill, David Kunzle, Judith O'Sullivan, David Richter, Jerry Robinson, Randall Scott, Art Spiegelman, Frank Stack, Robert J. Stolzer, Bruce Wheltle, Joseph Witek, and cat yronwoode. Without their support and, of course, the associate editors who worked tirelessly to support the journal from the start—Shelley Armitage, Robert C. Harvey, M. Thomas Inge, and Richard Samuel West—none of this would have been possible.

For the revival of *INKS* and the support to make this volume happen, we are indebted to the leadership of the Comics Studies Society, especially to its founding president, Charles Hatfield, and to the team at The Ohio State University Press under the directorship of Tony Sanfilippo, who have been terrific to work with at every stage in this process. We look forward to many years of *Inks* and comics studies at the Press to come.

INTRODUCTION

THIS VOLUME COMMEMORATES the work of the pioneering journal *INKS,* the first scholarly journal devoted to the diverse field of comics studies. It would be followed by others, of course, beginning with the *International Journal of Comic Art,* which has been edited since its inception in 1999 by John Lent. Today there are a variety of journals devoted to the field, including, beginning in 2017, a new *Inks* which will serve as the journal of record for the Comics Studies Society, the first national learned society for the field. But the original *INKS* was there first.

Firsts are important—especially for those who love comics. Devotees of the form spend countless hours of study and debate over "firsts": from the first newspaper comics character or the first female superhero to the first use of the term *graphic novel* or *web comic.* Some of these firsts, like Superman in 1938, end up launching entirely new fields and industries; others serve as roads not taken, moments in the history of the form whose recovery today might allow us to rethink what is possible in the future.

INKS in its own quiet way was both of these kinds of firsts. Too far ahead of its time, it nonetheless proved that comics studies in every way justified and demanded a peer-reviewed scholarly journal. *INKS* also offers an example of that second, road-not-taken kind of "first," and it is this vital aspect of the journal that keeps me returning to it repeatedly in the two decades since its run ended.

As will become immediately clear simply from skimming the contents of this volume, the version of comics studies in *INKS* does not closely resemble the field as it is currently constituted. In the United States today, comics studies is centered around the study of contemporary alternative comics (and the graphic memoir in particular) and on commercial comic book genres and history. Neglected almost entirely within academic scholarship have been newspaper comics, editorial and political comics, and (with the important exception of the aforementioned *International Journal of Comic Art*) global comics traditions outside of manga and *bande dessinée*.

When Lucy Caswell and her colleagues founded *INKS* in 1994, the impetus for the journal came from recent groundbreaking scholarship produced outside the academy (such as Richard Samuel West's 1988 *Satire on Stone*, Scott McCloud's 1993 *Understanding Comics*, and Robert C. Harvey's 1994 *The Art of the Funnies*). But they were also responding, as Caswell wrote in her introduction to the inaugural issue, to "the growing interest within academia by journalism historians, political scientists, art historians, sociologists and others." Beginning with the 1973 publication of the first volume of the magisterial *History of the Comic Strip* by art historian David Kunzle, the previous twenty years before the founding of *INKS* had seen a growing interest in the form within a wide range of traditional academic disciplines.

Over the intervening twenty years, however, the multi-disciplinary potential of the field did not develop as seamlessly or as quickly as Caswell and her colleagues foresaw in 1994. Today, however, the field having at last put down meaningful roots in several disciplines, there is every reason to believe the time has come when the promising vision with which *INKS* launched itself is now within reach. But like all goals worth pursuing, it will require work— beginning with reminding ourselves of the full range of comics with which we ought to be concerned and the methodologies with which we must be familiar.

This selection from *INKS* serves as such a reminder. Commercial comic books are represented in this volume by Christian Davenport's pioneering study of African American superheroes. The prehistory of the graphic novel is addressed by David Beroná's history of the wordless book tradition that begins with the work of Frans Masereel. The emerging alternative comics scene of the 1990s is highlighted in the selections gathered here by an essay on Gilbert Hernandez's early work by Charles Hatfield, today the founding president of the Comics Studies Society and (in my humble opinion) the most important comics scholar of my generation. International comics are highlighted by

Lent's study of the influence of American comics on Japanese manga and an essay by Julia Andrews on the Chinese tradition of *lianhuanhua,* or linked picture books.

As is appropriate for a journal seeking to lay foundations for American comics studies, however, the vast majority of the essays in *INKS* are focused on the centuries-long traditions of newspaper and illustrated-magazine comics. This focus is reflected in the essays gathered in this volume: Oliver Harrington's meditations on his experiences as an African American cartoonist; Mark Winchester's history of the legal battles that roiled the landscape of early newspaper comics; Robert Harvey's portrait of the role of *Tribune* publisher Robert Medill Patterson in shaping the history of the serial daily strip; Thomas Inge's meditation on the significance of the discovery of George Herriman's mixed-race ancestry to our understanding of *Krazy Kat*; Rich West's study of Ding Darling's editorial cartoons on behalf of the ill-fated League of Nations; and Alan Fried's portrait of the short but captivating comics career of one of the form's great artists, Lyonel Feininger. These essays serve to represent the invaluable contributions to our understanding of comics history, which few have adequately addressed in the intervening years.

It is sometimes the case that old-timers like myself worry, unfairly, that scholars new to comics studies think that comics began with *Maus* (something Art Spiegelman himself has preached against in his interviews and lectures on comics history). The truth is that younger scholars must focus their scholarly energy on topics for which there is a likely venue for publication. Repeatedly over the years, I have encountered young scholars in the Billy Ireland Cartoon Library & Museum's Lucy Shelton Caswell Reading Room poring over old issues of *INKS* and wondering about the lack of venues for scholarship of its kind. This volume serves as a reminder of the range of which our field is capable. It also serves, for me, as a reminder of my responsibility as I prepare to take up the new *Inks*—to balance the continued development of all we have accomplished as a field in the last twenty years with the need to begin repaving the roads-not-taken mapped out by the original *INKS*.

I confess, I find myself somewhat daunted by the latter charge. After all, there are good reasons for the focus our field has taken—starting with the obvious one that these two decades have witnessed a remarkable and concentrated period of intellectually and artistically ambitious publications, self-contained works that translate well into classroom environments and which are reasonably well-served by questions we have been trained to ask of other narrative forms.

Further, other comics forms present unique challenges. The vast majority of newspaper comics and commercial comic books, for example, were produced for mass audiences—not the kinds of audiences that an academic discipline perennially anxious about credibility is eager to highlight. Perhaps the greatest challenge is presented by the fact that the overwhelming preponderance of comics are serial. Indeed, in the case of some comic book series and newspaper comic strips, the serial storytelling extends across generations (and of course, often across media as well). This presents unique classroom challenges, of course, but also challenges for the scholar. How does one master, analyze, or even *read* forty years of *Love & Rockets*, let alone eighty years of *Superman*, or a century of *Gasoline Alley*?

And then, of course, there is the most neglected comics form of all: editorial comics. In *Understanding Comics*, McCloud valiantly attempts to get us all off the hook by privileging the sequential "comic" over the single-panel "cartoon." For some of us, in a book that has withstood intense scrutiny and critical challenges for more than twenty years, this particular proscription has proved increasingly unconvincing. But being unconvinced has not resulted in a flurry of new scholarship on editorial and political cartooning. Far from it.

Ours is a field devoted to a form with a rich global history, one that in the United States alone extends back at minimum to the comic magazines of the mid-nineteenth century, and, when we include political cartooning, back to Ben Franklin's 1754 "Join or Die" cartoon in his Philadelphia newspaper. We dedicate ourselves to the study of a form that has appeared in magazines, newspapers, comic books, mini-comics, and in numerous digital forms in the twenty-first century. And yet we teach and write about the smallest fraction of this long tradition. The time is ripe for us to take up the torches lit by the academic and public scholars of *INKS* and allow them to burn as bright as those currently lighting the field's way into the future.

In *INKS* one sensed the ambition to enfold all of comics into the pages of its richly designed pages. I could well be wrong, but I suspect that twenty years ago Caswell and her colleagues were motivated both positively and negatively by the rise of the "graphic novel," which offered both greater visibility for the form but also concomitant danger of relegating to the margins other comics traditions. *INKS* was an attempt to maintain a larger ecosystem of the emerging field, one that, had the journal been allowed to survive longer than its four years, might have maintained the balance we must now work twice as hard to restore.

Of course, it is never too late. "Firsts" call us back to them, both to honor the foundations they laid for us and to hear and respond to the messages we did not hear at the time. This volume adapts its title from Will Eisner's contribution to the journal. Here Eisner writes, "Reading a comic requires a certain contract between the reader and the author." I hope that these essays similarly serve as a kind of contract for those committed to the study of the comics form, one that encourages a new generation of scholars to pick up their pens. As editor of the new *Inks: The Journal of the Comics Studies Society,* I cannot wait to see what you all discover along the way.

Jared Gardner
Columbus, Ohio
May 2016

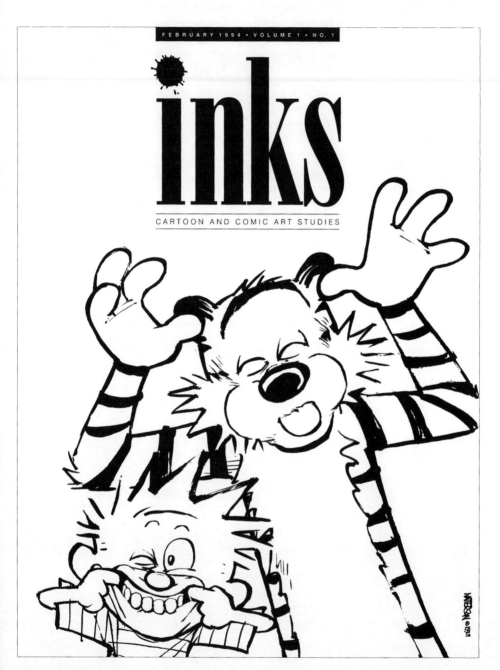

FIGURE A. Bill Watterson

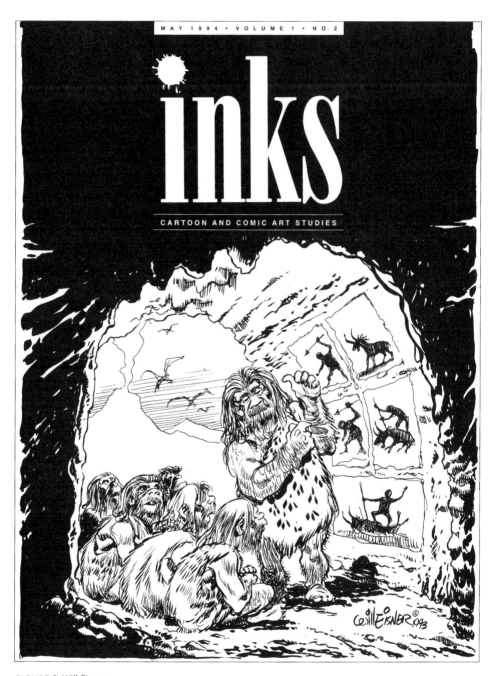

MAY 1994 • VOLUME 1 • NO. 2

inks

CARTOON AND COMIC ART STUDIES

FIGURE B. Will Eisner

NOVEMBER 1994 · VOLUME 1 · NO.3

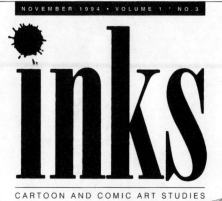

inks

CARTOON AND COMIC ART STUDIES

ISSN: 1071-9156

FIGURE C. Arnold Roth

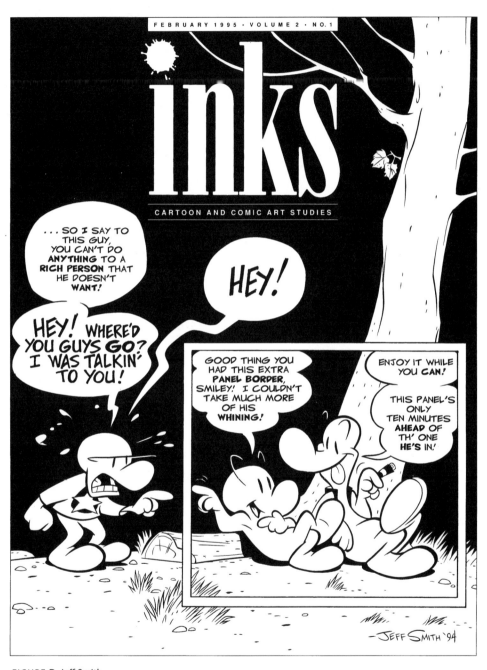

FIGURE D. Jeff Smith

MAY 1995 • VOLUME 2 • NO. 2

inks

CARTOON AND COMIC ART STUDIES

FIGURE E. Etta Hulme

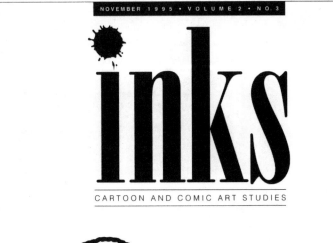

FIGURE F. Charles M. Schulz

MAY 1996 · VOLUME 3 · NO. 2

FIGURE G. Wiley Miller

NOVEMBER 1996 · VOLUME 3 · NO. 3

inks

CARTOON AND COMIC ART STUDIES

FIGURE H. Nicole Hollander

MAY 1997 · VOLUME 4 · NO. 2

inks

CARTOON AND COMIC ART STUDIES

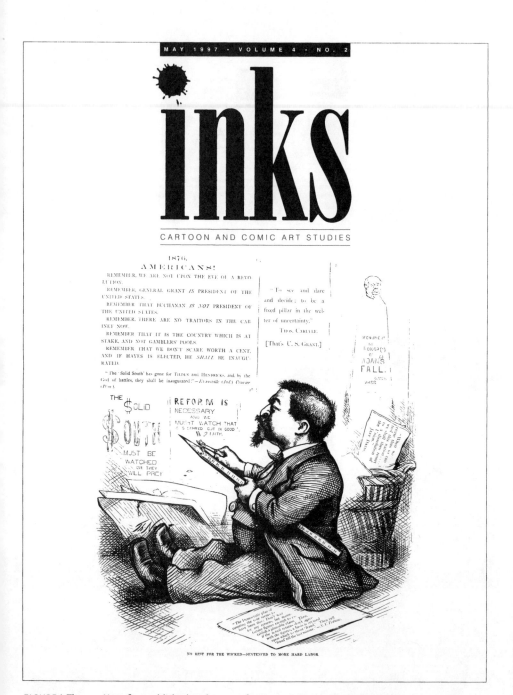

FIGURE I. Thomas Nast, first published as the cover for *Harper's Weekly*, December 2, 1876

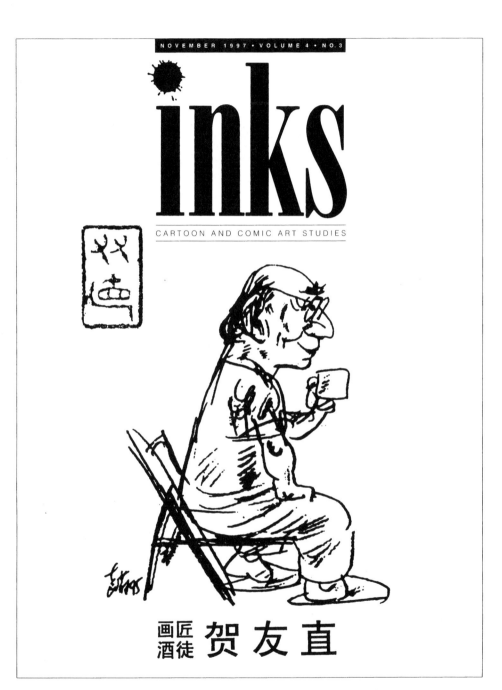

NOVEMBER 1997 · VOLUME 4 · NO. 3

inks

CARTOON AND COMIC ART STUDIES

FIGURE J. Adapted from the business card of He Youzhi, a leading contemporary Chinese cartoonist, and used by permission. Beneath his self-caricature, the characters read, "He Youzhi, artisan and drinker."

ESSAYS

Comics and the New Literacy
An Essay

WILL EISNER

THE COMICS, that long underrated and misunderstood art form, has emerged from its literary closet as a "third" reading medium and it is here to stay. As used in this essay, the term *comics* refers to sequential graphic narrative such as is usually found in comic books or graphic novels. Now the major media spectrum includes printed text, film, and comics.

Reading was mugged on its way to the twenty-first century. Teachers acknowledge that students become "reluctant readers" by the seventh grade. The print medium is under threat. The decline in reading proficiency threatens our unquestioned dependence on printed text. If we look about, we can quickly see what has happened. Printed text has lost its monopoly to another communication technology. Film (including video) has become the major competitor for readership and is the communicator of choice. With its limited demand on a viewer to acquire skills, film makes the time-consuming burden of learning to read seem obsolete. What has happened?

Clearly the drift has been toward electronic instruments that provide information, entertainment, and artificial experience through a combination of sound and imagery. But let us not waste time on ways of controlling its patronage. We have no choice but to accept it. Television, the primary disseminator of film, has become the major source of information for many and it will soon become the electronic library in most American homes. Evidence shows that television watching has increased as literacy has decreased. Clearly film and video are influencing reading habits.

How we read has been changing. Viewers "live" through countless lifelike experiences of ordained duration as they watch TV where artificial situations and contrived solutions become integrated into the audience's mental inventory. The actors become "real" people. Most importantly, watching film establishes a rhythm of acquisition. It is a direct challenge to print. The reader, accustomed to the pace of film, grows impatient with long text passages. He or she is used to acquiring stories, ideas, and information quickly. As we know, complex concepts become more easily digested when reduced to imagery.

But electronic dominance is not total. Printed communication is still a viable and necessary medium. In fact, it is responding to the challenge of electronic media by accommodation. A partnership of words with imagery has become the logical permutation. The resulting configuration is called comics and it fills the gap between print and film.

Comics are admittedly a mutant based on the earliest form of written communication. Their mix of text and image neatly satisfies the current reader's need for accelerated acquisition of information. They are capable of dealing with both instruction and storytelling. Comics are a formidable teaching tool and can cope with subject matter of considerable sophistication.

The impact of comics on literacy or the process of reading is worth examining. Because of their intelligent conventions and flexible structure, they are a valid reading vehicle in the traditional sense, and with the addition of their universal visual ingredient, they become a cross-cultural medium that transcends language barriers. Learning how to read a comic is an easily acquired skill. Comics are a disciplined arrangement of words and images, which require reader participation and involvement. Comics employ both image and text interdependently and require a reasonable word vocabulary. The fundamental difference between comics and illustrated text is that the imagery in comics is intrinsic to narrative content and employs analogous images in sequence as a language. Unfortunately, this ease of reading gave comics a reputation for usefulness confined to people of low literacy and limited intellectual accomplishment. Encouragement and acceptance of this medium by the educational establishment has been less than enthusiastic. For a long time, comics were not employed for much more than simple entertainment. The predominance of art and the traditional comics format bring more attention to its form than its literary content. It is hardly surprising, therefore, that comics as a reading form were always assumed to be a threat to literacy, as literacy was defined in the pre-visual/electronic era.

During the 1950s and 1960s, when schools were confronted with the competition of comic books for the attention of younger readers, the desperation to preserve traditional reading skills became acute. But no longer do educators question the prevalent use of capital letters in dialogue balloons. The "reading" of the comic book is the important thing. Eloquence of language or its special ability to transmit deep and abstract concepts still retains its potency even when written in capital letters and integrated with sequential images.

Today, comics attempt to deal with sophisticated subject matter. One major element of comics that has always provoked resistance to its acceptance as serious reading is imagery. I believe, however, that images are a reflection of experience. Because experience precedes analysis, the intellectual digestive process that results from reading comics takes place at a more rapid pace.

Narrative imagery has had a long history. Primitive images evolved into a symbol-code alphabet that ultimately became written language. Later, images were sidelined to serve as supporters of text. The technology of set type made printed books a universal medium. Historically, pictures in books were employed to make printed prose more attractive. But when the image is isolated and required to function as a narrative, another standard for it arises. Its employment must conform to a discipline tied to traditional reading. An image does have limitations. Images do not easily articulate abstractions and are not easily employed in the expression of complex thought. An image does, however, have the advantage of defining in absolute terms. It shortcuts the process of delineation that occurs when words are translated and converted into imagery in the brain. Images do transmit with the speed of sight.

Reading a comic requires a certain contract between the reader and the author. Intellectual participation by the reader is mandatory. The comic begins with the concept of sequentially arranged images and words printed to emulate in structure the written sentence of text. The reader must then contribute the intervening action, time, place, and ideas that are implied between the images. Words, in the form of dialogue or descriptions of time and place, are read within the image flow.

Comic art is a form of impressionism. It relies on images that are reduced to extreme simplicity. Usually the cartoonist employs an economy of realism to convey emotion, evoke humor, or, by exaggerations of anatomy, to simulate heroic action. For adventure stories, the art is often more rendered. The text, mostly dialogue, seeks to emulate real speech and is encapsulated in balloons, a necessary device to deal with space and sound. Comics depend on the stereotype and cliché to evoke comprehension drawn from common experiences. Their actors must be caricatures if they are to be recognized. The sequence of events is shown by selected segments taken from a seamless flow of action. The comic book reader quickly digests the suspended animation implicit in an ongoing action that gives intellectual meaning to the whole. The frames (or panels) punctuate the flow and provide the sense of time. Drawing style and skill of draftsmanship have an effect on the transmission of the idea and on the impact of its content. Because of the amount of space normally employed by this medium, the content must often be accommodated to it by a certain brevity.

A critical fact is that the reader is expected to supply the intervening action implied by the images, which depict either the start or the end of an action. This problem can be compared to the one facing a playwright who depends on stage setting, dialogue, and the skill of the actor—with the advantages of sound, live action, and real time. The playwright enables the audience to witness reality. With film, the viewer is a passive spectator of recorded reality. In comics, the audience views implied reality and the reader must interpret the meaning of postures and gestures, which, despite the limitation of a "frozen" image, try to convey subtle internal feelings. The arrangement of these postures and gestures in accordance with a common reading convention is the cartoonist's control over telling the story and the progression of reading.

Comics are not a substitute for reading text. They will not make words obsolete. In fact, text is an integral ingredient of comics, and complexity of content often determines the ratio of pictures to words. The graphic treatment of letters and words often reinforces their partnership in the cognitive process. This is a reading experience in every sense. Comprehension of the message is, of course, impaired by the inability to read the text of a dialogue or narrative, but the skilled deployment of images generally provides clues to word meaning. Success in teaching foreign languages via comics testifies to this. No one really knows for certain whether the words are read before or after viewing the picture. We do know that they are not read simultaneously. While modern comics begin with a typewritten script, the process of composing each page gives a certain primacy to the image or visual elements. Obviously, the skill of the artist has a great deal to do with the product. Modern comics are most often produced by a writer-and-artist team, and a failure in coordination sometimes affects clarity and readability. Nevertheless, most teams have grown more secure in their craft and the scope of subject matter and the quality of content have expanded.

From works relying heavily on text with static pictures to strongly evocative pictures with limited or no text, comics have matured to address more sophisticated experiences and dramatize complex themes. Comics have now established a niche in the library of printed communication and are a testimony to the durability of printed reading material. In the United States alone, the number of specialty comic book shops grew from one hundred to four thousand between 1970 and 1992. This growth and the huge volume of titles published and bought annually are ample evidence that comics are a reading medium whose time has come. Comics belong to the new literacy.

View from the Back Stairs

OLIVER HARRINGTON

EDITOR'S NOTE

[*From original publication*] This essay is adapted from a presentation by Oliver Harrington at The Ohio State University's 1992 Festival of Cartoon Art. The life of this extraordinary cartoonist has been remarkable in many ways: He was forced to abandon his homeland because of racism; he was isolated by the Cold War; and he has fought injustice with his art for more than sixty years.

Harrington describes his early life in this essay. In addition to his studies at the National Academy of Design, he graduated from Yale University in 1939 with a bachelor of fine arts degree. His panel cartoon *Bootsie,* which chronicles the life of an ordinary man living in Harlem, began in 1933. Political and social commentary were integral to this feature from its beginning, and *Bootsie* eventually appeared to a wide readership in the *New York Amsterdam News,* the *Baltimore Afro-American* and the *Pittsburgh Courier.* During World War II Harrington served as a war correspondent for the *Pittsburgh Courier* in North Africa and Europe. After his discharge, he had a variety of jobs—journalist, cartoonist, book illustrator, and baseball outfielder—until he became director of public relations for the National Association for the Advancement of Colored People (NAACP) in 1948.

Because of his outspoken efforts against racial discrimination, opponents began to label him as a communist. In 1951 he was warned by a friend who was an army intelligence agent that, for his own safety, he should leave the country. Because he was concerned for the future of the NAACP as well as his own well-being, Harrington left for Europe three weeks later. Except for a two-week trip to the United States in 1972, Harrington did not return to his homeland again until he was honored with an exhibition at the Museum of African American History in Detroit in April 1991.

Harrington lost everything for the second time in his life when he was trapped in East Berlin when the Berlin Wall was erected. He had travelled to East Berlin to discuss illustrating a series of books and, because he lacked the proper visas, he was unable to leave the city. *Bootsie* ceased publication in 1963, and Harrington found new outlets for his work in several European magazines, especially *Eulenspiegel,* and in the *People's Daily World,* a New York City tabloid with 72,000 readers. *Soul Shots,* a portfolio containing sixteen of Harrington's *Daily World* cartoons, was published in 1972. At the time of this publication, Oliver Harrington continued to live and work in Berlin.

The illustrations that accompany this article are from the 1958 collection titled *Bootsie and Others* (New York: Dodd, Mead) and are reprinted by permission of Oliver W. Harrington.

WHAT I HAVE IN MIND IS sharing my well-seasoned thoughts about cartoons and, I suppose, life in general. In this America—mine as well as yours—are the most creatively inventive, technically developed, and prolific cartoonists in the world today. At least that is my own unbiased opinion. Their mastery did not come about as a gift from heaven, or even from the benedictions of ranking politicians, though you may sometimes be given that impression. The truth of the matter is that this comes about as a result of certain time-proven natural laws, which indicate that when human beings of many different cultures and experiences are joined together in one society, the result is a more creative and more productive society.

This is recognized, rather superficially I am afraid, when one talks about the great American melting pot. My own personal experiences have convinced me of this. I am an American, born in America, but completely rejected by this melting pot. Irish Americans, Greek Americans, German Americans, Lithuanian, Finnish, and Polish Americans are part of the mix, but African Americans can forget about it.

"Doctor Jenkins, before you read us your paper on inter-stellar gravitational tensions in thermo-nuclear propulsion, would you sing us a good old spiritual?"

FIGURE 1. From Oliver Harrington, *Bootsie and Others* (New York: Dodd, Mead, 1958). Reprinted with permission.

Fortunately for my own mental health, I worked a kind of self-therapy while I tried to open the doors of countless art editors, where the words NO BLACKS ALLOWED were hanging. For about sixty years I have been locked out, black-balled, Jim Crowed, or whatever terminology is currently fashionable. All of the terms simply mean that the American cartoon industry shut its doors on me with a bang. It is a pity that I am not a baseball player. With statistics like that, I would certainly merit a few lines in the *Guinness Book of Records*.

I was born in a sneeze of a place called Valhalla in Westchester County, north of New York City. As far as I have been able to track down, the place got its name from a bunch of Prussian troops left stranded on the beach when their commander, the British general Lord Howe, scuffled to get his fleet out of narrow Long Island Sound before George Washington got there. When I arrived two centuries or so later, there was no trace left of paradise.

That was 1912, and near Valhalla a system of dams and reservoirs was being constructed. Most of the laborers were European immigrants who spoke little, if any, English. Since labor was scarce in those days, even African Americans were hired, among them my father.

Barracks-like tenements were thrown up as fast as the land plots were acquired by the state. Through some natural human process, ghettoes sort of formed themselves. The immigrant groups sought out their own. These groups separated themselves because of language differences. There was no friction because there was no communication. No friction meant no racism, but that came later.

My childhood impressions were of immense patches of dearly-loved woods. We were a bunch of exuberant kids who climbed what to us were mountains. We discovered huge caves, dark and mysterious. Caves with glistening sheer walls. With hearts beating like trip-hammers, we scaled the walls, holding each other up to get around the outcroppings, keeping a tight grip on the little ones. Some nights we sneaked out of the windows of our sleeping homes to meet in the caves, where we built fires. In the flickering light we told ghost stories, which often scared us into wetting our pants. Often we heard low growls of thunder overhead, rolling over the Hudson River Valley. Washington Irving must have heard the same thunder when he wrote his creepy but beloved tales. I distinctly remember all of my little friends from our uniquely joined ghettoes, and, although I can *visualize* every tree and rock in that area, I cannot remember which among those little faces were white and which were not.

When I was about nine, my family moved a few miles south to what is now quakingly called the South Bronx. By this time our family had increased to one tiny girl and four boys, plus, of course, my two awfully hard-working parents. The South Bronx slum was, again, a unique ghetto. It was in fact several small ghettoes joined together, some even meeting each other on the same street. Our street, Brook Avenue, which naturally was all black, was shared only with the Sheffield Farms milk company stables, which were on the opposite side of the street. How we envied those sleek-coated horses in midwinter, in their warm stalls, with clouds of evaporating steam flowing out of the doors.

The local elementary school, PS 35, was not segregated and more than 80 percent of the kids came from immigrant families. In my sixth-grade class there were only two African American kids, me and a strapping giant, Prince Anderson, who stood head and shoulders above the rest of us. According to the class grapevine, Prince came from someplace vaguely called Fluvanna County, where there were no schools for black kids. Prince must have been dragged from his ideal situation when his parents came north. The school bureaucracy was obviously stumped with the situation, and so, they pushed him into the first open classroom door they saw, hoping that the good Lord would somehow straighten things out.

Our teacher was a Miss McCoy, a tall, pasty-faced vixen who seemed to have devoted all of her attention to her weird hairdo. I always felt oddly apprehensive in her presence, watchful and alert. Was this the birth of intuition? I have heard it said in similar situations that it was probably paranoia. All I can say to that is—in the case of black folks—thank God for paranoia.

One bright morning Miss McCoy ordered us, the perpetually grinning Prince and me, to the front of the class. Pausing for several seconds, she pointed her cheaply jeweled finger (with what I think she considered a very dramatic gesture) at the trash basket and said, "Never, never forget. These two belong in that trash basket!" The white kids giggled rather hesitantly and then fell out in peals of laughter. For those kids, it must have been their first trip on the racist drug.

I stumbled backward in shocked resentment, aware of the growing pain in my chest. Prince only grinned, but I noticed that his eyes had suddenly narrowed. It was several days before I managed to pull myself together. Gradually, I felt an urge to draw little caricatures of Miss McCoy in the margins of my notebook: Miss McCoy being rammed into our local butcher's meat-grinding apparatus; Miss McCoy being run over by the speeding engines on the nearby New York Central Railroad tracks. One, which I worked on all through arithmetic class, really grabbed me. It showed Miss McCoy disappearing between the jaws of a particularly enthusiastic tiger. I began to realize that each drawing lifted my wounded spirits a bit higher. I did little sketches of the people around me, not from life as I learned later to do in art class, but from memory. Miss McCoy never caught me at it, but I began to dream of becoming a cartoonist.

I remember the best time of year in the South Bronx was the autumn, October and early November when the ochre-tinted light faded. Streaks of ethereal blue-grey mist swirled about our tenements, seeming to bring with them a tantalizing and ancient smell of wood smoke. I would light our kerosene lamp and lose myself in the books I had borrowed from the nearby public library. I know now that those books gave me wings. Those wings were giving me a hope that was to be lifesaving. With them I was able to soar over those ghetto walls. It was after many soaring flights that I realized a deep truth: Walls—regardless of whether they are the walls of American-made black ghettoes or the almost forgotten walls of Auschwitz—imprison the bodies of people, but never their minds.

In my travels I have been almost blessed as a result of having met miraculous survivors of the Nazi death camps—those most scientifically developed examples of the ghetto-erecting mentality, with its ethnic final solutions. One of those survivors, who became a close friend, was the great Czech cartoonist Leo Haas. By the early 1940s he was a well-known cartoonist in Prague and he was also Jewish. In Auschwitz, Leo owed his good fortune, if it can be called that, to the fact that the man selected by the Nazis to paint signs had just died of starvation. An hour after he arrived at Auschwitz, Leo was pulled out of the line headed for the gas chamber and told that he was now a sign painter. He managed to survive for two years before the camp was liberated. It was then discovered that Leo, under the very eyes of the supposedly super-efficient master race, had managed to sketch (between signs, of course) the most damning evidence of the Nazi horrors visited upon the *Untermensch*, the scientific Nazi word for so-called inferior races.

Let me tell you now how cunningly insidious these inhuman theories can be. I myself, an African American public school pupil living in the South Bronx slum ghetto of the largest city of America, New York City, had been infected with the deadly virus of racism without realizing it.

When I was ten or eleven years old, I began putting out a newspaper. It was not a real newspaper, but it looked like one. It was painstakingly printed by hand, divided into six columns with small drawings representing news photos. The paper had eight pages with headlines on the front page and it hit the streets, or perhaps I should say that it hit the eager eyes of my schoolmates, once a month.

In one column I wrote about Jewtown, the usual term used to describe a certain part of the Bronx community. A few days after it appeared, one of my teachers, a Mrs. Linsky, asked me to stay for a few minutes after school. That was, I still think, the most significant day of my life. Mrs. Linsky fixed her gentle dark eyes upon mine, and this shook me up because I saw affection and interest, sincere interest. She explained the evil purpose lurking behind terms like Jewtown and Niggertown. I made the association quickly. My mother was Jewish, a Hungarian from Budapest. I felt dizzy, as dizzy as I had been when a hard-hit baseball had taken a bad hop one day so that instead of landing in my frayed first baseman's mitt, the ball landed just above my right eye. I could say nothing for a few moments. When I started to say something, she gently put her fingers on my lips. "You see, Oliver," she said, "people often say things without thinking. In this way they harm other people without meaning to harm them and one day that becomes a habit." After that day we talked about many things until one day I shyly showed her some of my drawings. She stared at them for a long time. Then she leaned forward in her chair, placing one hand softly on my shoulder. "Oliver," she said, "they are so very good, your drawings. Never believe anyone who says they are not." But there was such a sadness in her eyes as she spoke.

Of all the people on Brook Avenue, our postman was the most fascinating. I must have made a hundred sketches of him. Watching him, I became aware that he had a deep perception about what people needed more than the letters and bills in his mailbag. He would lift folks up with a wildly funny joke or the latest spicy but harmless gossip. The meanest, hardcussingist old malcontents who hung out in the corner pool parlor rushed to the door, smiling with out-stretched hands, when the postman walked by with a good word for each of them.

Every Saturday night a rent party was held in the flat of some family chosen by their neighbors. The idea was to help them get the month's rent together. Admission to these parties was half a buck. Once you got past the no-nonsense-looking sister who collected the entrance fee, you found your-self in the front room faced with a mass of card tables, the kind with folding legs, loaded with steaming platters of trotters (better known as pig's feet), hog maws and chitterlings, and succulent pig ears. Paper plates became buried under these delights, which also cost half a buck. On each table stood a bowl of hellish hot sauce, which was free but taken at your own risk. In the next room, usually the bedroom, where an innocent-looking grandfather-type sat on the bed, you could buy a glass of guaranteed made-on-the-premises gin for two bits. Huge jugs of the stuff were stashed under the bed near the old gentleman's slippered feet.

Once past this rocket-fueling station, the happy revelers sort of sailed into the room where the action was underway, and there at the piano was—

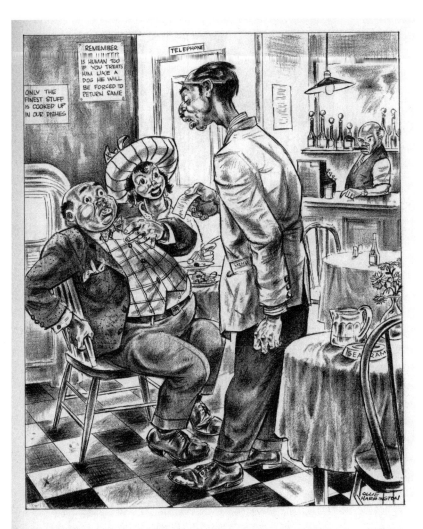

"Brother Bootsie sir, the news broadcast just said that Brother 'No-Mercy' Brown excaped from the penitentiary tonight. So the manager just sent over the bill, thinkin' that you and Mrs. Brown might prefer to clear the premises . . . before your coffee!"

FIGURE 2. From Oliver Harrington, *Bootsie and Others* (New York: Dodd, Mead, 1958). Reprinted with permission.

always—the postman. What he did with that piano, an upright, was, in the words of one lady, which I can still remember, sinfully delightful. He did have a little help: Placed on top of the piano within easy reach was a jar kept filled to the brim with the same bathtub gin, but for him it was free.

We kids of the neighborhood in our creaking beds listened to the sounds of irrepressible joy at simply being alive and warm and loving. Sadly though, once in a while, this mood changed abruptly. Some innocent misunderstanding would occasionally cause an explosion of emotions, followed by shrieks from the offended, shattering window panes, smashing borrowed furniture, and more shrieks when the happily alert cops stampeded in. Perhaps it was an unconscious respect in the presence of great art, but no one ever laid a hand on the piano-thumping postman.

But he had a problem. Her name was Ethel. No matter how diligently the local root people applied their divining skills in uncovering the nature of his problem, they never had a clue. It must have been a whopper, though, because one fine day our postman split and no one knew what had happened. But not for very long, because ghettoes seem to have a great attraction for bad news. Rumors that the piano-thumping postman was cooped up in alimony jail were being whispered all along Brook Avenue. As a matter of fact, the good Reverend Pasley, who was also the local barber, bricklayer, and undertaker, preached a sermon about it in his basement barbershop–church.

I need to explain about alimony jail, although it must seem unbelievable these days. Alimony jail was the annex to the very aptly named Tombs Prison in downtown New York City. In alimony jail reclined all of those otherwise upright citizens who had either neglected or simply failed to pay their monthly alimony payments. The rough part was that these people were held until they were all paid up, including the amount that had piled up while they were cooped up. As a result of this bureaucratic louse up, there were a number of poor bastards who were being held for the rest of their lives. This was the very real prospect facing the former Brook Avenue favorite. Here is where the unbeatable spirit of a thousand Brook Avenues reveals itself.

Finding the peace and tranquility of alimony jail a bit nerve-wracking and undoubtedly with Ethel in mind, the postman began composing songs and lyrics. One of them was called "My Fate Is in Your Hands." I have forgotten the details of how it all came about, but that song became the jazz hit of the year. It earned enough to spring the new-born songwriter from alimony jail, for a while at least. But the music business being what it is, and the new songwriter being black, the predictable result was that in a few short months, the cash had run out, the alimony due had run up, and again our postman was run in. Then he came up with another hit. It was called "Your Feet's Too Big." That hit

"Bootsie, tell me again how lucky I am to have a boy friend like you . . . an' brother, you better convince me!"

FIGURE 3. From Oliver Harrington, *Bootsie and Others* (New York: Dodd, Mead, 1958). Reprinted with permission.

was part of a cycle of in again, out again, and, eventually, out for good. You may have guessed by now that the Brook Avenue rent party mailman was Fats Waller.

To me that tale is simply another legend like those legends that lifted my boyhood mind high over ghetto walls. Fats Waller would put down his mailbag and exchange tales with my father. Some of them were not true, but that did not matter. These stories created a reality that did not exist outside the ghetto. This spirit is needed in America more and more every day. It can be summed up in the snickered-at word *brotherhood*. Throughout the world in which I have wandered—Europe, Mongolia, the Caribbean, Scandinavia, and Siberia—a world filled with death squads and murderous so-called security forces, I have realized that countless disk jockeys worldwide try, perhaps unconsciously, to keep despair at bay by filling the ether with Fats Waller's music.

The magic I am talking about lives within the walls of America's ghettos, but those walls must come down so that this remarkable energy can be released into the now sluggish and polluted melting pot. Make no mistake about it; this would be no great humanitarian act. It would be an act to salvage the dreams of Thomas Jefferson or Abraham Lincoln—or of Martin Luther King Jr.

I graduated from high school in 1929. People in New York streets and busses whispered about how awful things were. Back in the South Bronx, we whispered about how times were as they always had been in our ghetto. For more than a year after graduation, I read endlessly and continued with my drawings of what went on about me. We ignored the hunger as we always had. I was restless and I began to read about art schools. For one thing, my leaving home would mean a bit more food on my family's table. The decision was not easy. The fact was that I was scared as hell. I walked a bunch of miles to where a black person might find a place to lay his head. That meant the next ghetto: Harlem.

In those days, Harlem was the most dazzling place imaginable. I found a room at the Harlem YMCA for two dollars a week. I began working at an employment agency, doing tiny drawings on mimeograph sheets, informing Harlemites of the wonderful opportunities in store for them in second-hand, green metal filing cabinets in the cubby holes of the agency's cellar. I met types of people I had known nothing about. They did not exist on Brook Avenue. There was an optimism that was unbelievable. It was at the end of a period called the Harlem Renaissance.

I earned extra money ($8 per game) playing on a semi-pro baseball team where I got to be a star slugger, but not because of any innate ability. The team was owned by a gangster called Bumpy Johnson. He and his friends always sat in the bleacher behind the batter. I dared not strike out. In addition to hitting the ball, every two weeks I had to have a bag filled with clothes—soiled or clean—because Bumpy also owned a laundry.

There were great dangers in Harlem and I was not prepared for what I saw. I had never had a drink on Brook Avenue. Langston Hughes told me that I did not have to drink the stuff if I did not want it. He suggested ginger ale. I never became a great drinker because of my memories of ghetto drunks.

Langston Hughes was one of my father figures, a wonderful and protective man. He explained some of his ideas about why ghetto people laugh so much, why Prince Anderson in that school grinned all the time. He said it was laughing to keep from crying. It still is, and it creates a vibrant form of humor—intangible, myth-like, and oddly stimulating.

I walked to the National Academy of Design every day to study under drawing people like Leon Kroll, a leading painter, and Charles Hinton, a leading draftsman. In order to stay in the Academy, I really had to work. I loved what I was doing. It was very academic with drawing from casts. This training was most valuable, and it is never absent from any of my work.

I discovered the Harlem poetry of Claude McKay and the novels of Bud Fisher and Langston Hughes. These writers were not then widely recognized because they were black. There were also moments when I began to wonder how I could express the horror I saw. This is when I began doing the *Bootsie* cartoons. They were cartoons of the life around me. I did not have to think up gags. The gags thought themselves up for me. I just had to go into a gin mill, sit on a stool, and I had a hundred gags in half an hour.

There were tragedies, too. I moved to the eleventh floor of the YMCA where the "regulars" lived. One of the other roomers was a man who often came to my tiny room to talk about science. His name was Charlie Drew, a doctor who worked at one of the foundations in New York. He was obsessed with the wonders of nature. Black truck drivers and fishermen, other regulars who lived at the Y, would listen in awe as Charlie talked about outer space or creatures to be discovered in the oceans.

In his laboratory, Charlie was doing experimental work on developing blood plasma from whole blood. He made fantastic advances that were not known by very many people in the United States—or any place else, for that matter. But Winston Churchill knew about them. Churchill sent the British embassy in New York City instructions, and they telephoned the eleventh floor of the black YMCA and asked Charlie Drew to come to the embassy. Charlie was, of course, skeptical about the invitation. I was a great practical joker and he naturally thought I had made the call. He contacted the embassy and they

"Body all achin' and wracked with pain . . . Tote that barge, lift that bale . . ."

FIGURE 4. From Oliver Harrington, *Bootsie and Others* (New York: Dodd, Mead, 1958).
Reprinted with permission.

confirmed the invitation. Charlie went and was received by the ambassador. They flew him to London to help save the lives of people wounded at Dunkirk. After he returned to the United States, his draft board heard of his fame and sent him to the navy recruiting office in Washington. When he arrived, he was told that an error had been made and he should not have been invited to Washington. The experience made him so bitter that he swore that he would never speak to another white person. Years later he was invited to speak at a medical conference of African American doctors in Alabama. Because he did not want to have to deal with white people on the train, he drove his own car. It crashed during the night and Dr. Charles Drew died.

This story is a demonstration of the cost of racism. Such racism is destroying Europe now. Can we afford it? Do we know it must end? This is the only reason I continue to draw my cartoons: It is for me and for you—but mostly it is for our children.

Lyonel Feininger

A Kinder, Gentler Comic Strip

ALAN FRIED

COMIC STRIPS AND COMIC BOOKS have, from time to time, gotten a little too raucous, a little too violent, and, at times, a little too bloody.[1] Lyonel Feininger was an idealist who believed that children deserve well-drawn cartoon adventures with high-minded ideals. Feininger's achievements as an artist are known both to art historians and to a wider audience of art lovers because he helped found the Bauhaus movement and his work bridged cubism and German expressionism. The cartoons that first brought him widespread attention are far less known, although he devoted the years from 1898 through 1907 to creating editorial cartoons and a pair of noteworthy comic strips. Feininger was one of the first cartoonists who deliberately worked to elevate the notion, themes, and characterization of a comic strip for children. To understand the exceptional quality of Feininger's work, and to place it in context, it is necessary to recount briefly the familiar history of the comics and the critical resistance that the comics first met.

In 1895, Joseph Pulitzer's *New York World* created a phenomenon when it introduced Sunday supplements with color comic pages. Not to be outdone, William Randolph Hearst's *New York Journal* soon followed with its own supplement. These supplements were so successful, and they brought so many

FIGURE 5. San Francisco Academy of Comic Art Collection, The Ohio State University Billy Ireland Cartoon Library & Museum.

readers to newspapers, that they became a cultural institution. A dozen years later, one critic would write, "A newspaper without a colored press hardly considers itself a newspaper."[2]

The star of these early color comic supplements was, of course, the Yellow Kid, the creation of Richard Felton Outcault. Today, the Kid is popularly recognized as the first comic character because he established the importance of the comics to the commercial success of newspapers.[3] The Kid is also famous because he gave name to the form of sensational journalism that began at the turn of the century. In 1898, British journalist Margaret Banks explained the phenomenon for European readers, and she described the character that became its namesake as "an imaginary personage who is horrible, grinning, toothless, long-eared infant robed in an orange-colored frock and a tilted high hat." Although she could not explain the popularity of the *New York World* Sunday supplements, she did acknowledge it: "Bushel baskets of them were carried to the towering dome of the *World* building and from there thrown out to the four winds of heaven which carried them into distant regions and the circulation increased enormously."[4] As popular as these supplements were with the general public, they were the bane of many devotees of highbrow culture. As will be seen later in this article, much of the criticism came from such magazines as the *Ladies' Home Journal, The Printing Art, Outlook, Current Literature,* and *The Atlantic Monthly.*[5]

The end of the last century was not a friendly period for children. In the 1890s, the United States was one of the few Western nations that still permitted child labor. Without a minimum wage or other relief, immigrants and other poor families were forced to send their children into the mines, the mills, and the factories to work. Much as they are today, stories of child abuse were of particular concern to reformers. Such stories were not uncommon in the newly-sensationalized press. As early as 1897, The New York Society for the Prevention of Cruelty to Children saw the comic pages, with their garish representations of children, as particularly vulgar and harmful.[6]

Admittedly, the early strips often presented a world of manic agitation. As Blackbeard notes, "Following the popular vaudeville stage humor, the new comic strip humor was both vulgar and violent. Police nightsticks bounced off Happy Hooligan's head, tin-can hat or no tin-can hat, and dynamite planted by Hans and Fritz regularly blew the Captain and his cronies sky high."[7] Another popular concern of the time held that children and women were particularly susceptible to neurasthenia or nerve-disease. One reformer found the comic supplements particularly unnerving:

> Physicians generally are convinced there is entirely too much stimulation of
> the nervous system of children in our present life. . . . Ask any physician and

he will tell you that the precocious child, much in contact with adults and given to [Sunday supplement] picture absorption is more subject to night terrors. . . . The reason why night terrors are a little more frequent on Sunday and Monday nights . . . [is that] poring over the colored supplement of the Sunday supplement has been one of the absorbing occupations of the day of rest.[8]

Other critics were equally severe. Lindsay Swift wrote, "It is impossible to describe the vulgarity and insanity of their drawing and coloring," and questioned why newspaper editors would approve of such vulgarity and insanity. He closed his commentary by suggesting that comics "debauch the sensibilities and corrupt with wretched perversion."[9] The widely-popular *Ladies' Home Journal* editorialized:

Instead of helping to counteract the too prevalent tendency among children to irreverence and resistance to authority, these pictures and jokes actually teach our children irreverence and lawlessness by making cheap fun of age, dignity, good breeding and all the pieties and amenities which make the family the most sacred and important of all institutions.[10]

Yet even the *Ladies' Home Journal* did not think that the Sunday comics were past redemption. They noted that the International Kindergarten Union, recognizing the low ideals of child and home life that these supplements spread over the country, had recently (i.e., in 1905) proposed a concerted effort to secure a wholesome page in place of the present comic section; it urged families not to buy papers that issued comic supplements and to press upon editors the duty of securing good writers and illustrators of stories for children.[11]

If any newspaper would be prone to accept the idealistic appeal of the Kindergarten Union, it was the *Chicago Tribune*. From its inception in 1847, the *Tribune* had built a great reputation of personal accountability in journalism. From 1855 until his death in 1899, publisher Joseph Medill transformed the newspaper into a powerful voice for classic conservatism. He had helped found the Republican Party and created the boomlet that elected Lincoln, helped revive the city after the Great Chicago Fire, was elected mayor of Chicago, and helped to bring the 1892 Columbian Exposition to the city. While Medill made political and journalistic history, his daughters and their in-laws helped create an era of elegance in Chicago society. Medill's daughter Katherine was married to Robert Sanderson McCormick, the nephew of Cyrus Hall McCormick.[12] Robert McCormick would become ambassador to France,

Russia, and Austria. Katherine and Robert's son, Joseph Medill McCormick was editor in chief of the *Tribune*. As historian John Tebbels wrote in 1947, "The sons and daughters of the Medills and the McCormicks built their Chicago empire in the eighties and nineties and interpenetrated every aspect in the city's social and business life in the early decades of this century."[13]

Thus, the *Tribune* might have been seen as one of the most likely newspapers to pioneer decency in comics. Nothing tawdry or vulgar would ever be printed for children in its pages, but the task of recruiting respectable children's illustrators fell to a most unlikely newspaper editor. James Keeley was a hard-driving newspaper man in the spirit of the *Front Page*.[14] Keeley was born and raised in England by a very severe mother. She forced his father out of the house because of his drinking. Keeley emigrated to the United States alone at the age of sixteen. He first lived in Leavenworth, Kansas, (1883) and then moved to Chicago in 1889. He had been a news hawker in England and was a candy butcher on trains in the United States.[15] He came to Chicago in 1889 and immediately landed a job at the *Tribune* as a nighttime police reporter. In 1893 Keeley was named assistant city editor; in 1898 he was named managing editor; and he became editor and general manager in 1909. His predecessor in the post, Will Van Benthuysen, went to Pulitzer's *New York World*. Keeley was barely thirty-one when he took the position.[16]

Keeley's rough manner was not all that unusual among newspapermen, since most newspaper editors of the time were just as unrefined and rough-edged as the majority of their readers. They instinctively understood what their readers enjoyed in features such as comic strips because they enjoyed it as well. They simply had no use for what they saw as pretty flights of fancy that were so popular in socially-approved children's literature. They liked seeing cartoon bricks hit cartoon heads, and so did the paper-reading public.

Keeley was not only unlikely because his tastes tended toward the plebeian but also because he sought his artists in Europe. Keeley's biographer, James Weber Linn, describes the hard-bitten Chicago editor as knowing "little or nothing of international politics or European affairs," but he counted among his close friends Samuel Insull, head of Commonwealth Edison. Insull, a confidante of Robert W. Patterson (named president and editor in chief in 1890) and Medill McCormick (who briefly took over in 1910 when Patterson died), was a learned student of European affairs and undoubtedly tutored Keeley on the issues.[17] Despite Insull's best efforts, Keeley is remembered as a rough-hewn sort and thus it is particularly surprising that he was sent to Europe to find artists for the new *Tribune* supplement. Actually, it is more probable that Keeley's real quarry was Chicago bank president Paul Stensland, who absconded to Tangier with the funds of the Milwaukee Avenue State

Bank. In 1906, Keeley made his way to Paris, where he met Lyonel Feininger, and from there took the Sud Express to Tangier, where he caught up with Stensland and arranged for his capture.[18] Whatever Keeley's true travel intentions, he spent some of his time seeking cartoonists. He undoubtedly sought German cartoonists, in particular, for three very good reasons: a large part of the Chicago population was German; some of the most popular strips at the time were drawn by Germans; and German humor magazines were particularly popular and respected.[19]

One of the most popular strips at the time was *The Katzenjammer Kids* by Rudolph Dirks. Dirks began the strip at William Randolph Hearst's *Journal American* in 1897, where he was reportedly asked by editor Rudolph Block to create a strip that would compete with *The Yellow Kid* at Joseph Pulitzer's *World*. His strip was notable because it featured two of the roughest hooligans in comics. Although the *Katzenjammer Kids* was among the most popular of the *Journal American* cartoons, Dirks felt unappreciated by Hearst and tried to set up shop drawing the Katzenjammers for Pulitzer's *New York World*. Hearst successfully sued Pulitzer to prevent Dirks from taking the strip. The court ruled in 1914 that Hearst was allowed to publish the strip under its original title as illustrated by Harold Knerr, while Dirks could produce the strip under the name *The Captain and the Kids* for the *World*.

Dirks's hooligans, Hans and Fritz, were based on *Max und Moritz*, a popular illustrated story-poem about two boys who perform nasty tricks on people. Written by Wilhelm Busch in Germany in the 1840s, it was first translated into English in 1871.[20] Their victims are Widow Tibbets, who had laying hens (Max and Moritz eat them); Mr. Buck, the tailor (they cut his bridge across a deep pond while he is on it); the cleric Mr. Lämpel (they put gunpowder in his pipe); their Uncle Fritz (they put big bedbugs under his covers); the baker (they try to steal his cookies, but, instead, they get covered in flour and thrown into the oven); and a farmer (when they try to steal his grain, he has them milled). It is unlikely that the high-minded patrons of the *Chicago Tribune* had this sort of rough comic strip in mind for their children.

Foxy Grandpa, drawn by Carl Schultze, another German–American artist, was a popular comic strip of somewhat nobler intent. Albert Payson Terhune, of the *New York World,* told *Current Literature* that comic strips are "for the most primitive people on earth, children who have not yet developed a refined sense of humor." In describing the *Foxy Grandpa,* Terhune notes that, "The Foxy Grandpa series really taught a trenchant moral lesson. In bald language, it told of two bad boys who were always trying to get the best of a nice old man. But he always got the best of them. Punishment generally follows transgressions and in this respect they teach a valued lesson."[21]

It also seems apparent that the *Tribune* was intent on getting a German artist because German humor magazines were particularly successful. According to Ann Taylor Allen, some 2,100 magazines were formed in Germany between 1880 and 1900. The satirical press, or *Witzblatter,* was part of this trend. Although circulation information is somewhat inconsistent as to year, some data documenting their popularity is available. In 1890, *Kladderadatsch* had a circulation of 50,000, *Fliegenden Blätter* had a circulation of 20,000, *Ulk,* the humorous Sunday supplement of the liberal *Berliner Tageblatt,* had a circulation of 70,000 in 1908, and *Berliner Illustrierte Zeitung* had a 1914 circulation of 600,000.[22]

James Keeley met Lyonel Feininger in 1906 through a *New York Times* writer in Paris. By this time, Feininger had established his reputation as a political cartoonist and a talented illustrator. In a 1901 article, Berlin journalist and cultural critic Georg Hermann called Feininger "first among Berlin draftsmen."[23] Feininger's career as a professional cartoonist began in 1894, when he sold his first work to *Ulk.* The *Tageblatt* made him so well known that he was able to sell to other German magazines, including *Lustige Blätter, Berliner Illustrierte Zeitung, Sporthumor,* and others. During the 1890s and early 1900s, he drew hundreds of cartoons for these magazines, chiefly taking a liberal view of domestic and foreign political issues. He was a particular critic of the class system in Germany, and of its police, ultra-nationalism, and anti-Semitism.

Though he had received much of his artistic education in Germany and worked there all of his adult life, Feininger understood the American sense of humor because he was born and raised in the United States. Lyonel's grandparents, Adolph Michael and Lena Feininger, and his father, Karl, came to the United States after the German democratic revolution of 1848. When he was fourteen, Adolph and Lena sent Karl to study piano in Leipzig. Karl returned at age sixteen, settled in New York, married Cecilia Lutz (the American-born daughter of a Union army captain), and together they became successful stage musicians.

Lyonel Feininger was born in Manhattan on 17 July 1871, and was raised in a bilingual family in a primarily German–American neighborhood. At public school he learned English, and he studied the piano under his father's relentless direction, but he was more interested in drawing and art. Despite the boy's wishes, when Lyonel turned sixteen his father sent him to study music at the Leipzig Music Conservatory. His intended teacher was out of the country, so Lyonel's parents permitted him to attend the Hamburg School of Arts and Crafts instead. In 1888 he moved to Berlin while his parents went on their last concert tour together. Karl and Cecilia separated soon thereafter. At this time, though he was preparing for his entrance exams for the Koenigliche

Akademie in fine art, Lyonel devoted himself to doing caricatures. He wrote his American friend Francis Kortheuer, "I caricature almost all my spare time and have many fine caricature books from which I learn very much."[24] By June 1889, he was selling cartoons to German newspapers, including the *Humoristische Blätter.*

Although he would live in Germany from 1887 to 1936, Lyonel always remained connected to the country of his birth. That American connection, which proved so crucial for his success as a cartoonist, was maintained through his lifelong friendship with Alfred Vance Churchill, whom Lyonel met in 1889. Churchill, who was seven years older than Lyonel, opened the world of watercolors and landscapes to Feininger.[25] Kortheuer, also the son of a German–American musician, was Lyonel's other lifelong friend.

Karl Feininger visited his estranged family in Berlin in 1890 and decided that Lyonel was hanging around with too many bohemians, so he enrolled the young man in a Catholic school, St. Gervais in Liege, Belgium.[26] During his stay in Belgium, Lyonel became enamored with the art nouveau movement and gothic architecture that would figure so prominently in his later work.[27] Feininger first became aware of the work of Wilhelm Busch at this time. This is odd because the stories of *Max and Moritz* were popular in the United States when young Lyonel was growing up. He first mentions Busch in a letter to Kortheuer dated 8 March 1890:

> I am going to send you one of Wilhelm Busch's German karikatur books. They are not finely drawn but they are very full of humor and life. The American caricatures are the best in the world. You will see lots of them in *Judge* drawn by Zim [Eugene Zimmerman]. He is really wonderful and if you buy *Judge* look out for his drawings.[28]

By May 1890 he was drawing cartoons for the *Humoristische Blätter,* and Feininger wrote his friend Kortheuer, "When I go to America, I shall go to work for *Life* and try to earn a competence for myself."[29]

In May 1891, the young artist returned to Berlin to live with his mother, who rented a flat for the family. He enrolled at the atelier of the painter Adolph Schnabel, where he was encouraged to draw freehand sketches of nature. Through Churchill, he discovered the work of the American draftsman Joseph Pennell. As he saw there was a market for this style of work, he resolved to contribute to contemporary illustration in the United States. In October 1891, he returned to the Berlin Academy, but he found the teaching methods too constricting, so in November 1892 he went to Paris and stayed for six months. While there, he studied life drawing with the sculptor Filippo Colarossi.[30]

From June 1893 through October 1894, he began seriously to consider becoming a cartoonist and illustrator, and he first wrote down his thoughts about children's literature. His views are noteworthy because they seem to be a reaction to the Busch-style of childish mayhem. Feininger compares his artistic objectives with the work of popular German children's book illustrators such as Hermann Vogel and Ludwig Richter, who mainly did decorative illustration rather than telling humorous stories in the American way. In letters to Kortheuer he expressed admiration for the work of A. B. Frost, Frederick Burr Opper, and Peter Newell of *Harper's*.[31]

About a month later, he wrote to his friend, artist Alfred Kubin:

I am daily more impressed with the fact that I can do more good in America than here and that my country has the first right to my services. I am just thinking now of one thing: how to better the class of juvenile illustrated works and periodicals in America. There are so few artists who have the 'gemueth' [temperament] to patiently devote themselves to this work.

Our American illustrators are as a rule only such because they have the technique to draw. How few really go deep into delineation of character, humor pathos, rather than the mere outside accessories?[32]

In this same letter, he avers that he will try to not repulse children with his drawings, "My drawings for *Harper's* are slightly caricatured but in a way which I flatter myself does not cause repulsion but only vividness to the characterization."[33] Clearly, a decade before he would be approached by the *Chicago Tribune*, in the very early years of children-oriented newspaper cartoons, Feininger was conscious of setting his work apart from the kind of vulgar slapstick comedy that would soon gain popularity. In a letter dated 22 June 1894, Feininger declared that his mission was to introduce a whimsical cartoon style into the illustration of American children's books. He may have seen this as a way of getting back to his American roots.[34]

Happily, he found both a patron and an audience for his art. John Kendrick Bangs, the very popular children's author and editor of *Harper's Young People* magazine, was looking for an artist to illustrate a fairy tale with a Germanic theme. He contacted Feininger and hired him to illustrate a story entitled "How Fritz Became a Wizard." Bangs also commissioned illustrations for "Birthday Party in Topsyturvydom" and "The Old Settler in Zurich" for his magazine.[35] Feininger's biographer, Ernst Scheyer, seems surprised to find that these illustrations seem more reminiscent of E. A. Abbey's scenes of Shakespearean England than Vogel's fantasy of the German Middle Ages.[36] This is, however, hardly surprising. Although the boy may have grown up with many

FIGURE 6. Illustration by Lyonel Feininger, from "How Fritz Became a Wizard," *Harper's Young People* 15 (October 2, 1894): 820–822.

German books, his American education would have been far more strongly influenced by Abbey's Shakespeare than Vogel. In another way, Lyonel's childhood may have greatly influenced his quest for charm rather than sensation, since he grew up in an upper-middle-class household. His grandparents had owned a china shop in Germany, and their home was surely filled with delicate finery. His parents were among the leading musicians of the day. As first-generation immigrants, growing up at a time of strong xenophobia, they made every effort to identify themselves with the noblest of virtues. As demonstrated in Karl's letters to his son, they were driven by the highest artistic ideals.

Through the end of the decade, Feininger devoted himself to becoming a renowned cartoonist, aiming his whimsical work at adults. In 1895 he began drawing for *Ulk* and found a steady job with the magazine from 1897 through 1898, receiving a salary of 4,000 to 5,000 marks per year.[37] By contrast, some ten years later, the *Chicago Tribune* would pay him 24,000 marks to create cartoons for them. During the 1890s, he drew for the best German political, humor, and recreational magazines. In 1898, his sisters Helen and Bisa both died of consumption.[38] They had accompanied their mother to Berlin and had been his constant companions all of his life. After a year of heartfelt grieving, he was ready to settle down. In 1900, when Feininger was twenty-nine years old, Felix Strothman introduced him to Clara Fürst, the daughter of the renowned muralist Gustav Fürst. He stole Clara away from Strothman, who was her first beau, and married her in 1900. Because most of Feininger's papers were maintained by his second wife, Julia, little information is available about that first union. It is known that the couple had two daughters, Lorre and Marianne, and that Feininger kept in contact with the girls well after his marriage dissolved.[39]

During the period of his first marriage, Feininger's work was exhibited as well as widely published. His work appeared in some seventy issues of *Ulk* and almost every issue of *Lustige Blätter*. In successive years, he participated in the fifth, sixth, and eighth Berlin Secession exhibition and in another exhibition, the Grosse Berliner Kunstausstellung.[40] There may be signs in Feininger's work of the period that he was unhappy, as his drawings were notably angrier than his previous work. His earlier work featured light-hearted scenes of absent-minded professors, shy swains, and bad-tempered mothers-in-law. But in 1903 and 1904, he drew a caricature of an anthropomorphized runaway train, another of thieves in the night, and still another, of himself, trying and failing to build a summerhouse for his wife and daughters.

Not all of his troubles centered around the home. Feininger chafed under the strong direction that he received from his German editors. Alexander Moszkowski, editor of *Lustige Blätter,* described the process:

> The editor designs the drawings, establishing the content; often he stipulates this right down to the details and he expects the artist to follow these instructions. If an editor has a good imagination as well as an ability to draw, he will send a black-and-white or colored sketch as a guide. The method puts a certain constraint on the artist, although it prevents him from failing to produce what the editor needs—if the subject is a good idea—it guarantees him an effect.[41]

Then, in 1905, Feininger met the woman who was to most greatly influence his life and transform his artistic vision from that of a cartoonist to that of a painter. Julia Berg Lilienfeld was also an artist and also married. Feininger left Clara and the children to live with Julia, and they eventually married in 1908. Although Karl Feininger had also separated from his family, he felt obliged to give his thirty-four-year-old son some advice. His fatherly counsel, coming at the time when the artist would return to creating illustrations for children, provides an important window into the values and ideals with which the artist was raised. Karl Feininger expressed sympathy for his son's unhappiness, but he warned him not to defy the German laws and conventions against adultery. Instead, the father told the son to sacrifice his egoism for the sake of his art, "For without patience and lofty self-abnegation, you can arrive at nothing great either as a man or as artist."[42] Eventually, Karl Feininger changed his mind about Julia Lillienfeld and most willingly accepted her into the family.[43] From the moment that Julia came into his life, Lyonel Feininger worked to become a serious artist.[44] She encouraged him to begin doing lithographs and etchings. By becoming a cartoonist for the *Chicago Tribune*, Feininger was able to earn enough money to live in Paris and devote himself to learn his art under his old master, Colarossi.

The *Tribune* offered Feininger some 24,000 marks ($6,000) to create two comic strips: the first, *The Kin-der-Kids,* a kind of children's adventure strip and the second, *Wee Willie Winkie's World,* about a boy who wanders around in a magical land.[45] The two strips had clear antecedents in *The Katzenjammer Kids* and *Little Nemo in Slumberland.* Just a year earlier, the *New York Herald* had hired Winsor McCay to create its own gentle Sunday feature. Undoubtedly, Keeley and publisher Joseph Medill McCormick hoped a similar *Nemo*-style strip would be popular, perhaps popular enough to syndicate.[46]

As cartoon historian Dennis Wepman notes, there is little coherence in the story of *The Kin-der-Kids,* but a continuous thread of continuity linked its thirty-one rather self-consciously fanciful weekly installments in which their episodic adventures took them to England and Russia. In each case, Feininger had fun with the dialects of the supporting characters. Wepman's description of the kids is particularly striking:

> At the center of the strip's cast were the grotesque Kin-der-Kids themselves: the pompous Daniel Webster, who wore an under taker's crêpe-ribboned hat and was always engrossed in a book; Strenuous Teddy, who could break chains with his biceps and whose knowledge of jiu-jitsu enabled him to best whole teams of strong men; Pie-Mouth who ate so continuously that at one point he became a perfect sphere and had to be rolled like a ball. Accompanying them were an emaciated dachshund named Sherlock Bones and an Oriental wind-up toy, the "Clockwork Waterbaby," named Japanski.[47]

Blackbeard writes that *The Kin-der-Kids* was a complete comic strip in every way. It featured a recurrent crew of bizarre characters, an involved storyline based on dialogue exchange, and—a real innovation for the time—a full-fledged, frankly suspenseful week-to-week narrative continuity.[48] It also fits

FIGURE 7. Feininger had not yet left his career as a political cartoonist in Berlin when he drew *The Kin-der-Kids*. Daniel Webster warns a Russian anarchist that he is an American citizen.

the more rigorous criteria of David Kunzle, who defines the comic strip by the four following parameters: a sequence of images; a preponderance of image over text; a mass medium; and a moral and topical story.[49]

Rosemary Gallick suggests that Feininger continued the development of the popular child or "kid" strip genre of early twentieth-century comics and enlarged its scope and style, transforming the genre with his depiction of epic psychological struggles in a sophisticated international style.[50] Like Winsor McCay's *Little Nemo in Slumberland,* Feininger's *Kin-der-Kids* is an odyssey. Whereas McCay's elusive quest was pursued in the dream world or unconscious, Feininger's story takes place on the high seas.[51] Where McCay's fine line drawings are somewhat precious, Feininger's illustrations are rough enough to evoke laughter and fun. I found no evidence to support Blackbeard's assertions that the *Tribune* actually wanted pictorial, unconnected weekly gag humor in non-strip formats, this being somehow more elevated in their eyes than the Hearst-style stuff, but since Feininger was their big catch among the Germans, he was allowed to have his way.[52]

The international cast of *The Kin-der-Kids* was introduced with great fanfare on 29 April 1906, and the first adventure began on 6 May 1906. The boys depart New York "Triumphant in the family bathtub." Crying and waving good-bye, they take leave of the Statue of Liberty, setting sail on a universal sea, reminiscent of Feininger's own sailing for Hamburg in 1887. The exuberant adolescent males are pursued by the stern Aunty Jimjam. As the boys and their dog navigate the sea, Aunty Jimjam pursues them, with a bottle of castor oil in hand, in a balloon and an airplane. Whether she intends to use the castor oil as medicine or punishment is never made clear. Gallick writes that Feininger's status as a citizen of two continents found symbolic expression in his strips. *The Kin-der-Kids* bridges the id and ego, youth and age, male and female, duty and self-expression through the interaction of the airborne Aunty Jimjam and the nautical boys.[53]

The story, such as it was, made little sense, but the graphic style and the rudimentary attempts at cartoon characterization placed Feininger's work among the most interesting experiments in the early days of the new medium. His surreal artwork reflected that *The Kin-der-Kids* was clearly the work of an original and highly inventive artist. In his second strip, *Wee Willie Winkie's World,* Feininger replaces word balloons with printed legends that convey Willie's thoughts, a bit of a throwback to pre-Outcault days. It does, however, present the idea of an ever-changing landscape, a concept that would later become a hallmark of George Herriman's *Krazy Kat*. Feininger's artistic themes were expressed in a simple geometric style that owes much to the tradition of the woodcut and anticipates his later work in cubism. Feininger's sense of design, which would later become a hallmark of his more serious work, is evident in the strips themselves. When Feininger first started painting (1910–1919), he often portrayed over-sized and sharply-angled people almost as part of the architecture.[54]

It is known that Keeley helped name the two strips,[55] but the name of the first had a special significance that has been, heretofore, overlooked. Clearly the *Kin-der-Kids* were named to suggest the German-style *Katzenjammer Kids*. William Randolph Hearst suggested the name "Katzenjammer" to Dirks, but, according to Scheyer, there was nothing German about them except the names [*Katzenjammer* was German slang for hangover, literally meaning a cat's wail].[56] Until now, scholars have noted that the word *Kinder* is German for *children* and left it at that. No one has mentioned the obvious English aspect of the name. The strip that Feininger developed for the *Tribune* was not about hooligans, it was about sweeter, gentler "kinder" kids. Clearly, from the intent of the *Tribune* to create a strip that would mollify the critics and from Feininger's own stated intentions as well as his work to that date, the *Kin-der-Kids* was a

FIGURE 8. Feininger's second strip, *Wee Willie Winkie's World,* harkened back to the days when word balloons were not used. *Chicago Tribune,* August 19, 1906. San Francisco Academy of Comic Art Collection, The Ohio State University Billy Ireland Cartoon Library & Museum.

new kind of comic strip, a carefully crafted, graphically pleasing feature involving good (if somewhat strange) kids in exciting adventures.

Feininger remembered his treatment by German editors with some distaste. On Christmas Day in 1912, he reflected in a letter to his friend Alfred Kubin, what torment it was to try to meet the editor's demands even halfway. Thinking back, he noted that his deal with the *Chicago Tribune* seemed to have liberated him from the world of German magazines. The contract from Chicago made it possible for him to move to Paris and "meet up with the world of art" and abandon cartooning forever. In that same letter, he noted how uncommercial his work was becoming.[57] For their part, the *Tribune* found little interest for Feininger's work coming from their syndicate clients, and reader demand did not warrant the long-distance negotiations. Modern readers should not dismiss Feininger's cartoons because he could not find an audience at the turn of the century. As often happens, great artists, especially those who perform in a popular vernacular, often go unacclaimed until after their deaths.

ENDNOTES

1. While violence has virtually disappeared from the newspaper comic pages, it still reigns in comic books. John Leo, "Good Drama, Not the Krazy Kat Kind," *U.S. News and World Report* 120 (February 26, 1996): 22.

2. Ralph Berengen, "Humor of the Colored Supplement," *The Atlantic Monthly* (August 1906): 269–73.

3. David Kunzle traces the history of the true comic strip to late eighteenth-century England, but he notes that captioned pictures and word balloons can be found in post-Renaissance work. David Kunzle, *History of the Comic Strip: The Early Comic Strip* (Berkeley: University of California Press, 1973), 1:1–3.

4. Elizabeth Banks, "American Yellow Journalism," *The Living Age* 218 (September 3, 1898): 640.

5. See, for example, "A Crime Against American Children," *Ladies Home Journal* (January 9, 1905): 5; Lindsay Swift, "Atrocities of Color Supplements," *The Printing Art* (February 1906): 34; "Cultivating Dreamfulness," *Outlook* 62 (1907): 1538; Ralph Berengen, "Humor of the Colored Supplement," *The Atlantic Monthly* (August 1906): 269–73.

6. "Society for Prevention of Cruelty to Children Issues Annual Report," *The New York Times*, November 24, 1897.

7. Bill Blackbeard, *Comic Strip Art of Lyonel Feininger* (Northampton, MA: Kitchen Sink Press, 1994), 3.

8. "Cultivating Dreamfulness," 1538.

9. Swift, "Atrocities of Color Supplements," 34.

10. "Crime Against American Children," 5.

11. "Crime Against American Children," 5.

12. Though Cyrus McCormick died in 1884, his wife, Nettie, was one of Chicago's preeminent social leaders. She lived in a grand mansion that was recognized as one of the great town

houses of the Gilded Age. Under the widow's charming direction, the house became the center of Chicago society. She was one of the largest contributors to the Presbyterian Church and she helped found the McCormick Theological Seminary. John Tebbels, *An American Dynasty: The Story of the McCormicks, Medills and Pattersons* (New York: Greenwood Press, 1947), 68.

13. Tebbels, *An American Dynasty*, 68.

14. Ben Hecht, *The Front Page* (New York: Covici-Friede, 1933)

15. Teenage boys who peddled candy, tobacco, newspapers, and other items were called candy butchers.

16. James Weber Linn, *James Keeley, Newspaperman* (Indianapolis: Bobbs Merrill, 1937), 97.

17. Linn, *James Keeley, Newspaperman*, 116–17.

18. Linn, *James Keeley, Newspaperman*, 127–38.

19. In 1900, the population of Chicago was 1.7 million people. Germans—that is those who were born in Germany or those who considered themselves of German stock—accounted for some 428,000 or about a quarter of Chicago's population. "Chicago's Growth over the Century," *Chicago Daily News*, January 17, 1976; "People of Chicago, Who We Are and Who We Have Been: Census Data on Foreign Stock and Race, City of Chicago Development and Planning," *Chicago Daily News*, January 17, 1976.

20. Charles T. Brooks's translation of 1871 can be found in *Max and Moritz: With Many More Mischief-Makers More or Less Human or Approximately Animal*, ed. H. Arthur Klein (New York: Dover, 1962).

21. "Sounding the Doom of the Comics," *Current Literature* (December 1908): 630.

22. Ann Taylor Allen, *Satire and Society in Wilheimine Germany: Kladderadatsch and Simplicissimus 1890–1914* (Lexington: University Press of Kentucky, 1974), 29–37.

23. Ernst Scheyer, *Lyonel Feininger: Caricature & Fantasy* (Detroit, MI: Wayne State University Press, 1964), 85.

24. Feininger's letter to Kortheuer, 29 July 1888, American Archives of Art, Washington, DC.

25. By 1904, Churchill would become professor of history and interpretation of art at Smith College and later director of art at that same institution. Alfred V. Churchill, *Lyonel Feininger: The Early Years, 1889–1910* (London: Marlborough Fine Art, 1987), 31.

26. Feininger's letter to Churchill, November 1890, American Archives of Art, Washington, DC.

27. Scheyer, *Lyonel Feininger*, 27–28.

28. Scheyer, *Lyonel Feininger*, 41.

29. Feininger's letter to Kortheuer, 28 August 1890, American Archives of Art, Washington, DC. Partially quoted in Ulrich Luckhardt, *Lyonel Feininger* (Munich: Prestel-Verlag 1989), 9.

30. *Lyonel Feininger: The Early Years*, 33.

31. Feininger's letter to Kortheuer, 10 March 1894, American Archives of Art, Washington, DC. Scheyer, *Lyonel Feininger*, 64, 66.

32. Feininger's letter to Kubin, 4 April 1894, American Archives of Art, Washington, DC.

33. Feininger's letter to Kubin, 4 April 1894.

34. Feininger's letter to Kubin, 22 June 1894, American Archives of Art, Washington, DC.

35. Kenneth Bangs, "How Fritz Became a Wizard," *Harper's Young People* 15 (October 2, 1894): 820–22.

36. Scheyer, *Lyonel Feininger*, 41.

37. Feininger's letters to Kubin, 3–6 April 1894, American Archives of Art, Washington, DC.

38. *Lyonel Feininger: The Early Years*; Feininger's letters to Kubin, 3–6 April 1894, American Archives of Art, Washington, DC.

39. Feininger papers, Houghton Library, Harvard University, Cambridge, MA.

40. Luckhardt, *Lyonel Feininger*, 16–17.

41. Luckhardt, *Lyonel Feininger,* 11.

42. Karl Feininger to Lyonel, 29 April 1906, Feininger papers, Houghton Library, Harvard University, Cambridge, MA.

43. For instance, in a letter dated 4 October 1908, he congratulates Lyonel on his marriage to Julia.

44. Lyonel to Julia Berg, née Lilienfeld, 10 February 1906, as cited in June Ness, ed., *Lyonel Feininger* (New York: Praeger, 1974), 70. (Listed as letters to Julia Feininger, but they lived in common-law marriage until 1908. They had a son, Andreas, in 1906.)

45. Feininger's letter to Kubin, 10 February 1906, as cited in Ness, *Lyonel Feininger,* 70.

46. Blackbeard, *Comic Strip Art of Lyonel Feininger,* 4.

47. Dennis Wepman, *Encyclopedia of American Comics,* ed. Ron Goulart (New York: Facts on File, 1990), 217.

48. Blackbeard, *Comic Strip Art of Lyonel Feininger,* 4.

49. Kunzle, *History of the Comic Strip,* 1–3.

50. Rosemary Gallick, "The Comic Art of Lyonel Feininger, 1906," *Journal of Popular Culture* 10 (1977): 667–75.

51. Judith O'Sullivan, *Great American Comic Strip* (Boston: Little Brown, 1990), 51–52.

52. Blackbeard's assertions appear on page 5 of *Comic Strip Art of Lyonel Feininger,* his collection of Feininger reproductions. For a better discussion of the origin of weekly continuity, see Kunzle's *History of the Comic Strip.*

53. Gallick, "The Comic Art of Lyonel Feininger," 669.

54. In Luckhardt, see for example, *The Red Clown,* 1919 (103); *Trumpeters I,* 1912 (70); or *Newspaper Readers II,* 1916 (97).

55. Scheyer, *Lyonel Feininger,* 41.

56. Martin Sheridan, *Comics and Their Creators* (n.p.: Cushman, Hale & Flint, 1942), 58.

57. Ness, *Lyonel Feininger,* 36–37.

Was Krazy Kat Black?

The Racial Identity of George Herriman

M. THOMAS INGE

GEORGE HERRIMAN (1880–1944), creator of the comic strip *Krazy Kat,* has been recognized by many as America's greatest cartoonist.[1] The poetic complexity and the visual power of his work have generated considerable commentary and appreciation over the past five decades, but since the 1970s, a new element has been added to the discussion since it was discovered that Herriman may have been of African American ancestry. Thus, some critics have determined to classify Herriman as a black who passed for white in a racist society and to analyze his art from an ethnic perspective. The purpose of this essay is to reexamine the evidence for this conclusion and to question the validity of this approach.

When the *Dictionary of American Biography* decided to include Herriman in its third supplementary volume in 1970, they invited Arthur Asa Berger to prepare the entry.[2] Berger had just published *Li'l Abner: A Study in American Satire,* the first book-length study of an American comic strip. When Berger began to gather the scant material on Herriman, he wrote for a copy of his birth certificate to the Board of Health in the city of New Orleans. When it arrived, it contained some new and intriguing information. The document certified that George Joseph Herriman was born on 22 August 1880, but following his name was the racial identification of "colored." The father, George Herriman Jr., was listed as a native of New Orleans and the mother, Clara Morel Herriman, a native of Iberville, Louisiana. Further research into the federal census of 1880 for New Orleans revealed that the parents were designated "mulatto."

Nothing in the printed record had contained such identification, although there had always been some uncertainty about his racial origins. Accounts by friends had suggested that he was perhaps French or Greek, especially because of his handsome Adonis-like appearance. His 1944 death certificate, on file with the Los Angeles Department of Public Health, identified him as "Caucasian" and listed the birthplaces of his father and mother as "Paris, France," and "Alsace-Lorraine," respectively. This information was supplied to the coroner by Herriman's daughter Mabel.

Berger announced his discovery in an article for the *San Francisco Chronicle* on 22 August 1971 (coincidentally on the ninety-first anniversary of Herriman's birth) called "Was Krazy's Creator a Black Cat?" He went on to speculate:

> Since Herriman never was identified as a Negro, it seems likely that he was "passing" for white, which explains his remarkable reticence and the fact, curiously enough, that Herriman was almost never photographed without a hat. Herriman's mother and father were both mulattos, so it would have been eminently possible for him to pass, if that were his desire.

Berger also engaged in an interpretation of the comic strip in the light of this new evidence:

> . . . two of the basic themes in *Krazy Kat* are "the victory of illusion over reality" and the problem of "submission and dominance." In the light of Herriman's passing, and the psychological difficulties this passing must have entailed, it is understandable that such themes would show themselves in the strip. For both of these considerations had a direct relevance to Herriman's own life, which involved the victory of illusion (his being white) over reality (the fact that he was colored).[3]

When black writer Ishmael Reed read this article, he was pleased to reclaim one more major figure for the history of African American contributions to American culture. Thus, he dedicated his book *Mumbo Jumbo* to "George Herriman, Afro-American, who created *Krazy Kat*."[4] This information was soon disseminated through various publications about the comics and was repeated in 1986 in the first book to be devoted to Herriman's life and career, *Krazy Kat: The Comic Art of George Herriman* by Patrick McDonnell, Karen O'Connell, and Georgia Riley de Havenon. The authors add a confirming report by an unidentified source: "The always private Herriman, who never publicly divulged any information about his personal life or background, once told a close friend that he was Creole, and because his hair was 'kinky' thought he might have some 'Negro blood.'"[5] A similar piece of anecdotal evidence was provided in a letter to the *Comics Buyer's Guide* by catherine yronwode, which came from her stepfather, who once dated Herriman's daughter in Santa Monica in the 1940s:

> ... he said that she had told him she and her father were "colored people passing for whites." He told me that she said Herriman always wore a hat to conceal his kinky hair and that he told inquisitive people he was "Greek," to explain his dark skin. This was a family story in my household long before I knew that anyone on Earth still remembered George Herriman or *Krazy Kat.*[6]

Most comics historians now routinely identify Herriman as an African American or a Creole.[7]

In the light of this new biographical information, as one would expect, critics began to examine *Krazy Kat* more closely for encoded messages and meanings, made irresistible by the fact that Krazy is a black cat, after all, who endures the violent subjugation of her lighter-toned love object and master Ignatz Mouse. Franklin Rosemont has found echoes of black swing bands, the blues, and jazz in the comic strip,[8] while Elisabeth Crocker has read it for postmodern resonances of race and gender issues.[9] In *The Art of the Funnies,* Robert C. Harvey finds artifacts of black life in the strip, especially a vaudeville routine using racial stereotypes from the days of minstrelsy based on the comedy of reversal. But he resists turning Krazy Kat into "an allegory about race relations."[10]

I was asked to write the entry on Herriman for the recently published *Encyclopedia of African-American Culture and History* from Macmillan, but after having done so, I have begun to rethink the easy conclusion that Herriman is properly designated an African American. That he was of mixed blood seems indisputable, but given the recent thought being applied to racial categories in this country, I am no longer convinced that this is the most meaningful designation for Herriman.

If Herriman thought he had "Negro blood," it did not seem to have much direct influence on his early art. That he was even insensitive to the issue is

FIGURE 9. 1912 portrait of George Herriman. Harry Hershfield Collection, The Ohio State University Billy Ireland Cartoon Library & Museum.

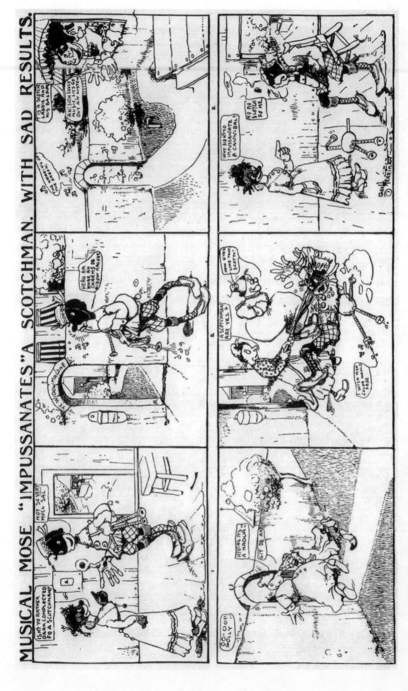

FIGURE 10. George Herriman, *Musical Mose*, February 16, 1902.

demonstrated in his easy reliance on the usual stereotyped portrayals of blacks in his cartoons—thick white lips, large rolling eyes, and heavy-handed use of dialect. One of his earliest sequential features was a three-part series about *Musical Mose* for the Pulitzer newspapers. In the first sequence of 16 February 1902, Mose attempts to "impussanate" a Scotchman, in a kilt and with bagpipes, only to be hosed down by the Widow Malone whom he is serenading. The Sunday strip is rife with racial humor at the expense of Mose—the widow calls him a "nagur"; he laments "I wish mah color would fade"; and his girlfriend, Sal, asks, "Why didn't yo impussanate a cannibal?"[11] This is strange humor for an African American passing for white, unless one argues that Herriman is unconsciously revealing his own fear of being found out. My guess is that he was not thinking very deeply about it and resorted to the standard racial humor of the day, as he did with the Irish, Jews, Italians, and other ethnic groups as well.

Black mammy figures appeared in his first comic strip features published in the *Seattle Post-Intelligencer* (such as *Rosy Posy* for 27 May 1906, and *Bud Smith* for 30 September 1906), as well as a Stepin Fetchit-style figure (*Major Ozone's Fresh Air Crusade,* 9 August 1906), albeit seven years before the black actor began his show business career. In several of the 1910 *Family Upstairs* sequences, the precursor to *Krazy Kat,* black characters appear, including several popular black boxing ring figures of the day in gross caricature, and on 5 December 1910, in the *Krazy Kat* feature that ran beneath the main strip, a blackbird serving as a train porter is called "Krazy Koon" by Ignatz.[12] The household in *Baron Bean,* a strip published from 1916 to 1919, had an Aunt Jemima-style cook one week in the kitchen named Fulginia, who pretty much went her own way despite her minstrel-show appearance.[13] One does not have to look very far to find examples of Sambos and shuffling coons in any of Herriman's features. What was he thinking when he drew them, and if he were concerned about racism, why did he include them?

How conscious was he of his racial background, and how did he view himself? What we think today may not be the same way he thought, and to whom should we defer? We have given up the notion that the United States has been largely a white, Anglo–Saxon society and have recognized that we are a multiracial or multiethnic nation. The population is so intermingled that clear identification for many is not possible, and racial purity has probably never existed here anyway.

The Creoles of Louisiana, presumably Herriman's stock, are good examples of the contradictions of racial categorization. According to the *Encyclopedia of Southern Culture,*

FIGURE 11. George Herriman, detail from *The Family Upstairs*, December 5, 1910.

Few ethnic terms in North American society have been as controversial or as sensitive as the term Creole. Coined by the Spanish and Portuguese who ventured into the New World, the word originally denoted individuals born in the colonies of European parents. Under the restrictions of this connotation, the term should have fallen from disuse with the cessation of colonial immigration.

Within Louisiana, the disparities between the predominantly Latin culture of the original settlers and the predominantly Anglo-Celtic culture of the late-eighteenth- and nineteenth-century newcomers served to encourage the perpetuation, evolution, and expansion of the term *Creole*. By the nineteenth century it had become synonymous with "native." In both the noun and adjective forms it embraced all objects indigenous to Louisiana, from cabbage to cotton and all people, regardless of hue, whose families were native to the Louisiana colony. Its application to people appeared in one of three forms: Creole, Creole *de couleur* [which denoted Creoles with African or Indian admixtures], and Creole Negro [which denoted blacks of unmixed ancestry]. By definition, the term was so inexclusive that it barred only those born outside Louisiana.[14]

Presumably, Herriman belonged to the second group, Creole *de couleur,* but it can be more complicated than that. Another scholar, Gwendolyn Midlo Hall, has noted,

> By the nineteenth century, the mixed-blood creoles of Louisiana who acknowledged their African descent emphasized and took greatest pride in their French ancestry. They defined creole to mean racially mixed, enforced endogamous marriage among their own group, and distinguished themselves from and looked down upon blacks and Anglo-Afroamericans, though their disdain stemmed from cultural as well as racial distinctions.[15]

Given the Herriman family tradition of claimed French ancestry, was it this kind of elite-minded family to which they belonged? The same author notes that in Louisiana, "The most precise current definition of a creole is a person of non-American ancestry, whether African or European, who was born in the Americas."[16]

A historian of Creole culture, Joseph Logsdon, has offered the following thoughts on the subject:

> I think you are on fairly safe ground in describing George Herriman as a New Orleanian with some African ancestry. Census takers erred more in declaring some persons white than in mistakenly declaring some mulatto or

black. Designation in New Orleans as "colored" meant apparent or declared African ancestry. In 1880, parents would have had much to do with the declaration of racial identity on a birth certificate. . . . What is unusual, but not unprecedented, is the name Herriman for a person of mixed racial ancestry in New Orleans. But I do know so-called black families with surnames such as Newman, Stern, Braden, etc.[17]

Another scholar, David Bergeron, who looked into the matter for me when he lived in New Orleans, reported:

"Mulatto" ought to mean that one parent was black and one white; but again the term seems not to have been applied in any consistent manner. One of my authorities speculates that Herriman's father was probably white and the mother, who was a Morel, black. He said that there are black Morels still living in New Orleans.[18]

No wonder that the *Encyclopedia of Southern Culture* concludes, "In consideration of the ambiguity that surrounds what is principally a question of evolving semantics, the safest definition of the term may well be the classic Louisiana compromise: A Creole can be anyone who says he is one."[19] And what happens, then, if one decides not to be a Creole and leaves this ethnic-linguistic briar patch behind? Is it possible to step beyond all racial classification, based mainly on law and custom, and simply be one's own person?

This brings us to what may be the most crucial concern in the matter of Herriman's racial identity. Anthropologists, biologists, and other scientists recently have largely abandoned concepts of race as meaningless and an outmoded method of classifying people.[20] The concept of race in this country is a myth developed specifically to support legal and social regulations for maintaining segregation between the free white European population and the descendants of African slaves. It has no basis in biology or genetics. Recent research indicates that more than 90 percent of so-called black Americans have some "white" genetic heritage, while over 10 percent of so-called whites have some African ancestry of which many are probably unaware.[21]

Herriman belongs to a large group of people who have fallen between the legally determined lines. These include Walter White, novelist and leader of the NAACP, who was categorized as black even though he was predominantly Caucasian and appeared so.[22] The cartoonist Oliver Harrington was born to a black father and a Jewish-Hungarian mother and in his early years was unaware that he was any different from the other children. Once discrimination and cruel racism were brought to bear on both of them, they became thoroughly assimilated into the black society of the time.[23] Some have had the liberty to make a conscious choice. I am reminded of the late scholar of American literature, Philip Butcher, who once told me that he remembered as a young man making a conscious choice to be a part of the African American community, although he could have passed, because he found it richer and more attractive than the alternative. And some have moved back and forth, like the talented writer Jean Toomer, whose light skin allowed him to grow up in the white upper-middle-class community of Columbia Heights in Washington, DC, but whose mixed parentage caused him to attend high school in the black community of Shaw. For those who asked him to identify his race, he wrote:

> Fourteen years of my life I had lived in the white group, four years I had lived in the colored group. In my experience there had been no main difference between the two. But if people wanted to isolate and fasten on those four years and say that I was colored, this too was up to them. As for myself, I would live my life as far as possible on the basis of what was true for me.[24]

The psychological impact of growing up on the color line has recently been discussed in the published memoirs of two academics, Gregory H. Williams, who grew up in Virginia thinking he was white only to discover at age ten that his father's relatives in Indiana were black, and Judy Scales-Trent, who grew up in a black community only to be assumed to be white all her life because of her appearance. Both feel they should have been allowed to claim both black and white heritage or escape society's need to force a choice on them.[25]

In Louisiana, where Herriman was born, the law stipulated that a person was to be identified as colored who was more than one thirty-second black. In fact, despite several legal challenges, that law was upheld in court as late as 1983.[26] Obviously, Herriman and his parents were light skinned enough to pass, and by leaving behind his Louisiana heritage, the choice was made for him. He grew up instead in the richly multiethnic community of Los Angeles with little awareness of African American society, culture, or consciousness. To simply conclude that he was "African American" is to accept as valid the scientifically and morally inappropriate categories of a racist society as reflected in the laws of segregation.

Probably, like Jean Toomer, Herriman was little concerned over these matters and knew that society's categories told him little about his essential identity. This may be reflected in an interesting *Krazy Kat* daily sequence of 1 January 1931. When Krazy and Ignatz are identified by an art critic as being "A Study in Black & White," they decide to switch colors on the pretentious dog. When he returns to find a white Krazy and a black Ignatz, again he

FIGURE 12. George Herriman, *Krazy Kat,* January 1, 1931, ©King Features Syndicate.

repeats, "A Study in Black and White." In other words, skin or fur color makes no real difference in Coconino County, nor should it elsewhere in the world. Rather than respond to the categorical assumptions of society, people should be allowed to create their own identities beyond the traditional identifications of race and ethnicity. Perhaps we should allow George Herriman that liberty.

ENDNOTES

1. See M. Thomas Inge, "Krazy Kat as American Dada Art," in *Comics as Culture* (Jackson: University Press of Mississippi, 1990), 41–47.

2. The entry was later assigned to Marie Caskey and published in *Dictionary of American Biography: Supplement Three, 1941–1945* (New York: Charles Scribner's Sons, 1973), 356–57.

3. Arthur Berger, "Was Krazy's Creator a Black Cat?" *San Francisco Sunday Examiner & Chronicle,* August 22, 1971, "This World," 35, 40.

4. Letter from Ishmael Reed to the author, 31 December 1972. Also see Ishmael Reed, *Mumbo Jumbo* (Garden City, NY: Doubleday, 1972), 12.

5. Patrick McDonnell, Karen O'Connell, and Georgia Riley de Havenon, *Krazy Kat: The Comic Art of George Herriman* (New York: Harry N. Abrams, 1986), 30.

6. catherine yronwode, letter in *Comics Buyer's Guide* 867 (June 29, 1990): 4.

7. See, for example, Richard Marschall, *America's Great Comic Strip Artists* (New York: Abbeville Press, 1989), 98; Judith O'Sullivan, *The Great American Comic Strip* (Boston: Little, Brown, 1990), 40; Ron Goulart, *The Encyclopedia of American Comics* (New York: Facts on File, 1990), 181; and Inge, *Comics as Culture,* 44–45.

8. Franklin Rosemont, "George Herriman," in *Surrealism & Its Popular Accomplices,* ed. Franklin Rosemont (San Francisco: City Lights Books, 1980), 58–64.

9. Elisabeth Crocker's essay, "'To He, I Am For Ewa True': Krazy Kat's Indeterminate Gender," appears only in electronic hypermedia format in the *Journal of Postmodern Culture.* For responses to her theses, see "Maybe We're All Krazy," *International Museum of Cartoon Art Inklings* 5 (Fall 1994): 6; Tom Heintjes, "Kooky Kriticism," *Hogan's Alley* 1 (Fall 1994): 8–9; and George Johnson, "Inside Academia: Krazy Kat Meets the Lit Crits," *The New York Times,* April 10, 1994, IV 3.

10. Robert C. Harvey, *The Art of the Funnies: An Aesthetic History* (Jackson: University Press of Mississippi, 1994), 179.

11. The strip is reprinted in McDonnell, O'Connell, and de Havenon, *Krazy Kat,* 36.

12. George Herriman, *The Family Upstairs* (Westport, CT: Hyperion Press, 1977), 49, 68.

13. George Herriman, *Baron Bean* (Westport, CT: Hyperion Press, 1977), 31–33.

14. Gary B. Mills, "Creole," in *Encyclopedia of Southern Culture,* ed. Charles Reagan Wilson and William Ferris (Chapel Hill: University of North Carolina Press, 1989), 426. Also see the definitions in Arnold R. Hirsch and Joseph Logsdon, eds., *Creole New Orleans: Race and Americanization* (Baton Rouge: Louisiana State University Press, 1992), 60–61 and passim.

15. Gwendolyn Midlo Hall, *Africans in Colonial Louisiana* (Baton Rouge: Louisiana State University Press, 1992), 158.

16. Hall. *Africans in Colonial Louisiana,* 157.

17. Letter from Joseph Logsdon to the author, 18 April 1992.

18. Letter from David Bergeron to the author, 22 March 1974.

19. Mills, *Encyclopedia of Southern Culture,* 427.

20. See Lawrence Wright, "One Drop of Blood," *The New Yorker* (July 25, 1994): 46–55; "Blood Not So Simple," *The New Yorker* (September 5, 1994): 8–10; and David L. Wheeler, "A Growing Number of Scientists Reject the Concept of Race," *Chronicle of Higher Education* (February 17, 1995): A8–A9, A15.

21. John George, "The Misnomer of 'Race,'" *Chronicle of Higher Education* (March 3, 1995): B6.

22. George, "The Misnomer of 'Race.'"

23. Introduction to *Dark Laughter: The Satiric Art of Oliver W. Harrington,* ed. M. Thomas Inge (Jackson: University Press of Mississippi, 1993).

24. Dana Hull, "D.C.'s Forgotten Native Son," *The Washington Post,* December 26, 1994, Bl, B4.

25. Robin Williams, "At the Racial Dividing Line," *Chronicle of Higher Education* (January 27, 1995): A17, A20. See also Gregory H. Williams, *Life on the Color Line* (New York: Dutton, 1995) and Judy Scales-Treat, *Notes of a White Black Woman* (University Park: Pennsylvania State University Press, 1995).

26. Art Harris, "Louisiana Court Sees No Shades of Gray in Woman's Request," *The Washington Post,* May 21, 1983, A3.

Litigation and Early Comic Strips

The Lawsuits of Outcault, Dirks, and Fisher

MARK D. WINCHESTER

THE QUARTER CENTURY following the Yellow Kid's debut saw several significant lawsuits involving the prominent cartoonists R. F. Outcault, Rudolph Dirks, and Harry Conway (Bud) Fisher. These cases are traditionally depicted as the prototypic conflict between a rebellious cartoonist and a greedy newspaper in a bitter court battle. In the model case usually described, the cartoonist loses control of the title and the ongoing feature, but retains the use of the characters under a new title or in a new feature. This perception of litigation involving early comic strips is widespread, with the newspaper left with the empty shell of the feature without its creator and the cartoonist winning the creative rights to the essence of the work.

In contrast to the mythology surrounding these cases as battles over ownership, they were actually argued and decided on issues of libel, trademark, unfair competition, and disputed contracts. Each case had its own merits and none follows the pattern reported in several comic strip histories. The opinions rendered in these lawsuits offer a wealth of information about issues relating to cartoon art, copyright, and trademark that are frequently overlooked in many studies.

The most legendary of all cartoon art-related cases are the *Yellow Kid* lawsuits between the *New York World* and the *New York Journal*. A substantial body of writing supports the idea of *Yellow Kid* lawsuits, but significant evidence places this notion in question. Contrary to popularly held belief, these cases may be just legend, because the reports of their existence are not documented. Several writers argue that there was a landmark case involving R. F. Outcault's *Yellow Kid*, and some expand the argument further to state that the case became a legal precedent for cartoon art ownership issues in later years.[1] Roy L. McCardell's 1905 "Opper, Outcault and Company" is the earliest source found that discusses the *Yellow Kid* lawsuits:

> There were lawsuits for breaking of contracts and for infringement of copyright brought by both papers, and the comic artists profited. The suits were of importance chiefly to the two papers engaged; but the Yellow Kid gained a place in literary history, albeit himself most unliterary.[2]

McCardell's brief reference to legal action does not mention an opinion resulting from the lawsuits nor does it imply that these cases were heard through to the point of a decision. He simply notes that there "were lawsuits . . . brought."

If there were lawsuits for the breaking of contracts and infringement of copyright, then the *New York World* must have sued Outcault specifically at a time when an entire staff might be purchased from one newspaper to work at another. If McCardell's story is accurate, then the *New York World* must also have sued the *New York Journal* for copyright infringement over the *Yellow Kid* property (with the *Journal* countersuing). However, at that time cartoon art was perceived as a static form (at best, illustrations linked by a common theme) rather than a dynamic serial feature where characters, relationships, and situations developed over time through a series of images.[3]

Edward Pinkowski's 1953 *Forgotten Fathers* elaborates on McCardell's story:

> When required to boost the Yellow Kid three times each Sunday, he [Outcault] almost quit the Hearst paper. He didn't know from one week to the next what his next comic strip would involve. The kid of his exuberant fancy began to fade. Luckily for him the courts, after a bitter legal battle between Hearst and Pulitzer, ordered Hearst to transfer the Yellow Kid to the *New York World*. Taking it off his hands saved the artist from going entirely dry.[4]

Bill Blackbeard expands Pinkowski's version:

> The furor kicked up by the widely publicized legal battle between the *World* and the *Journal* over the rights to the *Hogan's Alley* characters (which resulted in Outcault retaining the right to continue the characters and the

World holding control of the *Hogan's Alley* name and figures as well) irked him [Outcault] also.[5]

The flaws in Pinkowski's version of the story can be documented as a distortion of fact. Both Coulton Waugh and Stephen Becker note that Joseph Pulitzer hired George Luks to continue the feature because he had a legal right to do so, and neither writer suggests any litigation connected with this decision.[6] Furthermore, Pulitzer's *New York World* ended its regular use of *The Yellow Kid* prior to the cessation of the feature in the *New York Journal*. Another flaw in the concept of a "widely publicized legal battle" is that Outcault abandoned the location "Hogan's Alley" (*New York World*) for the new location of "McFadden's Row of Flats" (*New York Journal*). It is, therefore, very unlikely that any of the parties involved contested the use of "Hogan's Alley" as a location or as the title of the feature as mentioned above. Blackbeard supports the idea that Outcault retained the right to his characters, when evidence suggests that this would not have granted Outcault any rights over, or protections from, other artists who chose to draw the characters. As interpreted at that time, copyright protected specific drawings but did not protect an artist/creator from the use of established characters by someone else in his original drawings. At the turn of the century, a cartoonist was viewed as performing work for hire, selling services and a product to a larger corporate entity and being duly compensated by the corporation. Cartoon art was not distinguished from other forms of illustration and was subject to the protections offered for drawings and photographs that appeared in newspapers.

One of the more recent assertions about the significance of the alleged *Yellow Kid* case was made by Richard Marschall:

> Luks's valiant attempt at imitation notwithstanding, Joseph Pulitzer sued to stop Outcault from drawing the *Yellow Kid* for Hearst's *Journal*. The result of the notorious court case was that Outcault could draw his character for whomever he wished, while publisher Pulitzer could continue the *feature* with whatever artist he chose to employ. So New York had two Yellow Kids— one in *Hogan's Alley* in the *World* and one in *The Yellow Kid* in the *Journal*. (Since the legal issues revolved around likenesses and distinguishing characteristics, Luks's character for a few weeks wore bloomers instead of the gown and was once even green instead of yellow!)[7]

Marschall, like many of his predecessors, makes assumptions based on previous assertions without providing further documentation.

FIGURE 13. Detail from H. B. Eddy's "A Feast of Reason and a Flow of Sparkling Humor" (*New York Journal,* October 30, 1986, 2), an advertisement used to promote the *Journal*'s Sunday comic supplement.

Specific events in Outcault's career and the appearance of *The Yellow Kid* suggest that the existence of such a case is plausible, but the preponderance of evidence does not support it. Prior to moving from the *New York World* to the *New York Journal,* Outcault initiated copyright applications for designs of the Yellow Kid with the first of his three requests dated 7 September 1896.[8] Although he demonstrated concern regarding ownership of the character before the move, afterward there were several cartoonists drawing Yellow Kids: Luks' version of the feature ran in the *New York World,* Outcault's *Yellow Kid* feature appeared in the *New York Journal,* other *Journal* staff cartoonists exploited the character for a variety of other uses in that newspaper, and an

FIGURE 14. Charles Greening Bush's "Is He an Orphan?—Nit!" (*New York Journal*, November 6, 1896, 2) was inspired by a report in the *New York Telegram* of a "young person . . . found wandering aimlessly about Herald Square late Tuesday night. He wore a coat made of Evening Telegrams, and said he had shaken the Popocratic party. So far very little has been learned concerning his antecedents." The *Journal* added this illustration and the comment that "upon being reprimanded the Kid said: 'Naw; I was lookin' for de Herald's New High Water Mark.'"

unknown number of artists were contributing artwork for the non-newspaper-related enterprises. The *New York Journal*, for example, published Yellow Kid drawings credited to J. Campbell Cory,[9] Archie Gunn,[10] H. B. Eddy,[11] and C. G. Bush,[12] in addition to numerous uncredited Yellow Kid drawings for advertisements and illustrations. Similarly, the Yellow Kid was used as a

FIGURE 15. An uncredited drawing of the Yellow Kid from the *New York Journal* (October 24, 1896, 11) used to promote the want-ad section.

spokesperson in marketing many products, with Outcault and non-Outcault Yellow Kids sanctioned "by permission of *N. Y. Journal.*"

Outcault's claims (if they were made) would have been weakened by this permitted use of the character by other artists, since he and the *New York Journal* allowed other artists to use the character without reprisal or threat of legal action. If the *New York World* felt that Outcault's later work was an infringement of their property, then they would have been compelled to sue

FIGURE 16. The Yellow Kid made his first of six appearances in Richard Felton Outcault's *The Huckleberry Volunteers* on 16 April 1898 (page 12). This eleven-cartoon series in the *New York Journal* commented on the tense situation between Spain and the United States.

the multitude of companies employing the Yellow Kid to promote their products, a small complement of artists who executed the artwork, and the *New York Journal* for sanctioning this use.

Despite extensive use of the character, Outcault felt that his claims on the *Yellow Kid* rights were secure enough to be a definable property for trade or sale to others. On 4 February 1898, Outcault and Connor assigned the copyright for *McFadden's Flats* and *The Yellow Kid* to the McLaughlin Brothers,[13] just two days prior to Outcault's last regular *Yellow Kid* feature in the *New York Journal* on 6 February 1898.[14] Outcault's lax observance of copyright assignment presents another significant discrepancy because he did not stop using the Yellow Kid character later in drawings published in both the *New York Journal* and the *New York World*. Two months after assigning his copyright of the *Yellow Kid*, Outcault included the character in his series *The Huckleberry Volunteers* in the *New York Journal*,[15] and in the following month the character made one-time appearances in Outcault's *The Casey Corner Kids' Dime Museum* and *The Bud and Blossom of the Yellow Kid* in the *New York World*.[16]

To the litigious contemporary American society, it seems unthinkable that either the *New York World* or the *New York Journal* would let the other newspaper freely use the character of the Yellow Kid without the threat of legal action, but an extensive search for *Yellow Kid* lawsuits has not uncovered any cases related to that character.[17] There may have been a controversy with both newspapers agitated by the appearance of the character in the other newspaper, but its continued use by both newspapers demonstrates that neither party was successful in establishing that the other was using Outcault's creation unlawfully. Likewise, there is no evidence that a case was pursued to an eventual decision in a higher court; but it is possible that proceedings were initiated and an out-of-court settlement was reached prior to a decision. A case could have been heard in a lower court where the rendered opinions were not published. In any event, a *Yellow Kid* case did not establish a precedent for other cartoon art-related court cases. That honor was accorded to the *Buster Brown* decision of 1906, cited in several subsequent cases involving cartoon art, copyright, trademark, and ownership issues.

In the day-to-day process of publishing Outcault's work, the *New York World* registered his cartoons for copyright as a part of the newspaper and subsequently held proprietary rights to those specific cartoons and those specific titles. Anything that Outcault drew for another newspaper from that point on could not duplicate the *New York World's* published copyrighted drawings nor reuse their copyrighted titles. Any use of "Hogan's Alley" in the title or specific character names from the feature (if they appeared in the feature) could have been construed as copyright infringement. The likenesses of the characters were, however, not strictly protected by copyright and could be reused by any cartoonist or illustrator for any purpose as long as they were not an exact copy of a previously copyrighted drawing. Similarly, a photograph could be registered for copyright, although the subject of a specific photograph could not.

This resulted in occasions where two (or more) similar comic strips were published in different newspapers with different titles and subtle nuances but nearly identical premises, situations, and characters. In such a case, the owner of each title (for example *Hogan's Alley* and *McFadden's Row of Flats)* had the legal right to license subsidiary rights to those titles and characters for the purposes of commercial exploitation. When Outcault moved to the *Journal,* although he changed the location from "Hogan's Alley" to "McFadden's Flats," he retained the use of the likenesses of the characters, including Mickey Dugan, the Yellow Kid.

R. F. Outcault created *Buster Brown* to follow the success of his *Yellow Kid, L'il Mose,* and *Kelly's Kindergarten* features. The *Buster Brown* feature first appeared in the *New York Herald* on 4 May 1902. Outcault was persuaded to rejoin Hearst's *New York Journal,* ended the feature in the *Herald* on

31 December 1905, and restarted it two weeks later in the *Journal*. After Outcault left, the *New York Herald* published old *Buster Brown* installments, then
continued *Buster Brown* with artists other than Outcault.[18] As a result, Outcault sued the *New York Herald* to stop them from producing a feature even
similar to *Buster Brown*. The New York Herald Company, in turn, sued the
Star Company (the parent publishing company of the *New York Journal*) for
the trademark of the *Buster Brown* title and the right to continue the feature,
employing any artist of their choice.

In 1906 both cases were tried in the same court by the same judge, with
the New York Herald Company's case being heard first. The *Buster Brown* case,
New York Herald Company v. Star Company, was decided on the basis of trademark and trade-name issues (as opposed to copyright), as was *Outcalt [sic] v.
New York Herald*. In the first case the court held that the New York Herald
Company had the right to continue the use of the title *Buster Brown*, as it had
become an exclusive trademark of the newspaper through its published use
over a three-and-a-half-year period. The court noted that

> whether or not the original draughtsman of the so-called "Buster Brown"
> pictures was in the employ of the Herald is immaterial; concededly it bought
> them from him, paid for them, published them (whether with or without
> retouching, coloring, etc., is immaterial) and headed the page on which they
> were published with the words "Buster Brown."[19]

In favor of the *New York Herald*, the court issued a restraining order against
the *New York Journal*'s use of the title *Buster Brown*, noting that this restriction
included Outcault as well. The court concluded its remarks by noting that the
Star Company could continue the feature as long as they did not use the title
nor infringe on the previously published and copyrighted drawings:

> Mr. Outcalt [sic] or any one else whom the defendant may choose to employ,
> is entirely free to design, draw, color, and publish comic pictures of the same
> kind as those to which plaintiff has prefixed that title, provided only that they
> do not so closely imitate pictures already published and copyrighted as to be
> an infringement thereof.[20]

In the view of the court, the title (*Buster Brown*) and the individual published
drawings were subject to copyright, but the characters in general (including
elements of likeness, costume, and demeanor) were not tangible enough to
merit copyright nor trademark. Outcault and the Star Company were free to
use the character of Buster Brown but not the name or the title.

In *Outcalt* [*sic*] *v. New York Herald,* Outcault argued that he had the right
to exclude the *New York Herald* from use of the characters and the title, despite
the fact that he sold his artwork to the newspaper and they held the copyright
to his comic strips published in the *New York Herald.* The court noted Outcault's contention that the *New York Herald's* use of *Buster Brown* was

> unfair competition in trade for any one else to draw and offer for sale any
> other pictures in which, although the scenes and incidents are different,
> some of the characters are imitations of those which appeared in the earlier
> pictures which complainant sold to defendant.[21]

Although Outcault had sold his pictures to the *New York Herald* and they
"colored, copyrighted and published" his work, he held that he maintained the
creative rights to his characters.

> [Outcault,] although he never copyrighted them and did not acquire any
> right to the title in connection with newspaper publication, has, neverthe-
> less, some common-law title to individual figures therein displayed, which
> he can maintain to the exclusion of others, who depict them in other scenes
> and situations.[22]

The court was not sympathetic to Outcault's claim, noting that "it is sufficient to say that no authority is cited supporting this proposition, which
seems entirely novel and does not commend itself as sound."[23] His motion
was denied.

The existence of these cases further decreases the likelihood of the *Yellow Kid* case. Because Outcault was the creator of both the *Yellow Kid* and
Buster Brown, it seems inconceivable that any legal action initiated on behalf
of the former would not have been applied in the latter case. There were no
references to a prior case involving the *Yellow Kid* and Outcault did not claim
rights awarded in an earlier case. Therefore, it seems extremely unlikely that
there was a *Yellow Kid* case.[24]

In the *Buster Brown* cases, the court only recognized the composition and
execution of a drawing, refusing to entertain the idea of character (including
likeness and temperament) as a significant element of cartoon art. Outcault's
suit is notable as one of the first efforts for what is now termed *creator's rights.*
Outcault's failed bid was an unfortunate precedent for other cartoonists who
sought similar protection for their characters and artwork.

Two other cases directly involve *Buster Brown,* the 1907 *Outcault v. New
York Herald Company* and the 1908–1909 *New York Herald Company v. Ottawa*

Citizen Company. In the 1907 case, Outcault sued the New York Herald Company for $50,000 in damages on the grounds of libel. Immediately after Outcault left the newspaper to work at the *New York Journal,* the *New York Herald* republished an early *Buster Brown* comic strip. A few days after reprinting "The Buster and His Bath," the European edition of the newspaper published a letter critical of Outcault and the feature. The newspaper then reprinted the letter in the New York edition with editorial commentary.

```
                                    Hotel Lord Byron
                                    No. 16 Rue Lord Byron
                                    Paris, Jan. 10, 1906.
To the Editor of the Herald:
    What is the matter with Buster and Tige, children? I will
tell you. Mr. Outcault has evidently run out of ideas and no
wonder! But, unlike Mr. Gibson, he is not willing to attempt
something new. "The Buster and his Bath" that you saw in the
Herald last Sunday was one of the first of the Buster Brown
series and appeared in the New York Herald several years ago
when Buster was still somewhat raw and crude. This accounts
for the difference that puzzled you.
                                    "GRANNY."[25]
```

Instead of explaining that Outcault had left the *New York Herald* and that the newspaper was reprinting early installments of the comic strip, the newspaper announced that the feature was past its prime and used this as an opportunity to promote their other cartoon art features:

> Grumblers do not appear to realize that the sere and yellow leaf period must arrive for Buster as well as for all things. The power of the European edition has provided its readers with a new and exceedingly amusing pet, "Little Nemo," whose popularity here with young and old alike is boundless.
>
> Indeed, his adventures in Slumberland, the latest cataclysm provoked by Sammy Sneeze, and the agitated existence of those quaint little creatures, the Tiny Teds, form an amazingly popular feature of the weekly comic section of the European edition that more than compensates for the waning interest of Buster's pranks.[26]

Although the *New York Herald* had been uncharitable, the court found that Outcault failed to state a cause of action; the words that were considered actionable were sufficiently vague and did not constitute libel.

In the 1908–1909 case, the New York Herald Company, still holding the trademark for *Buster Brown,* sued the Ottawa Citizen Company for the illegal use of the terms "Buster Brown" or "Buster Brown and Tige" as the title to a comic section of a newspaper. The Canadian court acknowledged that the *Buster Brown* trademark was upheld in the United States with *New York Herald Company v. Star Company.* The court found that Canadian law did not protect the title or characters under trademark laws, since the feature was not used to promote a specific product but was an element of the product being sold. It was suggested that the New York Herald Company investigate copyrighting the character and seek protections on that basis.[27]

In contrast to the legal proceedings between Outcault and the *New York Herald,* the Outcault Advertising Company was successful in prosecuting cases involving companies' infringements on Outcault's copyrighted artwork. More than thirty lawsuits involved Outcault's firm and a conglomeration of other companies, including *Outcault Advertising Company v. American Furniture Company,*[28] *Outcault Advertising Company v. Harry Joseph Clothing Company,*[29] and *Outcault Advertising Company v. Young Hardware Company.*[30] Outcault also entered into legal battles over the theatrical rights to *Buster Brown* in the 1907 *Outcault v. Bonheur*[31] and the 1909 *Outcault v. Lamar.*[32] The use of the Buster Brown character was one of the most frequently contested issues in the early history of cartoon art.

The suit involving Rudolph Dirks had little to do with the ownership of *The Katzenjammer Kids* but was concerned with the contract between Dirks and the Star Company. In the 1914 *Star Company v. Press Publishing Company,* the Star Company (as publisher of the *New York Journal*) sued the Press Publishing Company (as publisher of the *New York World*) and cartoonist Rudolph Dirks, creator of the *Katzenjammer Kids.* The dispute centered on the exclusivity clause in Dirks's contract with the Star Company. After Dirks had a disagreement with the *New York Journal,* he went to work for the *New York World,* while theoretically still under contract with the Star Company. The Star Company sued to restrain Dirks from working for their competition, although they were no longer interested in publishing his work nor were they paying him in the interim. The court found Dirks's contract flawed in that the Star Company expected that it could keep the cartoonist off of their payroll as well as prevent his working for any other employer for the duration of the contract, thereby creating a master-and-servant relationship. The court found that the clause in question was "unenforceable by injunction" and that Dirks was free to work for whom he pleased.[33]

The most elaborate of the cases began in 1915, and concerned the ownership issues of Bud Fisher's *Mutt and Jeff.* Initially, the Star Company (*New*

York Journal) sued the Wheeler Syndicate to restrain them from using the title *Mutt and Jeff* in connection with the comic strip, maintaining their rights to the trademark of *Mutt and Jeff* and citing the *Buster Brown* case as a basis for this claim. The court found

> that the right of the Star Company to a trademark in the words "Mutt and Jeff," as applied to a comic section or strip, is so doubtful and the danger of deceiving the public is so great, that no preliminary injunction should issue.[34]

In August 1916 the Star Company continued to argue that it held a valid right to the trademark of the *Mutt and Jeff* title, although the courts could find no merit in their claims. In December 1916, the United States Patent and Trademark Office rejected a claim of the Star Company to cancel Fisher's registration of the words "Mutt and Jeff."[35] Four separate suits and countersuits[36] were eventually argued through the court system until they reached the United States Supreme Court in 1921. Ultimately, Fisher's rights to the trademark and trade name of *Mutt and Jeff* were affirmed, despite the extensive arguments and protestations of the Star Company.[37]

Throughout the cases described above involving comic strips, one major challenge to obtaining an impartial hearing was the courts' perception of cartoonists and their work. The opinions rendered regarded the cartoonists as "draughtsmen" or similarly skilled laborers with little creative input or control.[38] Throughout the early lawsuits, cartoonists were perceived as newspaper staff illustrators, who engaged in nonspecific and noncreative work. Above all, their work in newspapers was not highly regarded, and many people were hard pressed to describe the features as any form of "art." References to comic strips in legal opinions demonstrate this bias with great regularity. In one of the later *Buster Brown* cases, comic strips were described generally as "the nonsense that is produced by the brain of the man writing for the diversion of the idle that in truth is sold."[39] *The Katzenjammer Kids* fared little better in the definition offered by the courts:

> a series of horrible but apparently popular drawings representing the suppositious [sic] experiences in varying surroundings of certain nondescripts known as the Katzenjammer Kids.[40]

Mutt and Jeff was probably described in the most practical of terms, but the issues of the lawsuit were more serious than *Buster Brown* and the *Katzenjammer Kids*:

a series of five or six pictures arranged in a strip so as to cover the width of a newspaper page, and depicting the progressive development of a situation in which the oversized "Mutt" and the undersized "Jeff" are usually the only participants and in which the latter is usually the subject of maltreatment by the former.[41]

Each of the parties in the above decisions sought certain rights of ownership, but in several instances the courts were hesitant to affirm perpetual rights to characters in comic strips. In *New York Herald Company v. Ottawa Citizen Company*, the majority opinion of the court noted that comic strips "may be that kind of brain product that the copyright might amongst other things be extended to or that copyright might cover," however, the court was "quite sure it never was intended those sections should apply to such a thing."[42]

These lawsuits have been recalled and discussed by writers of comic strip history, but none appear to have been cited or quoted in those studies. The opinions rendered in these cases provide insight into the development of copyright and trademark issues in cartoon art. They also offer a unique view of the early years of commercially successful comic strips from the perspective of their creators and the challenges these cartoonists faced.

LEGAL SOURCES CITED

Caliga v. Inter Ocean Newspaper Company, 215 U.S. 182, 30 S. Ct. 38, 54 L. Ed. 150 (1909).

"Decisions of the Commissioner of Patents and of United States Courts in Patent Cases, Decision of the Examiner of Interferences: *Star Company v. Fisher* (Decided December 22, 1916)," *Official Gazette of the United States Patent Office*, 236, no. 1 (March 6, 1917): 283–85.

Fisher v. Star Company, 160 N. Y. S. 693 (App. Div. 1916), *aff'd* 188 App. Div. 964, 176 N. Y. S. 964 (1919), *aff'd* 231 N. Y. 414, 132 N. E. 133, 19 A. L. R. 937 (1921), *cert. denied* 257 U.S. 654, 42 S. Ct. 94, 66 L. Ed. 419 (1921).

New York Herald Company v. Ottawa Citizen Company, 41 Can. S. Ct. 229 (1909).

New York Herald Company v. Star Company, 146 F. 204 (N. Y. App. Div. 1906), *aff'd* 146 F. 1023, 76 C. C. A. 678 (2nd. Cir. 1906).

Outcalt [sic] v. New York Herald, 146 F. 205 (N. Y. App. Div. 1906).

Outcault v. Bonbeur, 120 App. Div. 168, 104 N. Y. S. 1099 (1907).

Outcault v. Lamar, 135 App. Div. 110, 119 N. Y. S. 930 (1909).

Outcault v. New York Herald Company, 117 App. Div. 534, 102 N. Y. S. 685 (1907).

Outcault Advertising Company v. American Furniture Company, 10 Ga. App. 211, 73 S. E. 20 (1911).

Outcault Advertising Company v. Harry Joseph Clothing Company, 51 Ind. App. 55, 98 N. E. 1005 (1912).

Outcault Advertising Company v. Young Hardware Company, 110 Ark. 123, 161 S. W. 142 (Sup. Ct. 1913).

Press Publishing Company v. Falk, 59 F. 324 (N. Y. App. Div. 1894).

Press Publishing Company v. Morning Journal Association, 33 App. Div. 242, 53 N. Y. S. 371 (1898).

Press Publishing Company v. Morning Journal Association, 41 App. Div. 493, 58 N. Y. S. 708 (1899).

Star Company v. Fisher, 257 U.S. 654, 42 S. Ct. 94, 66 L. Ed. 419 (1921).

Star Company v. Press Publishing Company, 162 App. Div. 486, 147 N. Y. S. 579 (1914).

Star Company v. Wheeler Syndicate, Inc., 91 Misc. Rep. 640, 155 N. Y. S. 782 (App. Div. 1915). 160 N. Y. S. 689 (App. Div. 1916), *aff'd* 188 App . Div. 964, 176 N. Y. S. 923 (1919), *aff'd* 231 N. Y. 606, 132 N, E, 907 (1921), *cert. denied* 257 U.S. 654, 42 S. Ct. 94, 66 L. Ed. 419 (1921).

Wheeler Syndicate, Inc. v. Star Company, 160 N. Y. S. 693 (App. Div. 1916), *aff'd* 188 App. Div. 964, 176 N. Y. S. 925 (1919), 132 N. E. 907 (1921).

ENDNOTES

1. References to these cases proliferate in cartoon and comics histories written from the 1940s to the present day, although none of the literature cites a specific case or information from periodicals contemporary to the controversy. Writers who claim this to be so include Roy L. McCardell, "Opper, Outcault and Company: The Comic Supplement and the Men who Make It," *Everybody's Magazine* 12, no. 6 (June 1905): 764; William Murrell, *A History of American Graphic Humor, I865-1938* (New York: Macmillan, 1938), 138; Edward Pinkowski, *Forgotten Fathers* (Philadelphia: Sunshine Press, 1953), 161–62; Bill Blackbeard, "The Yellow Kid," in *The World Encyclopedia of Comics,* ed. Maurice Horn (New York: Chelsea House, 1976), 712; Richard Marschall, *America's Great Comic-Strip Artists* (New York: Abbeville, 1989), 25; and Judith O'Sullivan, *The Great American Comic Strip: One Hundred Years of Cartoon Art* (Boston: Bulfinch Press, 1990), plate facing 148.

2. McCardell, "Opper, Outcault and Company," 764.

3. Cartoons were granted copyright protection for specific drawings (including the elements of style, form, and composition) but did not equally protect the more abstract concept of character. A character could be depicted by any artist without fear of reprisal or legal action as long as the use of the character fell within the definition of "fair use." For further discussion of these issues, see Bruce P. Keller and David H. Bernstein, "As Satiric As They Wanna Be: Parody Lawsuits Under Trademark and Copyright Laws," *ALI-ABA Course of Study: Trademarks, Unfair Competition, and Copyrights, November 4-5, 1994, Washington, D. C.* (Philadelphia: American Law Institute, 1994), 151–78.

4. Pinkowski, *Forgotten Fathers,* 161–62.

5. Blackbeard, "The Yellow Kid," 712.

6. Coulton Waugh, *The Comics* (1947; repr., Jackson: University of Mississippi Press, 1991); Stephen Becker, *Comic Art in America* (New York: Simon and Schuster, 1959).

7. Marschall, *America's Great Comic-Strip Artists,* 25.

8. Richard Felton Outcault, "The Yellow Dugan Kid," [design] 1896 copyright registration (50565), Copyright Division, Library of Congress, repr., O'Sullivan, *The Great American Comic Strip,* plate facing 148. Registered later that year were "Yellow Kid," [design] 1896 copyright registration (66463) and "Design of the Yellow Kid," [design] 1896 copyright registration (68735).

9. J. Campbell Cory, "Four Days More and the Political Campaign of '96 Will be Over," *New York Journal,* October 30, 1896, 5; J. Campbell Cory, "De're off in a bunch," *New York Journal,* November 2, 1896, 3.

10. Archie Gunn, "George Boniface as a Chinese Yellow Kid," [Yellow Kid caricature] *New York Journal,* November 5, 1896, 6.

11. H. B. Eddy, "A Feast of Reason and a Flow of Sparkling Humor," [advertisement illustration] *New York Journal,* October 30, 1896, 2; H. B. Eddy, "Out on Sunday," [advertisement illustration] *New York Journal,* November 6, 1896, 5.

12. Charles Greening Bush, "Is He an Orphan?—Nit!" [Yellow Kid caricature] *New York Journal*, November 6, 1896, 2.

13. Outcault and Connor, NY, copyright assignment of *McFadden's Flats* and *Yellow Kid* to McLaughlin Brothers (4 February 1898), copyright assignments (vol. 19, p. 131), Copyright Division, Library of Congress. The nature of Connor's relationship to Outcault is unclear, but he appears to have been a business associate of some stature. Unfortunately, Connor's first name was not recorded in any of the documents discovered to date, but his last name appears in at least two copyright notices attached to Outcault's work. (See R. F. Outcault, "Johnny Jones' School Days," *Cleveland Plain Dealer*, February 20, 1898, 27; R. F. Outcault, "Johnny Jones' School Days," *Philadelphia Inquirer* February 20, 1898, 40.) *Johnny Jones' School Days* was a precursor to Outcault's *Kelly's Kindergarten* (later *Kelly's Kids*) that appeared in Pulitzer's *New York World* (and syndicated in Pulitzer's *St. Louis Post-Dispatch*) from 16 October 1898 ("Opening of Kelly's Kindergarten for the Kids in Kelly's Roost—The New Teacher Makes Her Bow," *St. Louis Post-Dispatch*, comic supplement, 4) through 6 August 1899 ("A Mad Dog Disturbs the Summer Repose of Kelly's Alley," *St. Louis Post-Dispatch*, comic supplement, 4). Outcault's freelance work in this period (for the *New York World*, the *New York Journal*, and miscellaneous newspapers) has been described by Richard Olson as Outcault's "lost period" (letter to the author, 8 November 1994). The examples that appear in the *New York World* show Outcault working with several established techniques of cartoon art: the panoramic single panel, focused single panel, and multiple frames. A variety of subjects (including social classes, ethnic groups, generational groups, and animals) with several locations (including street scenes, exteriors, interiors, and country/pastoral scenes) are shown. The story or "joke" of the piece is related in numerous ways, such as the two-line joke at the bottom of the drawing, the "foolish questions" later used by Rube Goldberg and Al Jaffee, pandemonium panels, physical comedy, reversal of expectation, and juxtaposition. This part of Outcault's work also includes a significant precursor to *Buster Brown*—"Bobby Jones's Painful Impressions of his Day on Grandfather's Farm," *St. Louis Post-Dispatch*, August 20, 1899, comic supplement, 4—which is one of the earliest examples of an Outcault child getting into seven kinds of trouble, then atoning for his sins with a posted resolution at the end of the feature.

14. R. F. Outcault, "Yellow Kids of All Nations," *New York Journal*, February 6, 1898, comic supplement.

15. *The Huckleberry Volunteers* began in the *New York Journal* as a commentary on the sinking of the *Maine* and the impending crisis with Spain. The feature ran in the daily newspaper from 8 April to 22 April 1898. The Yellow Kid made his first appearance in this series in "An Old Acquaintance Meets Them in Cuba and Assumes Charge" on 16 April and made a total of six appearances in this series of eleven cartoons.

16. R. F. Outcault, "The Casey Corner Kids' Dime Museum," *New York World*, May 1, 1898, comic supplement, 4; Outcault, "The Bud and Blossom of the Yellow Kid," *New York World*, May 1, 1898, comic supplement, 7.

17. This writer searched indices for plaintiffs or defendants in cases possibly involving Outcault, Hearst, Pulitzer, McLaughlin, and Connor (as personal and corporate names); *New York Journal* (including *N. Y. Journal* and *Journal*), *New York World* (including *N. Y. World* and *Publishing Company*, parent publishing of the *New York World*); and *Evening Journal Association*, *Morning Journal Association*, and *Star Company* (parent publishing companies of the *New York Journal*). Indices searched include the Lexis and Westlaw databases and the American Digest System's *1906 Decennial Edition of the American Digest: A Complete Table of American Cases from 1658 to 1906* (St. Paul: West Publishing Company, 1911). While the publishing companies were named in a small number of cases as both plaintiffs and defendants and suits existed between the two, a *Yellow Kid* case is not among them. See *Press Publishing Company v. Falk*, 59 F. 324 (N. Y. App. Div. 1894); *Press Publishing Company v. Morning Journal Association*, 33 App. Div. 242, 53 N. Y. S. 371 (1898); and *Press Publishing Company v. Morning Journal Association*, 41 App. Div. 493, 58 N. Y. S. 708 (1899).

18. Although some comic strip histories and published legal opinions refer to other cartoonists drawing *Buster Brown*, none are credited with assuming responsibly for the comic strip. Richard Olson notes that the later non-Outcault *Buster Brown* installments in the *New York Herald* were unsigned and "clearly inferior" (telephone interview, 20 December 1994).

19. *New York Herald Company v. Star Company*, 146 F. 204 (N. Y. App. Div. 1906).

20. *New York Herald Company v. Star Company*, 146 F. 204

21. *Outcalt* [sic] *v. New York Herald*, 146 F. 205 (N. Y. App. Div. 1906).

22. *Outcalt* [sic] *v. New York Herald*, 146 F. 205.

23. *Outcalt* [sic] *v. New York Herald*, 146 F. 205.

24. It is, of course, possible that a *Yellow Kid* case was heard in court but did not have an impact on later lawsuits specifically involving Outcault. Recent reports have circulated about court documents relating to *The Yellow Kid*, but specific information about their contents has not been published.

25. *Outcault v. New York Herald Company*, 117 App. Div. 534, 102 N. Y. S. 685 (1907).

26. *Outcault v. New York Herald Company*, 117 App. Div. 534, 102 N. Y. S. 685.

27. *New York Herald Company v. Ottawa Citizen Company*, 41 Can. S. Ct. 229 (1909).

28. 10 Ga. App. 211, 73 S. E. 20 (1911).

29. 51 Ind. App. 55, 98 N. E. 1005 (1912).

30. 110 Ark. 123, 161 S. W. 142 (Sup. Ct. 1913).

31. *Outcault v. Bonheur*, 120 App. Div. 168, 104 N. Y. S. 1099 (1907).

32. *Outcault v. Lamar*, 135 App. Div. 110, 119 N. Y. S. 930 (1909).

33. *Star Company v. Press Publishing Company*, 162 App. Div. 486, 147 N. Y. S. 579 (1914).

34. *Star Company v. Wheeler Syndicate, Inc.*, 91 Misc. Rep. 640, 155 N. Y. S. 782 (App. Div. 1915).

35. "Decisions of the Commissioner of Patents and of United States Courts in Patent Cases, Decision of the Examiner of Interferences: *Star Company v. Fisher* (Decided December 22, 1916)," *Official Gazette of the United States Patent Office*, 236 no. 1 (March 6, 1917): 283–85.

36. *Star Company v. Wheeler Syndicate, Inc.*, 91 Misc. Rep. 640, 155 N. Y. S. 782 (App. Div. 1915), 160 N. Y. S. 689 (App. Div. 1916), *aff'd* 188 App. Div. 964. 176 N. Y. S. 923 0919), *aff'd* 231 N. Y. 606, 132 N. E. 907 (1921), *cert. denied* 257 U.S. 654, 42 S. Ct. 94, 66 L. Ed. 419 (1921); *Fisher v. Star Company*, 160 N. Y. S. 693 (App. Div. 1916), *aff'd* 188 App. Div. 964, 176 N. Y. S. 964 (1919), *aff'd* 231 N. Y. 414, 132 N. E. 133. 19 A. L. R. 937 (1921), *cert. denied* 257 U.S. 654, 42 S. Ct. 94, 66 L. Ed. 419 (1921); and *Wheeler Syndicate, Inc. v. Star Company*, 160 N. Y. S. 693 (App. Div. 1916), *aff'd* 188 App. Div. 964, 176 N. Y. S. 925 (1919), 132 N. E. 907 (N. Y. 1921).

37. For further information about the circumstances and relationship between Fisher and the Star Company, see Robert C. Harvey, "Bud Fisher and the Daily Comic Strip," *INKS: Cartoon and Comic Art Studies* 1 (February 1994): 14–25.

38. *New York Herald Company v. Star Company*, 146 F. 204.

39. *New York Herald Company v. Ottawa Citizen Company*, 41 Can. S. Ct. 229.

40. *Star Company v. Press Publishing Company*, 162 App. Div. 486, 147 N. Y. S. 579.

41. *Star Company v. Wheeler Syndicate, Inc.*, 91 Misc. Rep. 640, 155 N. Y. S. 782 (App. Div. 1915).

42. *New York Herald Company v. Ottawa Citizen Company*, 41 Can. S. Ct. 229.

Crusading for World Peace

Ding Darling, Woodrow Wilson, and the League of Nations

RICHARD SAMUEL WEST

JAY N. "DING" DARLING (1876–1962), longtime cartoonist for *The Des Moines Register*, is widely remembered as a conservative cartoonist, but close examination of his work in a variety of areas—the tariff, rights of labor, prohibition, the New Deal—reveals his politics to have been far more progressive than the average Republican and even more progressive than most Americans of his day. No issue exemplifies this progressive streak more fully than Ding's views on international disarmament and world peace. This paper examines Ding's work over a twenty-year period, from his earliest comments on the issue of peace between nations during the Theodore Roosevelt administration to the last gasps of the pro-League of Nations movement during the Coolidge administration.

Looking back on the pivotal years after World War I when the nation wrestled with the question of whether or not to join the League of Nations, one cartoonist—Ding Darling—emerges from the hot and furious debate as the league's most ardent champion. To say the least, this loyal Republican from the isolationist state of Iowa was not the most likely proponent of a Democratic president's plan to ensure international peace.

From the time he began cartooning in 1902, Ding aligned himself with Teddy Roosevelt, whom he admired in equal parts for his bold acts of leadership and for his physical courage. When TR vastly expanded the nation's parkland, Ding became an advocate for conservation. When TR attacked the nation's millionaires, Ding decried the greediness of the wealthy. When TR bolted the GOP in 1912, Ding became a Progressive, too. And when TR became a spokesman for preparedness in the early days of World War I, Ding pushed the issue in his cartoons.

But unlike TR, Ding was no jingoist. His first images of war came to him through his father, Marc Darling. The elder Darling had been brutalized by his participation in the American Civil War, and he did not romanticize the experience with his children. The respectable citizens of Sioux City, Iowa, where Ding grew up, valued physical courage and honored heroism, but they were circumspect people who did not go about looking for trouble. Trouble was easy enough to find in the Sioux City of Ding's youth because it was a wild, hard town, full of brothels and gambling halls. Rarely a week went by when the body of some poor soul did not turn up in the Missouri River. Ding appears to have been a product of all of these influences. He was not a physical coward, but neither did he lust for the fight. For instance, despite being the perfect age, there is no evidence that he ever considered enlisting in the armed forces during the Spanish–American War. While Ding never knew the activities of war, he fully appreciated its brutal cost.

And loss of human life was not the only cost of war. From his earliest days as a cartoonist, Ding railed against excessive military spending. In one 1909 cartoon, titled "The Great International Rat Hole," Ding pictured the dominant countries of the world dumping "Public Tax" monies into a hole labeled "For a navy that can whip everybody else's." Ding laments in the caption, "[They are] pouring hundreds of millions in annually, and it's no nearer full now than when they began."[1] At the same time, every international effort to curb the war impulse received his gentle support. When, for example, in August of 1911, England, France and the United States signed a treaty outlawing war, Ding greeted the idealistic agreement with hope, showing the three world powers marching arm in arm down the slope of Mount Olympus after having fitted a disgruntled Mars with a safety valve.[2]

In 1914, when war broke out in Europe, Ding drew the despairing cartoon, "After All, Civilization is Only Skin Deep." In it he pictured the primal instincts of Man, carrying the club of war, skulking through the edifices humankind created to art, science, learning, and brotherhood. In another cartoon titled, "Forever Going to School but Never Learning," Ding depicted the world as a schoolboy wearing a dunce's cap. Mars has him by the ear in an effort to get

THE GREAT INTERNATIONAL RAT HOLE

POURING HUNDREDS OF MILLIONS IN ANNUALLY, AND IT'S NO NEARER FULL NOW THAN WHEN THEY BEGAN.

FIGURE 17. Jay N. Darling, "The Great International Rat Hole," October 19, 1909.

him to pay attention to the lesson on the board, which reads: "War = death, paralyzed industry, endless sorrow, nobody's gain, famine, destitution, waste, misery."[3]

Not only had humanity never learned, but Ding believed it never would. In the cartoon, "From the Beginning of Time," he shook his head in disbelief at the "experts" who believed that this war, simply because of its unparalleled ferocity, would be the last.[4]

FIGURE 18. Jay N. Darling, "After All, Civilization Is Only Skin Deep," [1914].

FIGURE 19. Jay N. Darling, "Preparedness Invites War—Likewise Fire Escapes Invite Fire," October 15, 1916.

Inevitably, the fighting in Europe changed Ding's views on military spending. In 1915, he joined TR in the call for preparedness. In his view, the threat
posed by the violence and hatred gripping the European continent justified
such spending. Ding depicted the U.S. military as a shepherd fast asleep, oblivious to the animals representing threats to American security that were trampling on international laws and the rights of a neutral nation.[5]

But Ding and TR were in the minority. Most Americans saw the war as a
European crisis in which we had no stake, a crisis that we could easily avoid
if we only maintained neutrality. Stockpiling armaments did not strike most
Americans as a neutral act. Ding emphatically rejected this logic. To those
who argued that preparedness invited war, he showed a desperate soul pulling
down a fire escape because fire escapes make fires, burning up his umbrellas
because umbrellas make it rain, and shooing away the police because policemen bring burglars. In the final panel, Ding places the poor soul in an insane
asylum, where he comments in his own defense, "Why, I'm no worse than the
man who said preparedness invites war."[6]

The debate quickly polarized the nation, as Theodore Roosevelt became
identified as the nation's most outspoken belligerent and William Jennings
Bryan, Ding's *bête noir*, took on the role of leading pacifist. In his dozen or
so years as a cartoonist, Ding had never passed up an opportunity to ridicule Bryan. As Wilson's well intentioned but naive secretary of state, Bryan
gave him many opportunities, perhaps the choicest being his soft-headed
campaign for world peace in the midst of war. On the other hand, Ding was
always kindly disposed to TR's point of view, even when the former president's volcanic outbursts seemed to hurt more than help the cause they both
championed.[7]

Though TR held center stage on the issue of preparedness, by 1916 President Woodrow Wilson had become an advocate for preparedness too. Ding
did not vote for Wilson in either 1912 or 1916, but he did support the president
on occasion when he thought Wilson was right.[8] Wilson had joined the ranks
of preparedness advocates only reluctantly. Wilson, the man, was constitutionally repelled by acts of violence. Like Ding, he deplored the toll of war
and could make little sense out of it. But he had been won over to the issue of
preparedness over two years' time as he sought to execute his delicate policy
of neutrality. Though it was a political success, it posed vexing problems as
an economic theory: Wilson expected the British and the Germans to respect
America's right of commerce, but the maneuverings of war made that theory difficult, if not impossible, to execute in practice. Wilson was incensed
by Germany's decision to fire upon any ship that was found in the war zone,
but he sympathized with England's naval blockade of Germany, even though

IS THE ANSWER TO THIS AN INTERNATIONAL POLICE FORCE?

FIGURE 20. Jay N. Darling, "Is The Answer To This an International Police Force?" [1918].

FIGURE 21. Jay N. Darling, "The Python," [1918].

both practices disrupted American commerce. Clearly, the policy of neutrality would not hold indefinitely.[9]

Even before he asked for a declaration of war, President Wilson was devoting most of his thoughts to the type of world that should be created after the war was over—a vision that would justify the carnage and the madness. Ding drew his first cartoon on the subject of an international league during the 1916 campaign season. The cartoon depicted war as a robber, making off with the world's savings while "this old world" sits in the corner, bound, gagged, and bloodied. In the caption, Ding asks, "Is the answer to this [act of violence] an international police force?" Wilson, it appears, had already concluded that the answer was yes. Ding would arrive at that position more slowly.[10]

Meanwhile, the tone of his cartoons became increasingly belligerent. He was frustrated by America's—and particularly the Midwest's—isolationist tendencies and believed the country was in for a rude awakening. In January 1917 he pictured Uncle Sam looking on as the Rights of Humanity lay crippled on a roadside. Ding asked his audience what they expected of the United States: "Pharisee or Good Samaritan?" The war led many an artist to indulge in melodramatic images, and Ding was no exception. Increasingly, he was inclined to depict the German military machine as a python intent on swallowing the globe, or the German leadership as butchers, carving up the countries they invaded like meat in a slaughterhouse.[11]

In April, Ding got what he wanted, what he thought was America's only option: a declaration of war. The potency of the moment, however, gave him pause. Instead of glorying in the news or swaggering about the global stage, Ding struck a philosophical note. He proclaimed the U.S. renunciation of neutrality to be "Our First Victory." The cartoon featured a determined Uncle Sam unsheathing the sword of battle while his alter ego cringes on the ground, a cowering pathetic figure, protecting a hoard of gold. At the close of the war, Ding would write of that time that "we, as a nation . . . passed from a state of blind and selfish pacifism to one of active belligerency, righteous determination, self-sacrifice and glorious victory."[12]

Throughout the war, Ding kept the home fires burning by exhorting Americans to renounce pettiness and embrace the best within themselves. He showed soldiers of different classes sharing food with one another and commented, "Some of these days we'll learn to apply the same lesson at home." He pictured a mother waiting on the porch for a letter from her soldier son and reminded his audience, "Buying Liberty Bonds seems a simple matter when we consider the burdens others are carrying." When he overheard a Des Moines housewife at a party say she was tired of giving and giving, he funneled his outrage into the next day's cartoon. Titled "Tired of Giving? You Don't Know What It Is to Be Tired," he drew a portrait of a distraught mother and child sitting amid the bombed-out ruins of their home, exhausted, hungry, disconsolate.[13]

In the fall of 1918, as the war rushed toward a conclusion, Ding could not contain his optimism. In a cartoon that expressed sentiments diametrically opposite to the cynical one he drew at the beginning of the war, he asked, "Are we completing a cycle?" In the four-panel cartoon he reasoned: "Individuals used to settle their differences with the stone ax until they learned it was more profitable to co-operate and join together in clans. Clans fought each other for centuries until they found that through the medium of a state they could settle their differences without bloodshed. States attempted to settle their differences through the medium of the cannon and sword until they learned the advantage of national unity. Nations are now fighting the bloodiest war in history for supremacy. Is it not possible that out of it may come an international league to enforce peace?"[14]

The signing of the armistice in November 1918 marked the end of the military conflict and the beginning of a diplomatic war. The Paris Peace Conference would turn into one of the most tragic chapters of world history. During the two years that followed the armistice, President Wilson went from being regarded as a world savior and international man of peace to a bedridden old man, a political pariah even within his own party. Oddly enough, during this same period, Ding's estimation of and support for the president soared. By the time Wilson died in 1924, Ding had come to regard him almost as a mythic figure. For all of his love for the ideals and policies of Theodore Roosevelt, Ding exhibited his first passion for a president's position in his support for Wilson and the League of Nations.

Ding had to find a reason for the war. He could not justify the killing fields in Europe and the thousands of Americans, in particular, who had died there if the nation immediately abandoned what Ding regarded as its better self to return to the ruthless pursuit of money that had characterized the pre-war years. Wilson's vision of a league of nations in which the nations of the world could resolve their disputes through debate and arbitration spoke to Ding's need to impose purpose on the carnage.[15] He found a political justification for the league as well. War debts, boundary disputes, and other problems in Europe cried out for a league. In one cartoon, he shows old Mrs. World surrounded by dozens of screaming, fighting children, some of whom look up in surprise at the efficient-looking, well-dressed woman, labeled "League of Nations," who has appeared at their door. Ding's comment: "The sooner we can engage a governess the better."[16]

While Ding was expressing a majority sentiment, there was a vocal minority, headed by several influential Republicans in Congress, who were steadfastly opposed to the notion of a league. They believed the league would compromise America's independence, and they attacked it by employing xenophobic and partisan appeals. Ding was fully conscious of the threat that they posed to Wilson's dream, and he began hitting at them with frequency. Some of his cartoons ridiculed. To those Republicans who faulted Wilson for not including any leading Republicans in the peace delegation, Ding pictured the houses of Congress as back-seat drivers hectoring Wilson with one directive after another. Ding suggests that this was "probably the reason he didn't want 'em along on the trip to Paris." Some of the cartoons cast opposition to the league in monumental terms. On Christmas Day 1918, Ding juxtaposed the star of Bethlehem with a star representing a "League to Enforce Peace," and asked, "Will some new Herod of national ambition or political jealousy destroy this one, too?"[17]

Splits among the allies soon soured the proceedings in Paris, and even members of congress who supported the league began talking about amendments. Ding characterized congressional objections as absurd, arguing that the covenant provided more than enough latitude to accommodate any of our national interests. When the league was finally born in April, Ding celebrated the achievement by comparing it to the old hen in the barnyard who defies all skeptics and hatches a chick after all.[18]

When Wilson returned home in July, he received a hero's welcome. Ding characterized the event as "the end of another momentous chapter," but allowed that history would probably need "100 years or so" to pass a mature judgment on the proceedings. Still, that did not stop Ding from wading into the debate that ensued upon Wilson's return. He knew Wilson's league was in for trouble. Just after welcoming him home, he showed Wilson as a transatlantic traveler being stopped at customs for a baggage search. The agents are the leading league opponents and they make a big mess of all his luggage contents, much to his dismay.[19]

Republican leadership in Congress seemed intent on foiling what had become perceived as the president's peace treaty, and Ding chalked up their balkiness to petty politics, plain and simple. Ding stood with the increasingly intransigent Wilson in rejecting all attempts to qualify America's participation in the league, even those posed by moderate Republicans who were sincere supporters of the concept of a league for peace. Ding characterized the debate as one between extremists who wanted to kill the league and moderates who wanted to alter it. Neither path had Ding's support; he believed it was just fine as it stood. Ding outlined the debate in a two frame cartoon titled, "Removing the Adenoid to Improve the Breathing." In the top frame, he pictured a crazed Senator William Borah from Idaho lining up the blade of his axe with the neck of a little girl in hair bow and petticoats, labeled "Peace Treaty." In the bottom frame, he showed the more moderate Republicans Taft, Hughes, Lodge, and Root, as surgeons preparing to operate on the little girl. Ding's caption: "It is generally conceded that Doc Borah's method of removing the adenoid just below the necktie is probably unnecessarily severe. But that a slight operation by specialists would be both painless and beneficial." To this, Ding depicts Wilson explaining to the eager surgeons, "But the child hasn't any adenoids."[20]

In the summer of 1919, Senator Henry Cabot Lodge emerged as the leading opponent to the league. Ding considered him a pompous, self-righteous man (much as Lodge's supporters viewed Wilson) and he portrayed the senator's imperiousness in a number of cartoons. In the clownishly sad, "The Art Student's Masterpiece and the Professor's Criticism," he showed Wilson presenting Lodge with his "Peace Treaty" painting of the Goddess of Peace. Lodge hurrumphs that it "needs touching up in a few places," so he relieves the president of his palette and brush and proceeds to ruin Wilson's masterpiece.[21]

By the end of the 1919 legislative session it became clear to all but the most starry-eyed that the United States was not going to enter the league. When civil strife broke out in Poland and the league responded feebly, American opponents of the league took this as an indication of inadequacy. Ding took umbrage with this logic. In "There! Didn't We Tell You It Wouldn't Work?" he showed Europe beckoning to the league fire department to go douse the flames engulfing Poland. The league fire engine crew is ready to roll, except for one small detail: the fire engine is missing its right rear wheel, labeled "U.S. League Membership." Uncle Sam is passively watching the disaster unfold, using the wheel as a seat. Flanking Uncle Sam are league opponents Lodge, Borah, Hearst, and others, who taunt the frustrated fire crew, "Ha-Ha-Ha! Why don't you go put out the fire?"[22]

Ding, like Wilson, hoped the 1920 presidential campaign would become a referendum on U.S. membership in the league. But the Republican candidate, Warren G. Harding, danced around the issue, advocating greater participation in the World Court but not in the league. The Democratic candidate James M. Cox talked up league membership, but he seemed to do so without conviction. Harding was urging America to return to its isolationist roots and avoid foreign entanglements. Cox, in turn, tried to paint the Republicans as robber-baron elitists, awash in ill-gotten gains. Ding brought both candidates to task for sidestepping the league issue, and he seemed despondent when Harding won in a landslide.[23]

Despite the election results, Ding did not give up hopes for international peacekeeping efforts. In April 1921, league opponent William Borah began to promote the idea of a US–UK naval disarmament conference. Somewhat

THE ART STUDENT'S MASTERPIECE AND THE
PROFESSOR'S CRITICISM

FIGURE 22. Jay N. Darling, "The Art Student's Masterpiece and The Professor's Criticism,"
[1920].

FIGURE 23. Jay N. Darling, "There! Didn't We Tell You It Wouldn't Work?" [1920].

unconventionally, he viewed international disarmament as a logical extension of his isolationist politics. With the war over, Ding reverted to his earlier position on weapons spending, arguing that it was a waste of money. Ding drew Uncle Sam at a ticket window, considering his summer vacation options. One travel poster promotes "the Great Armament Race" at rates of "$3,000,000 a day and up!" The other extols the "International Disarmament Beach" as "quiet, inexpensive" and "$3 a day board & room." As Uncle Sam ponders his options, the American taxpayer/porter struggles under the weight of Uncle Sam's luggage, labeled "War Taxes."[24]

After the Senate unanimously passed Borah's bill, President Harding upped the ante by calling the global powers to a disarmament conference to discuss all forms of disarmament. Ding reacted to the news with joy, depicting Harding as David stunning the Goliath of world armaments with his disarmament conference pebble.[25] When the conference convened in Washington in November, Secretary of State Hughes shocked the participants by proposing sweeping reductions in U.S., British, and Japanese navies, along with a ten-year construction "holiday." Ding traveled to Washington for the opening proceedings and was heartened by the mood there. As the conference continued its work at year's end, Ding was inclined to give the first nine months of the Harding administration high marks, especially for its disarmament work.[26]

The conference ended in February with much to show for its efforts. Conference participants adopted three treaties: the Hughes proposals (with modest alterations), a treaty outlawing poisonous gas and submarine warfare, and a treaty that legitimized the status quo in the Pacific, which had the effect of blocking further Japanese expansion for a decade. Ding was particularly supportive of the Pacific treaty, believing it effectively outlawed unrest in the Pacific for the near future. Congress was not so enthusiastic, particularly the isolationists, who were concerned about entangling alliances, and some of the Democrats, who were loath to accept the idea of a Republican administration success.[27]

Ding was growing tired of such partisan rancor; he said as much in a four-panel cartoon he drew in March. The cartoon sequence begins with Wilson and Miss Democracy proudly sending off their little girl, labeled "League of Nations," with spring lilies for the Republican neighbors next door. Instead of welcoming the child, the Republicans batter her with bricks and stones. Then the GOP leaders send forth their little boy, "Arms Treaties," with a bouquet of flowers for the Democrats, who, of course, respond with an assault of their own. Ding's comment: "These family feuds may be great for family pride but they're kind of tough on the children."[28] Eventually the treaties were ratified with lukewarm Democratic support and amendments that stated that they carried no obligation to defend other nations.

FIGURE 24. Jay N. Darling, "These Family Feuds May Be Great for Family Pride but They're Kind of Tough on the Children," March 10, 1922.

On the other front, U.S. participation in the league, not much had changed. Generally, the Harding administration ignored the league, though in 1922 it did begin sending "unofficial observers" to league conferences of interest, particularly those in the areas of health and sexual issues. Even though public support for some kind of involvement in international peace-keeping efforts remained high, most politicians and newspaper barons considered it a bad idea. Ding expressed his frustration with this line of thinking in his cartoon "Millions of Boys to Fight but Not One Delegate for Prevention." In the face of war, said Ding, the overweight stay-at-homes couldn't send off young doughboys to the fighting fast enough. The politician intones "We'll win if it takes every boy in America," and the editor chimes in, "We should have ten million men over there right now." Ding commented bitterly, "With what generous idealism we gave the lives of the boys to the practical job of stopping bullets. . . . But what practical hard-headed businessmen we become when a small contribution of intelligent counsel is desired for the sake of prevention."[29]

Harding had made positive noises about membership in the World Court during the campaign, but had done nothing his first two years in office to make it happen. In 1923 Secretary of State Hughes finally put before Congress a bill for U.S. participation in the World Court, with four reservations involving financial obligations and prerogatives. Harding died in August 1923, before action was taken on the reservations. When Coolidge pressed for passage of the bill, Ding applauded. His cartoon shows Coolidge, the stationmaster of Isolationville, flagging down the World Court locomotive for passenger Uncle Sam. While Coolidge works, however, Lodge and his senate cronies use reservation nails to hammer Uncle Sam's coattails and luggage to the platform floor. Ding, mixing his tenses, ambiguously captions the cartoon, "Begins to Look As If We Never Would Get Out of This Jerkwater Town." From this it is difficult to say if Ding believed the United States would finally escape "Isolationville," or if Uncle Sam would be stuck on that platform forever.[30]

In the end, however, it was Coolidge and not Congress that added one fatal reservation to the World Court membership proposal: that the United States not be bound by opinions rendered by the court without U.S. consent. Congress passed the bill, with all five reservations, but the other member nations of the court refused to accept Coolidge's fifth proviso, arguing that it cut to the very heart of the court's ability to enforce its decisions. Coolidge responded by saying the issue was not negotiable. His intransigence—and later world events—would forever make the matter of U.S. participation in the World Court and the league moot. Two years after his pro-Coolidge "Isolationville" cartoon, Ding drew another town, "World Peaceville," in which he abandoned all hope for progress toward peace. The World Peaceville railroad station is boarded up, the real estate office is closed, and the landscape is dotted with signs announcing the good intentions of the United States and Europe who have purchased lots but will now never build on them.[31]

Ding's hero, Wilson, slipped out of the national spotlight in March 1921, but Ding did not forget him. When the ex president died in February 1924, Ding drew not one but two memorial cartoons to the crusader for world peace: The first showed a stricken Wilson and a grieving Angel of Peace, driving away the specters of Death, War, and Hatred. It was titled "That Peace Which in Life was Denied Him." Two days later, he drew one of his most powerful cartoons. It featured a vignette of a shepherd's mountain-top cabin in the midst of a lashing snowstorm. A black wreath hangs on the cabin door, and a staff labeled "International Leadership" lies abandoned in the snow. Surrounding the vignette is a forbidding snowscape, crowded with bleating sheep, lost in the driving storm and sure to perish. In his caption, Ding lamented: "And no shepherd has since come forth to take his place."[32]

Ding would draw cartoons for another twenty-five years. He would live through another world war and applaud Franklin D. Roosevelt's efforts to establish the United Nations, but he would never again feel as hopeful as he did in the heady days following World War I when a shepherd appeared in the guise of Woodrow Wilson, intent on leading the world into an era of peace.

ENDNOTES

1. Jay N. Darling, "The Great International Rat Hole," *The Des Moines Register and Leader,* October 19, 1909, 1.

2. Jay N. Darling, "No More Blowups," *The Des Moines Register and Leader,* August 15, 1911, 1.

3. Jay N. Darling, "After All, Civilization Is Only Skin Deep," and "Forever Going to School But Never Learning" reprinted in Darling, *Condensed Ink* (Des Moines, IA: The Des Moines Register and Leader, 1914), 98, 120.

4. Jay N. Darling, "From the Beginning of Time," reprinted in Darling, *Condensed Ink,* 105.

5. Jay N. Darling, "Under the Hay-cock Fast Asleep," *The Des Moines Register and Leader,* June 2, 1915, 1.

6. Jay N. Darling, "Preparedness Invites War—Likewise Fire Escapes Invite Fire," *The Des Moines Register and Leader,* October 15, 1916, 1.

7. See Jay N. Darling, "The Dreamer," *The Des Moines Register and Leader,* March 23, 1916, 1 and Jay N. Darling, "An Interruption in the Shopping Expedition," *Des Moines Register and Leader,* April 19, 1916, 1.

8. Jay N. Darling, "Making Sure They're Clean" and "There Was a Chicken in That Egg After All," reprinted in Darling, *Condensed Ink,* 31, 85.

9. August Heckscher, *Woodrow Wilson: A Biography* (New York: Charles Scribner's Sons, 1991), 359–433.

10. Jay N. Darling, "Is the Answer to This an International Police Force?," reprinted in Jay N. Darling, *In Peace and War* (Des Moines, IA: The Des Moines Register, 1918), 56.

11. Jay N. Darling, "Pharisee or Good Samaritan?," "The Python," "The Butchers of Potsdam," reprinted in Jay N. Darling, *Aces and Kings* (Des Moines, IA: The Des Moines Register, 1918), 8, 10, 14.

12. Jay N. Darling, "Our First Victory," reprinted in Darling, *Aces and Kings*, 16.

13. Jay N. Darling, "Some of These Days We'll Learn to Apply the Same Lesson at Home," "Buying Liberty Bonds Seems a Simple Matter When We Consider the Burdens Others Are Carrying," "Tired of Giving?," reprinted in Darling, *Aces and Kings*, 32, 69, 51.

14. Jay N. Darling, "Are We Completing the Cycle?," reprinted in Darling, *Aces and Kings*, 97.

15. Jay N. Darling, "Is It Possible We Will Go Right Back to It?," *The Des Moines Register*, November 14, 1918, 1.

16. Jay N. Darling, "The Sooner We Can Engage a Governess the Better," *The Des Moines Register*, November 16, 1918, 1.

17. Jay N. Darling, "Back Seat Driver," *The Des Moines Register*, December 2, 1918, 1; Jay N. Darling, "Will Some New Herod of National Ambition or Political Jealousy Destroy This One, Too?," *The Des Moines Register*, December 25, 1918, 1.

18. Jay N. Darling, "A Big Hole in the Barn for the Big Cat and Then a little Hole for the Little Cat," *The Des Moines Register*, March 4, 1919, 1; Jay N. Darling, "The Old Hen Seems to Have Hatched Something Out of the Doorknob After All," *The Des Moines Register*, April 16, 1919, 1.

19. Jay N. Darling, "The End of Another Momentous Chapter," *The Des Moines Register*, July 12, 1919, 1; Jay N. Darling, "No European Trip Is Quite Complete 'Till You've Been Through the Ordeal at the Custom House," *The Des Moines Register*, July 14, 1919, 1.

20. Jay N. Darling, "Removing the Adenoid to Improve the Breathing," *The Des Moines Register*, August 4, 1919, 1.

21. Jay N. Darling, "The Art Student's Masterpiece and the Professor's Criticism," reprinted in Jay N. Darling, *The Jazz Era* (Des Moines, IA: The Des Moines Register, 1920), 49.

22. Jay. N. Darling, "There! Didn't We Tell You It Wouldn't Work?," reprinted in Darling, *The Jazz Era*, 57.

23. Jay N. Darling, "Delivering It to the Wrong Door," *The Des Moines Register*, September 10, 1920, 1.

24. Jay N. Darling, "Let's See Now, Where Should We Spend the Summer?" *The Des Moines Register*, April 23, 1921, 1.

25. Jay N. Darling, "David, Goliath, and the Little Pebble," *The Des Moines Register*, July 13, 1921, 1.

26. Jay N. Darling, "There's Plenty More Big Game in the Woods for Those Who Know How to Shoot," *The Des Moines Register*, December 16, 1921, 1.

27. *The Des Moines Register*, January 23, 1922, 1.

28. Jay N. Darling, "These Family Feuds May Be Great for Family Pride but They're Kind of Tough on the Children," *The Des Moines Register*, March 10, 1922, 1.

29. Jay N. Darling, "Millions of Boys to Fight but Not One Delegate for Prevention," *The Des Moines Register*, April 24, 1923, 1.

30. Jay N. Darling, "Begins to Look As If We Never Would Get Out of This Jerkwater Town," *The Des Moines Register*, May 30, 1924, 1.

31. Jay N. Darling, "The Deserted Village," *The Des Moines Register*, April 19, 1926, 1.

32. Jay N. Darling, "And No Shepherd Has Since Come Forth To Take His Place," *The Des Moines Register*, February 4, 1924, 1; February 6, 1924, 1.

Picture Stories

Eric Drooker and the Tradition of Woodcut Novels

DAVID BERONÄ

An artist must have more than technical virtuosity to sustain a complete book without text; he must have wide creative range and total artistic integrity as well. This makes the whole book the work of art.[1]

—Lee Kingman, "High Art of Illustration"

The only two techniques that really are of artistic importance are rarely or never mentioned in essays and books upon the graphic techniques. They are those of pictorial imagination and sharp-sighted, sensitive draughtsmanship.[2]

—Williams M. Ivans Jr., *How Prints Look*

WITH THE PUBLICATION of Eric Drooker's *Flood! A Novel in Pictures,* the public was invited back to a form—the woodcut novel—whose rich tradition was an essential link in the development of pictorial narrative in the comic arts. Not constricted by any language barrier, this early form of cartooning without text or word balloons was available to every reader. Themes of alienation; mechanization; the return to a more pure, primitive society; and human annihilation were addressed in woodcut novels. This universality of human experience, the essence of cartooning, owes much to early woodcut novels. The revival of this form and these themes by Drooker, in his own unique picture stories, brings back the full dramatic power of black and white pictures without words.

With the revival of the woodcut in the early part of the twentieth century, a small number of book illustrators—notably the Belgian Frans Masereel and the American Lynd Ward—successfully introduced their "woodcut novels" to a curious public.[3] Though it is possible to concentrate on the enormous contributions of Masereel and Ward as strictly book illustrators, the focus of this article is on their woodcut novels, dismissed by many as being merely, on one hand, "experimental"[4] and, on the other hand, "inspired and innovative."[5] Although both Masereel and Ward were prolific and heralded book

FIGURE 25. Woodcut (3½ × 2¾ in.) by Frans Masereel from *Passionate Journey*, first published under the title *Mein Stundenbuch* (Munich: Kurt Wolff Verlag, 1919). Note the white streaks on the hero's coat and pants, an identifying trademark of Masereel.

illustrators,[6] their woodcut novels were the means for each man's personal vision to reach beyond the conventional relationship of the illustrator and the book. These woodcut novels, exempting the written word, combined technical prowess of wood engraving with inventive visions that had as their major themes social satire and the role of the artist in society.[7] Not regarded as book illustrations or print albums, these remarkable books remained relatively ignored by the bibliophiles and the graphic arts community until noted by Scott McCloud as "missing link[s]" and "powerful modern fables, now praised by comic artists, but seldom recognized as comics."[8]

In 1917 Masereel published his first set of woodcuts in book format rather than the traditional print albums of the day. The first two of his twelve woodcut novels were entitled *Debout Les Morts* (*Arise Ye Dead*), with ten woodcuts, and *Les Morts Parlent* (*The Dead Speak*), a series of seven woodcuts. Both these novels, similar to the woodcuts of his contemporary Käthe Kollwitz, represented the human devastation and the suffering of the victims of World War I.

Masereel's most successful and unique woodcut novel of 167 blocks was published in 1919 under the title *Mon Livre d'Heures* (*Mein Stundenbuch* in German). Thousands of copies were sold throughout the world, including two American editions under the titles of *My Book of Hours* and *Passionate Journey*.[9] In his extensive preface to the German edition, Thomas Mann captured the mood and spirit of Masereel's work:

> As you go through these pages, immerse yourself in the great riddle of this dream of life here on earth. It is as nothing, since it ends and dissolves into nothingness. Yet everywhere in this nothingness, quickening it to life, the infinite is at hand! Look and enjoy and let your joy in contemplation be deepened by brotherly confidence.[10]

This woodcut novel portrays the experiences of a young man entering a city. He is a witness and, later, a participant in all the experiences that life offers from the tragic to the comic. The skill with which Masereel is able to weave the emotional ties between the reader and the main character on black and white blocks with dimensions of only 3½ × 2¾ inches is noteworthy. Masereel's original monochrome technique disregarded light and shadow in favor of flat, legible images. "A face may be half black and a coat half white if the composition requires it. This accounts for those typical masculine figures wearing black garments with broad white streaks—an original device of Masereel's which is a badge of his style."[11] The reader's focus on the hero is highlighted not only by this device but also because of the limited expression of the subject's background in each block. The simple style, however, is misleading. Masereel captures the heart of the reader in much the same way as other cartoonists in the display of the magic of sequential art with less, rather than more, realistic representation of the action. He gives us a picture of a macadam street and allows us to walk down it alone, at our own pace, and with our own set of experiences.

Masereel continued to produce his woodcut novels portraying his concern for society's ills. "I find people's minds are so confused today that no one can make head or tail of anything, and in this outrageously technological consumer society people seem more and more mad, and no longer able to tell which way up they are."[12] Most notable among the later woodcut novels was *La Ville* (*The Town* or *The City*), with 100 blocks. Masereel gouged out pictures

FIGURE 26. Engraving on lead plate (2¾ × 2¾ in.) by Otto Nückel for *Destiny: A Novel in Pictures,* published under the title *Shicksal* (Munich: Delphin Verlag, 1930). Vigorous hatching allowed Nückel to sustain the somber mood of the plot.

of urban decay where vulgarity seemed to be the norm of the masses who lived in a hostile, industrial environment similar to the satirical vision that his friend George Grosz depicted in *Ecce Homo.*

In contrast to the theme of social satire, Masereel saw the artist delivering the human race like a prophet from this "confused" society to the just world of art. "Art seems to me to be the most universal religion of our time, and the artist its principal messenger. The artist is a witness of his time, but he can also be an accuser, a critic, or he can celebrate in his works the uneasy greatness of his day."[13]

In 1930, following the tradition of Masereel's woodcut novels, a realistic and psychological novel in pictures appeared called *Shicksal (Destiny: A Novel*

FIGURE 27. Wood Engraving (4½ × 4 in.) by Lynd Ward from *Wild Pilgrimage* (New York: Harrison Smith and Robert Haas, 1932).

in Pictures) by the German Otto Nückel. This realistic tale of seduction and betrayal pitted a woman against the abuse and corruption of a hypocritical society similar to those depicted in the realistic novels of Émile Zola. Nückel used lead plates, "which are almost indistinguishable from wood,"[14] instead of wood blocks for his pictures. With single white-line composition, dominant areas of black, and vigorous hatching, Nückel sustained the focus of action in each plate. The rough texture of his technique sustains the somber mood in this dramatic plot with more than 200 plates, resulting in a monumental piece of social and artistic importance. Although Masereel was able to successfully capture the private world of his heroes' dreams and aspirations against a backdrop of urban decay, Lynd Ward suggests that Nückel "surpassed Masereel both in complexity of plot development and in subtle psychological interplay between characters."[15] Ward developed this psychological tension even further in his own woodcut novels.

In the 1920s Ward studied in Germany with the renowned wood engraver, Hans Mueller. Ward's wife, Mary McNeer, the celebrated children's writer, recollected that Ward had discovered the "stories in woodcuts" of Masereel and Nückel and was "fired with an intense wish to do one himself."[16] Just as Mann had earlier suggested the similarities of film and the woodcut novels of Masereel, Ward reasserted this comparison with his description of the creative process involved in the production of his own woodcut novels.

> It seems to start with an almost obsessive concentration on some aspect of the human condition that keeps nudging the imagination until somewhere within the microcosm of the mind a single figure emerges. This figure is seen fuzzily at first, then gradually acquires physical definition of character. Slowly the background elements come into focus, and the figure assumes an identity that seems to exist independently in time and space. Soon there is movement and things begin to happen. It is in many ways like a tiny motion picture projected inside the cranium. In the early stages, what takes place is not too clear, nor does it last very long. The machine soon runs out of film. But gradually in succeeding days, as the film is run again and again, more events take place, the story moves from stage to stage—and soon, without a conscious act on my part, a critical process begins to operate in which things are tried out and, if they do not work, are discarded.[17]

The result was the first of six woodcut novels, *Gods' Man,* published in 1929 with 139 blocks and simple chapter headings similar to those used by Nückel. Ward stated in the collection of his work, *Storyteller Without Words,* that *Gods' Man* and *Prelude to a Million Years*—"a kind of footnote to *Gods' Man*"[18]—are concerned with the role of the artist in the modern world and "with the difficulties he encounters in a world whose face, if not completely hostile, is not universally friendly either."[19] The novel was published in the same week that the New York stock market crashed.

Wild Pilgrimage, published in 1932 with ninety-five blocks, depicted the desire to return to a more simple life than that lived in most urban settings during the Depression era. The narrative began with a series of blocks that could have come from a setting for Fritz Lang's *Metropolis,* where individuals were overshadowed both physically and spiritually by an industrial complex. Ward explored the bitter struggle between master and slave and the heralded cry of support for socialism.

Besides political themes, Ward added a new device to the idiom of the woodcut novels that depicted the inside fantasy of a character (inner) and the outside reality (outer).[20] Once Ward established a familiar setting in the story, he changed the color of the printed block to an off red. The change in color also allowed him the creative freedom to express the psychological stirrings inside his characters without compromising the closure between blocks. The change from black to off-red was an indication to the reader to adjust from the outer to the inner world. The dream-like sequences in *Wild Pilgrimage* are some of the more disturbing within the tradition of woodcut novels. Ward takes the reader into the psyche of his hero, where the conflict with his outer world is resolved. When he brings his fantasy out into the real world, however, the result is tragic. Recognizing the irreconcilable difference of his inner and outer worlds, the hero chooses to live in reality and fight against injustice even when his decision costs him his life. The power of this woodcut novel is not only in the effective inner and outer device Ward unveiled but in the themes of the fraternity of workers and the price humans are willing to pay for equality.

The political climate of the 1930s was further depicted in the highly symbolic work *Song Without Words,* which was published in 1936 using only twenty-one blocks. With the looming threat of fascism, Ward addressed the risk of bringing children into a totalitarian state. He depicted the female as the child's guardian who wards off every threat to the child's life. Ward's skillful technique showed the extent to which wood engraving could successfully present the rich interplay of light and shadow with controversial metaphors that words could not approach in overall affect.[21]

The last of Ward's woodcut novels, *Vertigo,* was a long and complicated work, published in 1937. It also dealt with the Depression era and, more than previous works, resembles the work of comic book artist Will Eisner, who referred to his own graphic storytelling without word balloons as "images without words."[22]

Ward's focus on the social and political climate of America was imitated in 1940 by Giacomo Patri in his book, *White Collar: A Novel in Linocuts.* Patri adopted the device of the "inner and outer" worlds of Ward in his depiction of the effects of the 1929 stock market crash on the life of a white-collar worker and his family. Patri's pictorial background is minimal, centering his focus on the hero as he becomes aware of how organized labor can rebuild the American Dream into a reality for himself and his family. Patri's dream-like portrayal of his hero's inner struggle and disillusionment is similar to the dream sequences in Alfred Hitchcock's *Vertigo* or in the surrealistic set from Robert Wiene's *The Cabinet of Dr. Caligari.* Patri makes creative use of familiar icons and symbols such as the hourglass to successfully support the passage of time between panels. He also opens up his panels so that an object like a closed door or a book floats in white space on the page rather than inside the familiar boarders of the woodcut. This particular work had historical importance, with an afterward in the original 1940 edition by John L. Lewis and an introduction by Rockwell Kent. A few of Kent's remarks are especially relevant since they endorse the power of pictures, specifically a novel in pictures, in igniting social change.

> A million novels could be founded on that [1929] crash, all different in plot and characters yet all alike in common tragic theme of sudden poverty, disrupted homes, of broken lives, of final and irrevocable hopelessness. A thousand lifetimes would be spent in reading them. One story might epitomize them all: this story does.[23]

In the following decades an occasional resemblance to the woodcut novel surfaced,[24] such as the woodcut novels of James Reid, who published *The Life of Christ in Woodcuts* in 1930, and those politically and spiritually impassioned works such as *Thy Kingdom Come* by the Englishman Arthur Wragg.[25] Although the pen-and-ink work of Peter Kalberkamp's, *Mea Culpa*, published in 1990, and artists' books such as the 1988 parable in linocuts, *At the Beach*, by Babette Katz followed the spirit of the tradition, it was not until 1992, with the publication of Eric Drooker's *Flood!*, that the essence of the woodcut novel re-emerged.[26]

Drooker, whose cartoons are often published in *The Village Voice* and *The New Yorker*, is able successfully to display his themes of social satire and the role of the artist in American culture with a more modern point of reference. Like Masereel, Drooker's hope seems placed in our humanity and not our technology. His themes are presented on scratchboards in sharp, inventive lines with all the vitality of Ward's wood engravings. A scratchboard drawing is made by cutting a line through black ink, which is spread out over a white chalk-coated board. It imitates wood engraving because it scrapes away the black and leaves the white.[27] The striking similarities in both technique and themes bring back the wealth of this tradition, which has always skirted between the fine arts and cartooning. This technique allowed him to open the page even further for more expansive visual development of his themes, since the width of his panels ranges from 5/16 inches to 14 inches. Except for the sidesteps into fantasy, Drooker's *Flood!* (a compilation of three stories: "Home," "L," and "Flood") remains centered in the city, the hub of modern culture. In "Home," one lighted window in an ominous and looming city building immediately confronts the reader. Drooker shows in pictures the gradual desperation and confusion of an unemployed worker whose job skills are no longer viable in our market. With his scratchboard drawings, he is able to address the economic concern and alienation of the unemployed, who daily join the growing number of the city's homeless. Starting with a full page spread, a blue-collar worker discovers the factory where he worked has closed. In half-page spreads, we follow the worker as he walks through the city. The panels become jagged into quarter-page spreads, increasing the pensive, manic setting inside a bar. He leaves with a prostitute and, unable to pay, is booted out of the building. The belittled and now desperate worker roams hungry and aimless. The page separates into sixteen panels, and then sixty-four panels, and finally 256 panels on the page as the worker becomes little more than a stick figure who loses all sense of his surroundings until he is literally scratched out of existence.

Using McCloud's iconic abstraction scale,[28] what is especially noteworthy is the gradual digression of realism in the pictorial sequence of panels as the worker becomes more iconic. Drooker skirts close to the next inevitable step in McCloud's scale—the use of words and language—in this proclaimed "novel in pictures."

In the second part of Drooker's picture novel, "L," the hero travels into the depths of a subway system. He searches for escape like the hero in Ward's woodcut novel, *Wild Pilgrimage*: "When the crush of too many people in too small a space is finally more than one can take; when the noise and the smells of the city are at last too stifling to be borne. Then the urge to pick up and leave, to get away somehow, is irresistible."[29] Drooker's worker, however, is unable to leave the city, except in his own fantasy. He awakes from his fantasy not in a more compassionate and primitive society but in the same abrasive and hostile reality he sought to escape. Although Drooker does not change the color of his panels to indicate the jump from reality to fantasy, the possibility of the hero's escape from reality is plausible and allows for a greater impact and surprise ending. As the hero leaves dejectedly from the subway, the skeleton of a fish is highlighted, suggesting the remnants of our primitive past are no longer available in our culture except as an idle daydream.

In the final story, "Flood," Drooker explores our history and culture through the eyes of an artist. During a torrential downpour, the artist, who is offered an umbrella by a sage-looking man, returns to his room, where he is greeted by his black cat. Drooker uses the "inner and outer" world device of Ward in this story, using blue instead of off red. The artist begins to work with pen and ink in creating a story about a lone Eskimo who is trapped on the ice. The theme of primitivism in the previous story is repeated. Drooker, again, uses his skeleton or x-ray motif to express our most natural allegiance with all living things. The motif also exhibits our culture's intent upon disregarding death as part of our life cycle and the return to a more primitive and perhaps more fulfilling lifestyle. The deluge continues and has now begun to fill the artist's studio. We enter another vignette of a man hanging on the end of his umbrella. The wind seizes his umbrella. In a series of striking two-page

FIGURE 28. Scratchboard drawing (3¼ × 6 in.) by Eric Drooker from *Flood! A Novel in Pictures* (New York: Four Walls Eight Windows, 1992).

spreads, the man sails over the city to a dream-like amusement park. He is drawn to a sideshow where a muscleman, covered with tattoos, displays the brutal history of America's darker side, including the genocide of the Native American and the inhuman slave trade. Each picture is garnished with the icons of Fortune 500 companies and symbols of racism strung together with barbed wire and rope. This device of a story within a story is quite effective, and the strong images Drooker uses, like the best political cartoons, generate a heartfelt reaction.

The man, slumped over with the revelation of our culture's atrocities, roams through a maze of sterile modern buildings. He reaches a rally where a crowd is incited by a woman to rebel against the forces in power.[30] The crowd, bearing banners of musical notes, rises against armed guards whose uniforms bear the insignia of a dollar sign. A bitter battle ensues in which the rebels fight with musical instruments and sling shots against ensuing armored tanks as the floodwater rises and drowns both rebels and armed guards. We return to the artist whose studio is filling with water and whose reality seems to change into the color of his own pictorial fantasy. The action is now colored blue as the artist and his cat float inside the umbrella the sage gave him earlier in the novel. As the force of the rain streaks across the panels, the umbrella overturns and the artist drowns. The ending to this novel in pictures has similarities to Herman Melville's *Moby-Dick*, where Ishmael floats on Queequeg's coffin before he is taken aboard the ship named *Rachel*. The artist's cat, who now carries the heart icon and floats on the artist's body, is safely taken aboard an approaching ark by the sage who originally gave the umbrella to the artist and now appears to be a Noah-like figure. However, unlike Ishmael, who floats for an entire day and night with "unharming sharks, they glided by as if with padlocks on their mouths,"[31] the body of the artist is eaten by sharks as the ark slips between the last remaining vestiges of our civilization.

The icon of the heart and all that it represents—love, charity, or, perhaps, the most vital part of our own humanity—survives despite the eminent end of our culture by natural causes. Not only has Drooker brought back the richness of the tradition of novels in pictures, he brings what Ward originally sought to express with his woodcut novels.

> My search, then, is for something beyond affirmation—for an image or a combination of recognizable shapes and forms that on one level will say something very specific but that at the same time, on a different level, will achieve a sharing of feeling and understanding that cannot be explained in words or communicated in any but visual terms.[32]

In contrast, David Bland, in his hallmark retrospective work on book illustration, wrote the following about woodcut novels:

> As an experiment it is interesting but it cannot be called a successful art-form because no picture can survive if it is made to carry too much meaning. Moreover the woodcut is not exactly a subtle medium and in order to convey meaning[,] gestures and expressions have to be greatly exaggerated, often with a faintly ridiculous air.[33]

Bland's reactionary attitude, however justified by convention, was happily disregarded by Masereel and Ward. What resulted was a tradition that has supported the rich picture book trade industry as well as the imaginative and fertile comic arts. With humanistic themes and images powerful enough to support the ideals of artists like Eric Drooker, picture stories remain the best ambassador for our world's humanity—a medium allowing access regardless of age or level of literacy in any country of the world.

ENDNOTES

A portion of this essay, titled *Worlds Without Balloons*, was presented for the "Comic Art and Comics" section of the Popular Culture Association in Chicago on 8 April 1994.

1. Lee Kingman, "High Art of Illustration," *Hornbook* 50 (October 1974): 98.

2. William M. Ivans Jr., *How Prints Look* (Boston: Beacon, 1943), 146.

3. As used in this paper, the term *woodcut* includes woodcut and wood engraving. A woodcut uses a block cut longitudinally with the grain of the wood running parallel to the surface. Wood engraving uses a block cut across the grain of a hardwood like boxwood. Lynd Ward's "woodcut novels" are, in fact, "wood engraving novels."

4. David Bland, *History of Book Illustration* (Berkeley: University of California Press, 1969), 395.

5. Scott McCloud, *Understanding Comics* (Northampton, MA: Tundra Books, 1993), 18.

6. An extensive bibliography about and catalogue for Frans Masereel by Pierre Vorms and Hanns-Canon von der Gabelenz is included in the comprehensive work of Roger Avermaete, *Frans Masereel* (London: Thames and Hudson, 1977).

7. On close examination, the heroes in Masereel's *Passionate Journey,* Ward's *Wild Pilgrimage,* and Drooker's "Flood" in *Flood!: A Novel in Pictures* have striking similarities to portraits of the respective artists. Although the actual events may be imaginary, this autobiographical device displays the active political role the artists see themselves playing in the culture.

8. McCloud, *Understanding Comics,* 18.

9. Windsor Art Gallery, *Tribute: Frans Masereel* (Windsor, ON: Art Gallery of Windsor, 1981), 23.

10. Thomas Mann, introduction to *Passionate Journey (Mein Stundenbuch): A Novel Told in 165 Woodcuts,* by Frans Masereel, translated by Joseph M. Bernstein (New York: Penguin, 1988). The preface by Thomas Mann is an enlightened discussion on Masereel and woodcut novels. Mann also refers to the role that film played in the development of Masereel's "novel in pictures." He comments that "Recently a film magazine published abroad asked me if I thought that something artistically creative could come out of the cinema. I answered: 'Indeed I do!' Then I was asked which movie, of all I had seen, had stirred me most, I replied: Masereel's *Passionate Journey.* That may seem an evasive answer, since it is not a case of art conquering the cinema but of cinema influencing art. . . . [Masereel] calls his books *romans en images*—novels in pictures. Is that not an accurate description of motion pictures?" Mann's assertion was later echoed by Will Eisner, who stated that "comics are movies on paper." Eisner's influence on many film directors is noted in M. Thomas Inge, *Comics as Culture* (Jackson: University Press of Mississippi, 1990), xix–xx.

11. Avermaete, *Frans Masereel,* 26.

12. Avermaete, *Frans Masereel,* 76.

13. Avermaete, *Frans Masereel,* 84.

14. Bland, *History of Book Illustration,* 411.

15. Lynd Ward, *Storyteller Without Words* (New York: Abrams, 1974), 21.

16. Mary McNeer, "Lynd Ward," *Bibliognost* 2, no. 2 (May 1976): 17–19.

17. Ward, *Storyteller,* 21.

18. Ward, *Storyteller,* 178.

19. Ward, *Storyteller,* 23.

20. Ward, *Storyteller,* 126.

21. Henry Hart describes one of the wood engravings in *Song Without Words.* "Woman, nude and with her back to the viewer, raises her arms in defiance of her enemy, death, symbolized by the face of an enormous skull. In the dark, eyeless hollows, two highlights seem to be irises, but in fact are two miniature faces, one of which is that of a high-hatted plutocrat, and the other, that of his uniformed minion. The teeth of this skull seem at first glance to be gravestones, but on closer inspection, prove to be miniature skyscrapers." Henry Hart, "Images vs Word." *Bibliognost* 2, no. 2 (May 1976): 27–31. A comparison of the verbal and pictorial description shows the dramatic impact of a picture over words.

22. Will Eisner, *Comics and Sequential Art* (Tamarac, FL: Poorhouse Press, 1985), 24.

23. Giacomo Patri, *White Collar: A Novel in Linocuts* (Millrae, CA: Celestial Arts, 1975), vii.

24. Besides the woodcut novels, there were many "novels in pictures" using other mediums such as lithographs or pen and ink. Art Spiegelman notes a "brilliant book-length parody of the form" [novel in pictures] titled *He Done Her Wrong: The Great American Novel (With No Words)*, published in 1930 by the cartoonist Milt Gross. Art Spiegelman, "Gloomy Toons," *The New York Times Book Review*, December 27, 1992, 9.

25. Inside a copy of Arthur Wragg, *Thy Kingdom Come: A Prayer in Black & White for Ourselves and the World Today* (London: Selwyn & Blout, 1939) was an original letter from the noted book illustrator Frank Brangwyn. His reaction to the social idealism of Wragg can be extended, in general, to most woodcut novels. "It [the book] is most stirring and mordant. I hope it may do good but my [experience?] is that to be moved by such vital illustrations of the shortcomings of man one has to have the moral sense of right and wrong, which seems to be more or less dead in our time. . . . Do not let the misery of the world hold you down for there is a lot of good. It is only that the teaching has been wrong. Let us hope for the best."

26. Eric Drooker, *Flood! A Novel in Pictures* (New York: Four Walls Eight Windows, 1992).

27. Meritt Cutler, *How to Cut Drawings on Scratchboard* (New York: Watson-Guptil, 1960), 11.

28. McCloud, *Understanding Comics*, 46.

29. Ward, *Storyteller*, 125.

30. The woman, similar to many Romantic paintings of women such as Eugène Delacroix's *Liberty Guiding the People*, may represent the personification of liberty.

31. Herman Melville, *Moby-Dick; or, The Whale* (New York: Dodd, Mead, 1922), 527.

32. Ward, *Storyteller*, 309.

33. Bland, *History of Book Illustration*, 395.

The Captain and the Comics

A Capsule History of the Medium in its Fourth and Fifth Decades

ROBERT C. HARVEY

IF CIRCULATION IS what makes a newspaper great (and that is surely one of the measures of greatness in newspapering), then Joseph Medill Patterson knew more about how to achieve that greatness than any other man of his time; in circulation battles in both Chicago and New York, he soundly defeated the champion of the previous generation, William Randolph Hearst. Like Hearst, Patterson recognized the importance of comics in selling newspapers. One of his first acts upon assuming control in 1912 of his patrimony, the Sunday *Chicago Tribune,* was to add to the Sunday funnies his favorite strip, Rudolph Dirks' *Hans and Fritz.*[1] But Patterson was otherwise much different from Hearst in publishing comic strips. Hearst purchased established or proven talent; Patterson developed talent. Hearst's success as a press lord had rested almost entirely upon the size of his bankroll (and that was derived more from inherited mining interests than the newspapers he published)—and Patterson's upon his uncanny understanding of what appealed to the ordinary citizen.

Despite his achievement in the realm of newspaper publishing (not to mention comic strip production), Patterson has received relatively little notice from the Boswells of journalistic moguls in America—particularly in comparison to Hearst, whose life and career have fascinated several biographers.[2] This essay attempts in a quiet way to correct the oversight. Here, then, I would like to begin by answering the question: What sort of man was it who so consistently pleased great numbers of readers of newspapers and comic strips? And along the way, we will look at some of the ways he shaped the comics his newspaper published. Because Patterson's career spanned the second most formative period in the development of the medium (the first decade embraced the all-important defining moments), his life in comics furnishes us with a microcosmic history of the American newspaper comic strip between roughly 1917 and 1940. In fact, given Patterson's pervasive influence on the cartoonists he worked with, he may even be seen as a catalyst in that history.

Patterson was born in 1879 to Chicago wealth and influence. His father was managing editor of the *Chicago Tribune*; his grandfather was founder of Lake Forest College and a satrap in the Republican Party. But Patterson would gain his extraordinary insight into human nature through the variegated experiences of a youth that his wealthy peers might say was misspent. He learned disdain for members of his class at Groton, a tony school for the scion of the rich and famous, where his classmates sneered at his midwestern accent. Henceforth, he had no use for snobs, young or old. And disdain fostered a reformer's spirit. Moreover, he acquired by the experience a dread of ostentation and show that lasted throughout his life.[3]

He entered Yale in 1897, interrupting his tenure there for a year to serve an apprenticeship in the family calling. But his baptism in journalism was not performed at the family font: when he went to cover the Boxer Rebellion in ancient Imperial China in the summer of 1900, he went as an aide to a reporter for Hearst's *Chicago American*. In China, he doubtless witnessed the last flaunting of old-style imperialism, the final flourish of traditional, pre-mechanized military campaigning, as the multinational force wound its way from Tientsin to besieged Peking under a rainbow of fluttering guidons—a wondrous sight, the mounted and trudging might of historic colonialism in full martial panoply.[4]

After his adventure in the East, Patterson returned to Yale, graduated in 1901, and joined his father's *Tribune* as a reporter. He found the work dull and left in order to throw himself into local politics, campaigning for municipal reform in Chicago. His performance eventually earned him a Republican seat in the Illinois House of Representatives in 1903. There he distinguished himself on at least one occasion by throwing an inkpot at the speaker of the House during a heated debate on streetcar franchises. Then, when Patterson learned that his election had been engineered by his father and Republican bosses, he resigned his seat, the fires of rebellion again banked.

Patterson next scandalized his paternity by switching parties and working for Edward J. Dunne's Democratic campaign for mayor of Chicago. When Dunne won, Patterson served in his administration as commissioner of public works. In 1906, he shocked his family once again: in a dramatic letter of resignation, he expressed a loathing for himself and all other wealthy persons who enjoyed the fruits of others' labors without working themselves and announced that he was becoming a socialist and that he would thereafter earn his own living. To that purpose, he became a dairy farmer and a writer, producing socialist tracts, plays (three of which were produced on Broadway), and novels (of which *A Little Brother of the Rich* was modestly successful); and in 1908, he served as campaign manager for Eugene Debs's bid for the U.S. presidency.

By 1910, however, Patterson had become disillusioned with socialism; the movement had too many talkers and too few doers. It was no more a practical means to the end of social reform than politics generally had proved. Coincident with his growing disaffection with socialism was the death of his father, Robert W. Patterson. The throne at the *Chicago Tribune* stood empty, and Joseph Patterson and his aristocratic cousin, Robert McCormick, took their places at it. The newspaper community watched with fascination as the cousins assumed management of their legacy; disruptive quarrels between the Pattersons and the McCormicks were a Chicago legend, and everyone expected the cousins to provide juicy entertainment by ripping the *Tribune* to shreds in a struggle for control. Everyone was disappointed. The cousins, it turned out, were the best of friends. Each regarded the other with genuine admiration and affection, and although they disagreed on some matters affecting the *Tribune*'s editorial stance, they were determined to end the historic family feuding. As a step in this direction, they made a unique arrangement on the editorial page: by the unprecedented device of alternating the top responsibility month by month, the Bourbon and the erstwhile Bolshevik shared editorial control while at the same time avoiding daily disputes. (They each also modified the extremities of their differing views so the paper would not have an editorial policy with a split personality.)

While the cousins shared overall control of the *Tribune*, each followed his own bent in choosing an aspect of newspaper management in which to concentrate his energies. McCormick devoted himself to the business side. To the editorial side, Patterson brought the perspective of a disillusioned idealist, a man born to power who had thus far been frustrated in his rebellious attempts to exercise it. He brought also the insights gained through his associations with state and city machine politicians and with blue-collar socialists and parlor pinks and through his modest success as a popular playwright and novelist. To these experiences, he would add those of war correspondent in

Veracruz during the Mexican troubles of 1914 and of commanding officer of Battery B during World War I.

When the United States entered the war, Patterson joined up. He turned down a commission in the Illinois National Guard, enlisting instead as a buck private, but by the time his unit (among the first called up as part of the famous Rainbow Division comprised of Guard units from all the states) was sent to France in February 1918, he had worked up the ranks to Captain, a title he would invoke the rest of his life. Battery B saw action in five major campaigns in 1918, spending about two hundred days of its thirteen-month tour in line service with little relief. Somewhere during the months of forced marches and rainy nights in muddy gun emplacements amid the stench of rotting bodies, Patterson was wounded. He was also gassed and spent time in a field hospital. But mostly, he was on the line with his unit. With status enough to have claimed a stateside job or a staff post, Patterson earned the regard of his men for being one of them, a volunteer in the mud with other volunteers. He often went on dangerous patrols when he could have sent someone else. Under fire, he showed more consideration for the safety of his troops than for his own, earning the affectionate nickname "Aunt Josie" because of his sometimes extreme concern for his men. (They also called him "Sloppy Joe"—a doubtless complimentary allusion to an eccentric negligence in dress that remained with Patterson all his life.[5])

Patterson may not have been one of the ordinary people, but he had been close enough to enough varieties of them to acquire an acute perception of their wants and needs. That understanding he would apply to building the circulation of the *New York Daily News,* which he launched after the War.

America's first successful tabloid, the *Daily News* was an epochal journalistic phenomenon. Its first issue hit the streets with 150,000 copies on 26 June 1919. Sales flagged that summer but picked up again in the fall and grew steadily thereafter. By October 1923 (only four and a half years after its launch), it had moved from last place among New York's eighteen daily papers to first in the nation, with a daily average circulation of more than 600,000. Patterson had learned much about building the circulation of a big-city newspaper while editor of the *Tribune,* and he applied those lessons in New York. Believing that people wanted more romance and adventure than their ordinary lives afforded them, Patterson produced an outrageous, sobby, glamorous sheet featuring sex and scandal, pictures and contests—a three-ring circus of sensation and entertainment. Tradition has it that it was a contest that doubled the *News'* circulation in the autumn of 1919—a limerick contest in which readers competed for the $100 prize by supplying the fifth lines to the four printed in the paper. Patterson attributed the growth surge that fall to New Yorkers' discovery of the convenient size of the *News*: the tabloid was easy for commuters to hold and read. But the contests went on—coloring contests, beauty contests, lucky name contests (based upon horoscopes), tongue twister contests, solve-the-mystery contests, and so on. Other features included columnists of every stripe (gossip, political opinion, health and beauty, sports), racing entries, movie listings, and comics. All attracted readers. And when the *News* added an eight-page, color comics section to its Sunday edition on 12 February 1923, circulation increased by 65,000 (up 20 percent), ringing testimony to the commercial power of the funnies.[6]

At first, Patterson managed the paper from his office at the *Chicago Tribune* in Illinois, employing both telephone and telegraph and making frequent visits to the New York offices. By 1926, the *Daily News* had achieved financial stability, and the Captain could restrain himself no longer. He moved to New York to assume direct daily control of the tabloid, retaining only a financial interest in the *Tribune*. At last, the somewhat uneasy editorial partnership the cousins had endured while sharing the helm of the *Tribune* was dissolved; now each cousin had his own paper and could follow his editorial instincts unencumbered by considerations of the other's view.

Patterson had been in command of the *News* all along, but now he was in the midst of its daily evolutions, where his on-the-spot decisions could influence every edition before the paper hit the stands. He took a cubbyhole office on the fourth floor of the building, but he spent most of his time stalking his staff in every department of the paper. By the time the Captain reached the building at about ten o'clock in the morning, he had already worked his way through every morning newspaper in New York City, and he brought this familiarity with the day's news to every stop on his rounds, expecting to find his editors similarly informed.[7]

Walking with a heavy, decisive step, Patterson first prowled the newsroom for an informal look at what was going on. Then he stopped at the city desk to discuss the day's news and to issue instructions about how it should be handled. He often discussed stories with the reporters assigned to them, and he never hesitated to tell them how to write their leads. A concise, thoughtful, and incisive prose stylist himself, the Captain liked short, punchy writing in both news stories and picture captions, and he gave bonuses for particularly telling paragraphs. He stopped at the picture desk to review the photos that were candidates for the day's issue and to order special coverage. Patterson was not good at visualizing, so later in the day his editors produced mock-up pages with photostats of the pictures pasted into position for his approval.

On Thursdays, Patterson made a lengthy visit to the Sunday department. A special chair was reserved for the Captain on these occasions, but Patterson was out of the chair as much as he was in it during the conference. A restless man, Patterson would squirm in his seat, crossing and uncrossing his legs and tilting the chair far back, clasping heavy, thick hands behind his head. Abruptly, he would get up, stretch, pace a bit, and then drop back into the chair. During these visits, Patterson would originate several stories, often discussing their treatment directly with the reporters or with the picture editor.

Late each morning, Patterson met in his office with editorial writer Reuben Maury and C. D. Batchelor to formulate the next day's editorial proclamations. Patterson and Maury talked, and Batchelor, the *News* editorial cartoonist, sketched while he listened. After the meeting, Maury would convert the Captain's pronouncements into the pithy colloquial language for which the *News* editorials became famous, setting a fashion for readable and easily understood editorial writing.

Patterson's constant presence in every department of the *News* heightened the normal tension that springs from meeting hourly production deadlines, but his vigilance also assured that the paper would be produced in exact accordance with his vision for it. Although he was aided by a succession of able editors and skilled reporters who translated his ideas into print better than he could, the *News* was very much a one-man paper. The superior coverage that the *News* gave the big stories of the twenties attested to the Captain's acute news sense. He anticipated the importance of Charles Lindbergh's solo transatlantic flight, for instance, just as he knew what the news value of a picture of Ruth Snyder being electrocuted would be. One fuzzy photograph of the blindfolded murderer seated in the electric chair as the deadly current coursed through her body sold a million extra copies of the *News*.

Keen newsman though Patterson was, the newsman was less important to the success of the *News* than the common man in him. The Captain prided himself on his celebrated grasp of human nature (particularly at its lower levels), and to buttress his opinions, he engaged in a unique kind of readership survey. Periodically, with editors and subeditors in tow, Captain Patterson led forays into the streets and subways of New York, peering over the shoulders of *News* readers to see what they were reading. On other occasions, Patterson would eat alone at cafeterias and automats, eavesdropping on the conversations at nearby tables to find out what the masses were thinking. Sometimes (legend has it) he would dress as a bum and mingle with the dregs of society in the Bowery. Scarcely scientific, this method of studying human nature probably did little more than confirm Patterson's opinions. But his opinions, judging from the success of the *News*, were unerring enough in themselves.

The subjects and their treatment in the paper were determined largely by instinct—Patterson's instinct. Writing a history of the *News* in 1969, Leo

McGivena, who had served in various promotional capacities on the paper since its beginning, made note of this vital ingredient of a newspaper's success:

> An editor is largely a creature of instinct—an instinct that assesses and calibrates the degree of public interest and response to a topic or event. He is often a hunch player, sometimes prophetic. He may sense a need to know, a ground swell of opinion or sentiment. He is part detective; an out-of-character act or utterance by a prominent person may indicate or predicate newsworthy consequences. Invariably he is an innovator . . . some editors are brief-blooming, do not outlast their early period. Patterson carried the *News* through the frivolous 1920s, the serious depressed thirties, the crucial World War II years, without ever losing the perspective of the public or its patronage.[8]

A *Chicago Tribune* editorial that appeared when Patterson died in 1946 denied that the Captain had a formula for the success of the *News*:

> What he had was something infinitely more precious, and that was a sure sense of what the masses of people, rich and poor, smart and dumb, were interested in and how to tell it to them. The Tribune-News comic strips disclose this understanding, but it should not be forgotten that what he did in developing these cartoons here in Chicago and later in New York offers merely one evidence of his ability to penetrate the minds and hearts of people. His whole paper and the feature pages of the *Tribune* as well tell the same story.[9]

Captain Patterson was undoubtedly interested in people and in what concerned them. But he was not one of them. He was a loner, psychologically withdrawn (partly out of the conviction that a publisher should have no close friends in order to prevent his feelings for them from coloring his judgments). He disliked shaking hands and avoided it when he could. And on occasion he displayed an unexpected shyness.

John McCutcheon, the *Chicago Tribune*'s editorial cartoonist for a generation, got to know Patterson better than most of the Captain's employees. Patterson took McCutcheon with him to Europe in 1915 to inspect the embryo of war, and the two spent several months together, sharing a cabin on the ship to France and a hotel room in Paris. On the trip across the Atlantic, they played dominoes by the hour and talked. McCutcheon, older than his companion and already long established as the star of the *Tribune*'s front page, was interested in discovering his new boss's philosophy. "He had a keen zest and curiosity about life, a great desire for firsthand experience," McCutcheon wrote years later. "He was intellectually honest, and though one might not agree with his opinions, one respected his courage in asserting them. I could not imagine Joe Patterson misrepresenting a fact although the truth might be awkward and have unpleasant consequences."[10] In France, the two indulged a common love of adventure one day at Villacoublay, when the French offered them a chance at flying in one of their new monoplanes.

After three months, Patterson left Paris and returned to Chicago. McCutcheon, who had traveled the world extensively, was sorry to see him go: "One could not have wished for a more interesting and companionable shipmate," he said. "In those days, Joe never asserted the importance which his position gave him, and it was not difficult to abandon the relation of employer and employee." The feeling was mutual: Patterson often said that McCutcheon was the only person with whom he really liked to travel. The two took several trips together in later years until the Captain moved permanently to New York. Curiously, before the Paris trip, McCutcheon heard through a mutual friend that Patterson was almost afraid to go with him because he liked him so much, and "he felt certain we would not come back friends. This was his way of saying that he considered himself very hard to get along with."

Although nothing in the *Daily News* was too trivial to evade the Captain's attention, he concentrated, as he had in Chicago, on improving and increasing the paper's feature material—including, especially, the comics. Because Patterson's forte was features, he also ran the Tribune-News Syndicate, which was therefore headquartered in New York. Arthur Crawford, whom Patterson had named head of the syndicate, was little more than an administrator; Patterson made all the important decisions for the operation. Day-to-day implementation of his decisions was entrusted to his assistant, Mollie Slott, who, in the normal course of events, became the de facto manager of the syndicate.

The war had interrupted Patterson's program for developing new comic strip features for the *Tribune*. Four years after adding *Hans and Fritz* to the Sunday lineup, he had introduced (in May 1914) William Donahey's *Teenie Weenies*, a Sunday feature aimed directly at kids. It was the first strip Patterson selected for its juvenile appeal—and it would be the last. The Captain quickly realized that comics, like everything else in a newspaper, had to attract adults; it was the adults who bought the papers. His next comic strip reflected this conviction. With this strip, it is often said, Patterson also invented the continuity comic strip. Maybe, maybe not. But even if he did not invent the story strip, Patterson certainly midwifed at its birth and nursed it into healthy infancy.

Patterson's inspiration for a comic strip that told a continuing story from day to day may have arisen from his earlier experiences while in charge of the Sunday *Chicago Tribune*. He started running a directory of current attractions in Chicago's movie theaters, and, noting the favorable reader response, he soon hit upon another way to capitalize on the popular fascination with the flickers. Making a deal with William Selig, the producer of one of the first movie serials, *The Adventures of Kathlyn,* Patterson began on 4 January 1914 to publish the written version of each week's installment the week before the film version appeared. Readers could win prizes by guessing the solutions to mysteries in each week's printed episode. *Kathlyn* ran for twenty-six weeks, and each week the *Tribune*'s circulation department had to increase news agents' orders by hundreds of copies.[11]

The lesson was not lost on Patterson. He continued to run written versions of serial thrillers, and the success of these features (together with that of serialized popular fiction, which he also published in the Sunday *Tribune*) doubtless lodged in a corner of his brain an idea that he would later introduce into the medium of comic strips. A basic ingredient of the installment stories he was publishing was *continuation*: readers, newspaper buyers, had to buy next week's Sunday *Tribune* to see how the stories came out. They had to go on buying the next week's edition as long as the story continued.

Comic strips that told continuing stories had been around long before Captain Patterson took an interest in the idea.[12] But even if he did not invent the concept, he helped refine it in a way that opened the door to the future, to continuity strips of exotic adventure. *The Gumps* made suspense the driving mechanism of the continuing story strip. And because *The Gumps* was syndicated and distributed to many papers around the nation, it had a greater impact upon the medium than any of the earlier attempts at continuity strips.

When Patterson began thinking about a new comic strip in early 1917, he envisioned a strip about real people who would become involved in situations with which *Tribune* readers could identify. Doubtless in conceiving the strip, Patterson harkened back to the novels he had written in his youth when influenced by the social realism of Theodore Dreiser. The strip would achieve both comedy and catastrophe by focusing on an average lower-middle-class family whose aspirations and adventures would mirror the ambitions and appetites of the *Tribune*'s readers as Patterson imagined them. In christening the strip family "the Gumps," Patterson employed a slightly derisive term that he and his sister, "Cissy," had applied as children to loudmouth adults.[13] In Andy Gump's case, the name was a self-fulfilling prophecy. To produce the strip, Patterson turned to the *Tribune*'s staff of cartoonists and picked Sidney Smith, a somewhat baffling choice. Smith was drawing *Old Doc Yak,* a silly slapstick romp about a goat and his son, Yutch—about as far from Dreiser's gritty realism as vaudeville is from Shakespearean tragedy. Whatever Patterson's reasons, Smith turned out to be an inspired choice.

Given Patterson's proprietary, almost paternal, feeling about *The Gumps,* it would be difficult to imagine Smith doing a continuing story without Patterson's approval—if not at his express suggestion. Although Smith offered a slight thread of continuity in the strip from the beginning on 12 February 1917 (the Gumps move into the house Doc Yak is renting, displacing the goat—and his strip—from the paper), he did not hit his stride with suspenseful reportage until February 1921, when Andy's millionaire relation, Uncle Bim, falls into the clutches of the Widow Zander, a gold-digging damsel whose marital intentions for Bim threaten Andy's hopes of inheriting his uncle's fortune (a preoccupation that animates many of Andy's soliloquies over the years). Once Smith warmed to his task, he soaped his stories with every sudsy bubble of melodrama he could squeeze out of his pen. He was able to prolong the Widow Zander affair for most of 1921 and into the next year, and that year, Andy Gump ran for Congress. The blowhard was in his natural element.

By this time, people were asking news dealers for "the Gump paper," not the *Chicago Tribune.* Reading the strip every day had become a habit, if not an addiction, among its readers. Suspenseful continuity as a device for building a successful comic strip was convincingly established. The next step was to make that suspense life-threatening and to make it seem real: the serious adventure strip realistically rendered by illustrators would achieve that goal in the 1930s. Meanwhile, the immense popularity of *The Gumps* helped establish the Chicago Tribune Syndicate, which later became the Chicago Tribune-New York Daily News Syndicate. Patterson's success with *The Gumps* was followed by similar success with the other strips he inaugurated during the next decade.

In 1919, he accepted a submission from Carl Ed, retitled it *The Love Life of Harold Teen,* and introduced it as a Sunday page on 4 May. At the time, it was the only comic strip about teenagers, and once the twenties began to roar with the exuberance of Youth, *Harold Teen* became a national pastime, popularizing such expressions as "shebas" (girls), "shieks" (boys), "Yowsah!" "Fan mah brow!" "pantywaist," and the like. Patterson also tinkered with a strip that his cousin had inspired in 1918, *Gasoline Alley.* Frank King drew the feature at the command of McCormick who thought (correctly) that the growing population of automobile owners would enjoy a strip about the problems people had with cars. Reflecting on the strip, Patterson decided all the talk about cars left out women readers' interests. "Get a baby into the story fast," he commanded the flabbergasted King, who protested that the main character, Walt Wallet, was a bachelor. It was then decided to have Walt find a baby on his doorstep—which he did on Valentine's Day 1921. With the arrival of Skeezix, the strip evolved its most unique feature: its characters aged. The children grew up, and the adults grew older. To King, this innovative aspect of his strip was simply logical. "You have a one week old baby, but he can't stay one week old forever. He had to grow."[14] By logical extension, so did everyone else in the strip. Patterson concurred. This attribute of *Gasoline Alley* added a dimension of real life to the strip, and King went on to convert everyday concerns about automobiles into a larger reflection of American life in a small town.

But a strip about small-town life wasn't entirely appropriate for the readers of the *Tribune* and the *Daily News*. Both were big-city papers, and although their readers may have enjoyed *Gasoline Alley* as a nostalgic interlude, the world these readers lived and worked in was far removed from King's comfortable idealization. When Patterson began looking for his next new comic strips after *Harold Teen,* he had his metropolitan readers foremost in his mind. For the working women, he found Martin Branner's *Winnie Winkle the Breadwinner.*[15] Introduced in September 1920, Winnie was the first of the post-World War I "liberated women" in the funnies, and her struggle to make her way in the world, supporting her father and mother and kid brother, Perry, made the strip a great attraction among women readers. The strip was so popular that it earned the *Daily News* its nickname: "the working girl's paper." Two years later, Patterson found a male counterpart for *Winnie* in a strip called *Bill the Office Boy,* by Walter Berndt. Patterson did not like the name of Berndt's thirteen-year-old protagonist, though, so Berndt grabbed a phone book, opened it, and saw a page of Smiths. So *Smitty* was born, appearing in print on 29 November 1922. To complete the comics lineup for big-city sensibilities, Patterson wanted something about the lower strata of society, roughnecks and connivers who made their way with their wits and pure gall, in total disregard (or ignorance) of the Puritan work ethic, books of etiquette, and every other refinement of social intercourse. When Frank Willard walked into his office one day in 1923, the Captain knew that he had found the man to limn the low life of the city. He described what he wanted, and Willard went off to develop that classic comedy of scheming, brawling, uncouth social pretension, *Moon Mullins.* As he would do repeatedly, Patterson named the title character, employing a term just then emerging into public consciousness—moonshine. The strip started on 19 June 1923, and Willard quickly surrounded his protagonist with kindred souls, con artists all—Lord and Lady Plushbottom, Uncle Willie and his wife, the cook Mamie. Moon's kid brother, Kayo, was the only realist (and he was a full-blown cynic).

Shortly after Willard was established in the Tribune-News stable, another novel concept for a strip crossed Patterson's desk and caught his eye. Sidney Smith's assistant, Harold Gray, had been submitting ideas for strips for months, but this, his latest, seemed promising to Patterson. Called *Little Orphan Otto,* the strip featured a cute gamin with curly hair. Close but not quite. "The kid looks like a pansy to me," Patterson growled. "Put a skirt on him and we'll call it 'Little Orphan Annie.'" It may have been the head of curls that did it, recalling to Patterson's mind the image of Mary Pickford in her early films.[16]

Patterson worked with Gray to plot the first few strips, telling the cartoonist to aim for adult readers. "Kids don't buy papers. Their parents do," Patterson explained. They devised a Dickensian tear-jerker of an introductory sequence: little Annie (smaller and therefore cuter at first than in her heyday) was forced to labor for her keep at the orphanage, which was as grim and oppressive as any Oliver Twist ever endured. Her fate was presided over by Miss Asthma, whose rotten disposition ringed every childish hope for adoption with a nimbus of gloom. The first strip appeared on 5 August 1924 and concluded with Annie's bedtime prayer: "Please make me a real good little girl so nice people will adopt me. Then I can have a papa and mama to love. And if it's not too much trouble, I'd like a dolly. Amen."

But Annie was not just a cute, sweet little girl. Gray quickly added dimension to her character: in the next day's strip, when a rude boy teases her, Annie wallops him in the kisser, establishing immediately that she has a certain independence of spirit in spite of her straitened circumstances. In a short time, Annie was a popular feature, and that spirit of independence that pervaded Gray's work eventually enlisted a devoted readership. At the end of the second month of the strip's run, Gray introduced the character that would shape the philosophy of independence into a political stance: Annie is adopted by Oliver "Daddy" Warbucks, a millionaire industrialist. Warbucks became Gray's example of the self-made man, the self-reliant individualist who made himself what he is through purposeful enterprise. Annie is often separated from "Daddy" and must find the means of survival, which she invariably does, following Warbucks's example of hard work and canny capitalism.

Oddly enough perhaps, Little Orphan Annie reached the zenith of its popularity during the presidency of Franklin D. Roosevelt, the man who encouraged people to look to government for help rather than exhorting them to help themselves by working hard and exercising diligently the principles of free enterprise. As Gray's exemplar, Warbucks could scarcely espouse self-reliance during the Roosevelt years without, at the same time, attacking FDR's policies. Little Orphan Annie became the first nationally syndicated comic strip to be unabashedly, unrelievedly, "political."

Some readers and critics—mostly avid supporters of Roosevelt's New Deal—saw Annie as a political mouthpiece for McCormick's conservative views masquerading as entertainment, a not-too-subtle indoctrination attempt by the Chicago Tribune. Not likely. While the strip's political diatribes during the thirties echoed McCormick's on the editorial pages of the Tribune, they did not, for a long time, reflect Patterson's views. And it was Patterson who ran the syndicate and directed the efforts of the cartoonists. With his eye ever on the common working people, Patterson sensed that most of his readers were behind Roosevelt. Moreover, his Socialist instincts, never fully abandoned, made him sympathetic to the worker's plight.[17] In the early thirties, the *Daily News* suddenly (and, remarkably, without any change in circulation or financial status) shifted its editorial ground. In a celebrated speech to his staff, Patterson announced, "We're off on the wrong foot. The people's major interest is no longer in the playboy, Broadway and divorces, but in how they're going to eat, and from this time forward, we'll pay attention to the struggle for existence that's just beginning."[18]

Almost alone among major newspaper publishers, the Captain supported Roosevelt and the New Deal. His support lasted through the thirties—until, in Roosevelt's lend-lease formula for aid to Britain, Patterson thought he saw the president tipping his hand. Once Patterson, a passionate isolationist and advocate of neutrality, thought Roosevelt intended to get America into the European conflict, he broke with FDR and became as bitter a critic of his policies as his cousin had been for nearly a decade. But from March 1933 until December 1940, the cousins disagreed on Roosevelt, and Patterson defended him as passionately as McCormick attacked him viciously. Meanwhile, Gray's orphan heroine went somberly about her business—reflecting her creator's opinions, born of both political conviction and narrative necessity.

Testimonials to the success of Patterson's strips began appearing almost immediately—in the usual flattering form. When *The Gumps* proved so popular, for example, other syndicates came up with their own "family" strips to sell to newspapers competing with those running Smith's melodrama. Thus we find *The Nebbs* offered by Bell Syndicate, beginning 22 May 1923; and from McNaught in 1925, Harry Tuthill's *The Bungle Family,* with more direct praise in the Gumpish upward aspirations and social criticism of its protagonist, George Bungle. Virtually all of the Patterson-guided strips were similarly aped.[19] Sincerely meant as all these encomiums doubtless were, they were to fade into insignificance in the face of similar praise that would be tendered the strip Patterson restyled from a submission by Chester Gould in 1931. *Dick Tracy* would be so widely imitated that it could correctly be said that the strip started an entire genre in the medium. Tracy himself would come to share a place in the history of detective fiction hitherto occupied in solitude by Conan Doyle's Sherlock Holmes.

Gould came to Chicago in 1921 to take courses in commerce and marketing at Northwestern University, but he had his eye on a cartooning career, and so he took night courses, too, in art. He began to bombard Patterson immediately with ideas for comic strips, keeping up the barrage steadily for ten years without success. Then he had his brainstorm: observing on every hand the lawlessness and corruption fueled by Prohibition, Gould decided to do a strip that would take on the criminal element. What was needed, he felt, was the kind of incorruptible cop who would shoot known hoodlums on sight. He promptly sat down to create just such a stalwart as a comic strip hero.[20] The hardboiled detective had been flourishing in the pages of such pulp magazines as *Black Mask* throughout the twenties. Gould appropriated the persona and, in visualizing his hero, gave him the chiseled profile he associated with Sherlock Holmes. Calling his hawk-nosed, razor-jawed private detective Plainclothes Tracy, Gould did some sample strips and shipped them off to Patterson in June 1931. He heard nothing for nearly two months. Then, on 13 August, he received a telegram:

YOUR PLAIN CLOTHES TRACY HAS POSSIBILITIES STOP WOULD LIKE TO SEE YOU WHEN I GET TO CHICAGO NEXT STOP PLEASE CALL TRIBUNE OFFICE MONDAY ABOUT NOON FOR AN APPOINT-MENT J M PATTERSON

Patterson began the interview by telling Gould his strip's title was too long. "Call him Dick Tracy," he said, "they call plainclothesmen 'dicks.'"[21] He also felt that the gangbusting activities of Gould's hero needed to be validated legally to prevent the strip's being accused of championing vigilantism, combating one sort of lawlessness with another. Tracy would not be a freelance operative; he would be a professional police officer. Patterson quickly outlined an introductory story that would provide both motive and legitimacy for Tracy's dogged crusade against crime. Tracy would begin as an ordinary fellow, but when his girlfriend's father is murdered by thugs and she is kidnapped, he would dedicate himself to her rescue and the hoodlums' apprehension. (Patterson named the girl, too—Tess Trueheart.) The police take advantage of Tracy's determination and enlist him in the plainclothes squad. Tracy infiltrates the gang, rescues Tess, and finally brings the crooks to book. Having proven his prowess as a hard-hitting crime fighter, Tracy becomes a career policeman. *Dick Tracy* began in the *News* and the *Detroit Mirror* (the Tribune Company's second tabloid undertaking) on Sunday, 4 October 1931. It appeared again the following Sunday, with the dailies starting the next day, 12 October.

Until the debut of Dick Tracy, the continuity strip had focused on one of two extremes, exotic adventure or domestic intrigue. Tracy brought the excitement of adventure to its readers' front doors when Gould's cop began fighting contemporary crime in everyone's hometown. Initially, the popularity of the strip sprang from its overt recognition and exploitation of the harsher realities of everyday life. Until Tracy, gunplay and bloodshed had been nearly taboo. Imitations began almost at once, and many of them disappeared pretty quickly.[22]

Gould's gratitude to and admiration for Patterson remained undiminished throughout a long career. "I owe everything that came to me in those days to the faith Patterson had in the strip," he once said.[23] Patterson's counsel did not end with their initial meeting. He continued to give advice—everything from broad plot outlines to tiny transitional maneuvers for getting from one story to the next, as he did with all the Tribune-News Syndicate cartoonists. Sometimes the ideas came to the cartoonists by memo or phone call. Sometimes they came out of the special forum Patterson conducted to nudge his strips to continued success.

Patterson had regular monthly meetings with his Chicago cartoonists, commuting from New York after he'd moved there permanently. (He once tried to get them all to move to New York where he could watch over them more conveniently. Gould avoided the directive by pointing to the relationship he had built up with the Chicago police department as a resource. Other cartoonists made similar cases for themselves, and a few actually made the move.) The cartoonists had offices along the same hallway in the Tribune building, and Patterson would call them all together in one of the offices. At these meetings, Patterson made suggestions about stories and characters and about whole ranges of reader-grabbing, suspense-building devices. He helped cartoonists fine-tune continuity and kept them abreast of his views on what would interest readers. If someone had drawn his story into a corner from which he saw no escape, Patterson would offer solutions. Patterson usually began by questioning each cartoonist about his progress and intentions on his strip's current story. Then the Captain would take his turn. "He would invariably have something to contribute," Gould recalled, "a story outline, a finale to a plot. He had a fantastic mind. He could talk to five cartoonists and give every one of them a terrific idea."[24]

Frank Willard agreed. "I worked for a syndicate manager once who got everybody in the place together once a week and jumped on a desk and gave us 'pep talks,'" he recounted. "In fact, I believe he was the original pep talker. He didn't give us any ideas, but, oh boy, how worn out we were after those pep talks. The guy who applauded the loudest got the most money, and I didn't get much as he found out who it was who gave him the bird. So I've never been accused of waving flags for the boss. But when you ask me what influenced me most in making *Moon Mullins,* I've gotta put the Captain in the Number One position, and I hope he never learns to draw, or I know about five or six comic artists who'll be looking for jobs."[25]

Patterson's letter to Berndt on 23 November 1923 is typical of the kind of direction he gave by written missive:

```
Dear Mr. Berndt:


I believe it would be proper to try an experiment. That
is, put a little pathos in the Smitty strip. This came
to me: Suppose Smitty is unjustly suspected of stealing.
Things disappear from the office, which he doesn't take, but
the boss, very much against his wish, is convinced of his
thievery and that Smitty is light-fingered. So, reluctantly,
he fires Smitty who goes home in disgrace and everybody
points the finger of scorn at him. Eventually, of course,
he is exonerated and all is well.


I believe that you could get some Jackie Coogan appeal by
this method.


Sincerely yours,
J. M. Patterson[26]
```

Patterson knew the value of comics in building the circulation of his newspaper, and he treated his cartoonists accordingly—always allowing for the fact that their value was even greater once they enjoyed the benefit of his own insights into the minds and hearts of readers. Mostly, his instincts were right. But sometimes he was dead wrong. Once in 1925 he yanked *Little Orphan Annie* when he disapproved of the direction in which Gray was going. Patterson thought Annie had no business leaving the Silos' humble farm to stay in Daddy Warbucks's sumptuous mansion. When she got mixed up in international finance and foreign intrigue, the Captain had had enough. But when the paper came out on 27 October without *Annie*, reaction from readers quickly told Patterson that he had made a mistake. He hastily reinstated the strip and apologized in a front-page editorial.[27]

On at least one other occasion Patterson revealed his fallibility. The take off of Zack Mosley's *Smilin' Jack* was so wobbly and prolonged as to suggest that the Captain's fabled instinct had bailed out to attend to other pressing matters while he was buying the strip. Mosley had heard that Patterson was taking flying lessons, so he concocted a light-hearted strip about instructor pilots and called it *On the Wing,* basing the incidents upon his own fearful experiences in learning to fly.[28] The strip started as a Sunday feature in a new, expanded comics section on 1 October 1933.

Five weeks after the strip started, Mosley got a telegram in Chicago from Patterson: "Change the name of *On the Wing* to *Smilin' Jack,*" it said. Mosley wired back: "The name of the main character is Mack not Jack." Patterson was not deterred by details: "Change name to *Smilin' Jack,*" he responded. "Naturally I did," Mosley recalled, "but I wondered what the readers would think when they saw that 'Mack' was suddenly 'Jack.'" Readers apparently thought nothing of it: not one complained when the new name appeared on December 30. (Mosley never found out why Patterson changed the name. Maybe the Captain was inspired by Mosley's own beaming countenance, the autobiographical nature of the strip, and the profusion of sound-alike names—Zack, Mack, and Jack.)

Those who remember *Smilin' Jack* doubtless recall a strip with lots of pictures of airplanes and a string of bizarre adventures, but it did not begin as an adventure strip—a fact of which Mosley had to be rudely reminded almost immediately. Shortly after the strip began, he insinuated some hair-brained adventuring into it, and Patterson promptly relieved him of any confusion he may have had about why the strip had been selected.

"You started off with true-to-life scared pilots," he explained. "But you are about to become imaginative. Stick to real flying. No shooting tigers from a cockpit. Keep up your flying lessons—and, so I can keep an eye on you, move to New York immediately."[29]

Properly chastised, Mosley dutifully packed himself and his wife off to the Big Apple, and *Smilin' Jack* continued for the next two and a half years as a Sunday-only feature about the high-spirited training field antics of a bunch of young pilots. Patterson eventually relented, and *Smilin' Jack* was convened to a seven-day adventure strip, the daily beginning 6 June 1936, and Mosley's aviator was thrust into one harrowing scrape after another for the next thirty-seven years.

Mosley proved himself adept at telling an adventure story—in his own haphazard, eccentric, almost zany, fashion. His off-hand plots were held together by a rapid-fire series of increasingly desperate situations from which Smilin' Jack extricated himself by a succession of maneuvers whose ascending ingenuity of contrivance gave every story the breathless spontaneity of catch-as-catch-can invention. Typifying Mosley's creative eccentricity perhaps is one of his most memorable characters, Downwind Jaxon, whose face we never saw.

In early 1939, Mosley was rushing to complete a batch of strips so he could take a vacation in Cuba. He needed a handsome skirt-chasing character, but since handsome men were difficult for him to draw distinctively, he could not come up with a good face quickly. Mosley decided to postpone the moment of creation until he returned from Cuba, but he had to introduce the character before he left. He faked it. When we first see Downwind, we see him almost from behind: only the side of his forehead and rounded cheek and chin are visible in a sort of profile. When Mosley returned two weeks later, he still could not come up with a face for Downwind, so he continued to draw him in profile as seen from behind one shoulder. Pretty soon, the mysterious Downwind began to draw mail. Patterson complimented Mosley on his perspicacity and suggested waiting about two months before showing Downwind's face. "Well, if it's getting such a good response," Mosley said, "how about never showing his face?" The Captain thought for a moment and then agreed. And so Downwind was condemned to a faceless existence.[30] Patterson's instinct convened Mosley's fumbling and groping into a firm grip on his readers, and letters asking for a glimpse of Downwind's permanently averted visage came in a steady stream for the next three decades.

The Captain followed his instinct again with Milton Caniff. And again, he was proved absolutely correct. In the autumn of 1934, Patterson was unhappy about the *Teenie Weenies*. For the expanded comics section that had been launched the previous fall, he had talked Donahey into using a comic strip format for the feature instead of illustrating a portion of storytelling text as he had done since the feature's inception. Patterson thought it was not working. Moreover, in Patterson's view, the big-city readers of the *Daily News* needed something livelier, something spicier than Donahey's children's feature. He decided that he wanted an adventure continuity, a genre just emerging on the nation's comics pages. Mollie Slott had been showing him clippings of *Dickie Dare*, an adventure strip from The Associated Press Feature Service that her sons followed and liked. So the Captain sent for its author, Milton Caniff.

As usual, Patterson knew what he wanted, and he quickly outlined his ideas to the young cartoonist. He specified an adventure strip with a young boy as hero (to appeal to young readers) but with plenty of pretty girls around, too (for the kids' fathers, those who bought the paper). The boy should have an adult sidekick, a rugged handsome fellow to handle the rough stuff and to romance the girls. Patterson urged Caniff to give his strip sex appeal but to confine the heartthrobs to daily strips—"Do the Sunday page for the kids," he said. The action should be set in the Orient, the Captain ordered. "Adventure can still happen out there," he said, recalling, perhaps, his own experiences in watching the sacking of Peking more than thirty years before.[31] There were still pirates active along the China coast, he added, and, referring Caniff to a book on the subject, he suggested that a beautiful female pirate might make a good villain.

Patterson did not give the young cartoonist much time to develop his concept. Within a week, he wanted to see some Sunday pages. (He needed a Sunday strip so he could drop the *Teenie Weenies* as soon as possible.) According to legend (of which Caniff was chief author), Caniff researched the Orient (about which he then knew next to nothing), developed characters, and wrote and drew up a couple of sample Sunday pages—all within a single week while also producing the next week's set of *Dickie Dare* strips and a week's worth of *The Gay Thirties,* the panel cartoon he was doing for The Associated Press. By way of research, Caniff consulted the book Patterson had recommended—*Vampires of the China Coast,* a lurid potboiler about a marauding pirate band—and several other works on the Far East that he found at The New York Public Library. Following another of the Captain's recommendations, he also read *Wuthering Heights,* where he found fully developed the theme of passionate but unconsummated and thwarted love. He recognized immediately that such a circumstance was perfect for dealing with a footloose romantic lead who was to encounter an endless parade of toothsome ladies, becoming involved with each of them but entangled by none. The frustration in an unrealized love affair would grip readers by building and sustaining suspense.[32]

At the end of a week, Caniff submitted a strip called *Tommy Tucker.* Patterson liked everything he saw except the name (as usual), so he asked for a list of alternatives; from that list, he picked "Terry," adding "and the Pirates" to create the strip's title. He then put the Sunday pages into production and told Caniff to produce a week's worth of dailies. The first Sunday page would not get into print for about two months, but Patterson wanted to start the daily strips immediately—the following Monday, 22 October, if possible; so Caniff concocted another storyline for the dailies, and Terry began that Monday.

With *Terry and the Pirates,* Caniff redefined the adventure strip genre. Inspired by the work of his studio mate Noel Sickles, Caniff developed an impressionistic style of drawing that suggested reality economically, with shadow rather than with painstakingly rendered particulars. To the realism of his graphic technique, he added realism of detail, striving for absolute authenticity in depicting every aspect of the setting for *Terry.* He polished the prose of his dialogues, and as speech balloons grew larger to accommodate increasingly sophisticated and complex plots, he resorted to cinematic techniques to rejuvenate visual excitement in the strip. But his signal accomplishment was as a storyteller: he enriched the simple adventure story formula by making character development integral to action-packed stories. Plots were character driven rather than imposed upon characters. His characters seemed to be real people, and we were as concerned about how they developed and their relationships to one another as we were about what happened to them.

It was undoubtedly the Dragon Lady that sparked Caniff's interest in character portrayal. In realizing Patterson's suggestion to make a beautiful pirate queen a villain in his story, Caniff struck a rich vein of creative ore in his own imagination. As he attempted to understand and portray the complexities of a villain who inspired both lust and loathing, he discovered the dramatic power of characterization. In the exotic locale Patterson had suggested, the cartoonist's creativity flowered. Patterson had supplied Caniff with the very material most congenial to his talent. More than congenial, it was to prove a uniquely prolific union, a conjunction of talent with material that continually stimulated it. Under the spell of his material, Caniff set new standards of excellence against which all subsequent adventure strips were measured.

But Caniff never attended Patterson's periodic meetings with the other cartoonists. In fact, his absence from these confabulations was a point of pride with him. Years later, when I was interviewing him for the biography I was writing, Caniff would insist that he had had only three interviews with Patterson about the strip—and two of them were those that resulted in the assignment and the selection of the strip's name.[33] In the twelve years he produced *Terry*, Caniff had no other story conferences with the Captain. Caniff repeated this assertion on a couple of occasions, as if his having enjoyed an absolutely free hand with the strip was validation of his own talent: he had been able to sustain the strip *without* any assistance from the medium's most highly regarded story editor and idea man. Caniff's insistence on this point also testifies to Patterson's own considerable talent.

But the Captain was not always right, and not every strip he touched was Midas-ized. None of the other strips he had introduced in the expanded comic section in 1933, for instance, lasted as long as *Smilin' Jack* or attracted as faithful a following.[34] Not that Patterson had suddenly, overnight, lost his grasp on the public pulse. He had launched other strips that had faltered and, finally, failed: Ferd Johnson's *Texas Slim* ran for only three years until it was discontinued in 1929.[35] Tack Knight's *Little Folks*, starting in January 1930, lasted only a little longer than Johnson's entry. The Captain was not infallible. Sometimes he picked losers. Sometimes he overlooked promising submissions. Take *Brenda Starr*, for instance.

Brenda is undoubtedly the most frilly-witted heroine in comics, and perhaps for that reason, Patterson wanted nothing to do with her. Brenda is the creation of one of cartooning's most celebrated female cartoonists, Dalia Messick. Messick, knowing that a woman cartoonist would have small chance of success in the male-dominated world of the thirties and forties, changed her name to Dale when she signed her cartoons, thinking that most editors to whom she submitted her work by mail would not suspect she was female. But by the time she got around to peddling her strip about a girl reporter to Patterson, he knew Dale was a woman. Patterson did not like the strip. He might be guilty of simple male chauvinism, or he could be accused of sexism. But anyone hoping to make the charge stick will have to explain Mary King and Mollie Slott. King was Patterson's first assistant on the Sunday *Tribune,* and he gave her credit for "at least half of every good idea I ever had."[36] He eventually married her (but not until 1938). Slott was Patterson's good right hand on Tribune-News Syndicate matters. It is doubtful that a rampant sexist would give such power and responsibility to women.

In any case, Slott overcame Patterson's objections to *Brenda Starr.* She prevailed upon the Captain to buy the strip. He agreed—but only so long as *Brenda Starr* would never appear in his newspaper, the *New York Daily News,* and it did not. Messick's chronically romantic newspaperwoman was introduced 30 June 1940 in the *Chicago Tribune*'s newly launched Sunday comic book magazine. Not until after Patterson's death in 1946 did the strip make it into the *News.*

No, Joe Patterson was not always right. To make the comic strips that he adopted succeed, he doubtless needed the chemistry of collaboration with just the right kinds of cartoonists. Willard was probably correct: Patterson was only half of a creative team. He was the spark that kindled the tinder, and without the proper combustible, the flame wavered and expired. In any case, the Captain's successes far outshone his misfires.

If not all of the strips he midwifed attracted the fanatical followings achieved by *The Gumps* or *Little Orphan Annie* or *Dick Tracy* or *Terry and the Pirates,* all of the others described acquired large and devoted readerships that garnered wide circulation and ran so long as to outlast their creators. Each of these strips is a unique creation. Each bears the individual signs of its cartoonist's creative personality, and they all carry the stamp of their co-creator's generative invention and imaginative intervention. Patterson's continued participation in the production of these strips helped assure their success and perpetuated his reputation. It is clear that he had a peculiarly valuable gift for knowing what his readers would like—for storylines, characters, incidents, and gimmicks. When his genius as a story editor and idea man was coupled with the genius of a graphic storyteller—when the cartoonist was another kind of genius—the combination produced strips of remarkable originality and longevity. For all the ideas and advice he gave his cartoonists, theirs were the individual creative talents that took his suggestions and made them into distinctive and memorable works of narrative graphic art. Patterson's ideas, valuable as they were, could not have flourished without them. To make the long haul, the cartoonists needed ingenuity of their own to complement his contributions, to put his notions into successful motion. But Patterson got them started and often kept them going.

ENDNOTES

This article appeared in somewhat different form as a chapter in Robert Harvey's *The Art of the Funnies* (Jackson: University Press of Mississippi, 1994). In addition to the works cited below, the author consulted Frederick Lewis Allen, *Only Yesterday: An Informal History of the 1920s* (1931; repr., New York: Harper and Row, 1964).

1. The reincarnation of Dirks's famed *Katzenjammer Kids*, the strip was later re-titled *The Captain and the Kids* in the national fit of anti-German feeling during World War I.

2. John Winkler's *W. R. Hearst: An American Phenomenon* (New York: Simon and Schuster, 1928) was published while Hearst was still a relatively young man. W. A. Swanberg, *Citizen Hearst* (New York: Scribner's, 1961) is among the standard biographies.

3. The details of Patterson's life are briefly sketched in several works, most of them about his cousin, Robert McCormick; among them are Joseph Gies, *The Colonel of Chicago* (New York: Dutton, 1979); Frank C. Waldrop, *McCormick of Chicago* (Englewood Cliffs, NJ: Prentice-Hall, 1966); Lloyd Wendt, *The Chicago Tribune: The Rise of a Great American Newspaper* (New York: Rand McNally, 1979). But in John Tebbel, *An American Dynasty: The Story of the McCormicks, Medills, and Pattersons* (New York: Doubleday, 1947) and in Leo E. McGivena, *The News: The First 50 Years of New York's Picture Newspaper* (New York: News Syndicate, 1969) we find more extensive biographical accounts. The best portrait of Patterson's personality that I have found is provided in the anecdotally rich *Tell It to Sweeney: An Informal History of the New York Daily News* (New York: Doubleday, 1961) by John Chapman, longtime drama critic for the paper, who joined the staff as a cub reporter in 1920.

4. The happiest phrases in the last two sentences are the felicitous confections of Richard O'Conner in *The Spirit Soldiers* (New York: Putnam, 1973), a rendition of the Boxer Rebellion.

5. McGivena, *The News*, 24.

6. McGivena, *The News*, 93.

7. Patterson's daily routine is outlined in Tebbel, *An American Dynasty*, 290–91 and in McGivena, *The News*, 291.

8. McGivena, *The News*, 25.

9. Tebbel, *An American Dynasty*, 302.

10. John McCutcheon, *Drawn from Memory* (New York: Bobbs-Merrill, 1950); pages 286–90 cover his adventures with Patterson and his remarks as quoted herein.

11. McGivena, *The News*, 19–20.

12. Winsor McCay's famed *Little Nemo in Slumberland* frequently continued a narrative from Sunday to Sunday, and Bud Fisher had done it from day to day at various times in the early days of *Mutt and Jeff*. These two strips were not alone. C. W. Kahles introduced *Hairbreadth Harry* in 1906, a Sunday strip that carried its story forward from week to week. Harry Hershfield used daily continuity in his *Desperate Desmond* (1910) and its sequel, *Dauntless Durham* (1913). But the Kahles and Hershfield strips were burlesques of melodrama rather than serious continuing stories.

13. Herb Galewitz, ed., *Sidney Smith's The Gumps* (New York: Scribner's, 1974), viii. The history of the strip is recounted in the book's introduction.

14. Herb Galewitz, ed., *Great Comics Syndicated by the Daily News-Chicago Tribune* (New York: Crown Publishers, 1972), ix.

15. It is not clear whether Patterson originated the idea for *Winnie,* or whether Arthur Crawford or Branner simply hit upon something Patterson liked. But since Crawford reportedly went looking for a cartoonist rather than for a strip, it is probable that he and Patterson had the concept in mind. Compare Stephen Becker, *Comic Art in America* (New York: Simon and Schuster, 1959), 74–75 and Martin Sheridan, *Comics and Their Creators* (1944; repr., New York: Luna Press, 1971), 189.

16. Bruce Smith, *The History of Little Orphan Annie* (New York: Ballantine Books, 1982), 8–9.

17. George Seldes, who attacks the "lords of the press" in his 1938 book by that name (New York: Julian Messner), praises Patterson as an employer on page 40: "Patterson treats his employees better than ninety or perhaps ninety-nine percent of the publishers in America. He is one of the few owners respected and liked by the Newspaper Guild. No one has ever accused him of double-dealing, nor have briefs charging violations of the law been filed against him. Some of the self-announced great liberal newspapers cannot make equal claims."

18. Tebbel, *An American Dynasty,* 258.

19. *Harold Teen* doubtless prompted the birth in 1925 of *Etta Kett,* King Features's teenage manners strip by Paul Robinson. *Winnie Winkle* obviously inspired Russ Westover's *Tillie the Toiler,* which King launched in 1921. *Little Orphan Annie* immediately provoked United Feature into getting Charles Plumb and Bill Conselman to do *Ella Cinders,* which appeared in 1925—less than a year after Gray's strip debuted. Two years later, Hearst entered two strips in the waif lists: *Two Orphans* and *Little Annie Roonie.* If two strips were better than one, so two orphans (a boy and a girl, both with blank eyeballs—and a dog) were better than one. Drawn by Al Zere, this double-trouble entry had a short life. But *Little Annie Roonie* (an echo of the original in title as well as heroine and constant canine companion) lasted longer.

20. The story of the genesis of Dick Tracy can be found in Ellery Queen, "The Importance of Being Earnest; or, the Survival of the Finest," introduction to *The Celebrated Cases of Dick Tracy,* ed. Herb Galewitz (New York: Chelsea House, 1970), xvii; Sheridan, *Comics and Their Creators,* 121–22; and John Culhane, "Dick Tracy: The First Law and Order Man," *Argosy* (June 1974): 20–21, 44–47.

21. Culhane, "Dick Tracy," 44.

22. Among the ones that lasted a reasonable time were *Dan Dunn* by Norman Marsh (1933), *Pinkerton, Jr.* by Charlie Schmidt (1933; becoming *Radio Patrol* in 1934), *Red Barry* by Will Gould (no relation; 1934), *Secret Agent X-9* (1934), written by Dashiell Hammett and drawn by Alex Raymond, who would achieve greater fame drawing *Flash Gordon* and, later, *Rip Kirby,* a detective strip that started in 1946; *Inspector Wade* by Lyman Anderson (1935), *Jim Hardy* by Dick Moores (once assistant to Gould; 1936), *Mickey Finn* by Frank E. Leonard (focusing on a policeman's family life; 1936), *Charlie Chan* (1938) and *Kerry Drake* (1943), both by Alfred Andriola, and so on. Virtually every comic strip about cops and robbers is a descendant of Dick Tracy (including, naturally, Al Capp's patent parody, *Fearless Fosdick,* in which Gould delighted, saying he was pleased to be the only cartoonist in the world who had a great comic strip artist for a press agent—absolutely free).

23. Galewitz, "Interview with Chester Gould," in *The Celebrated Cases of Dick Tracy,* viii.

24. Galewitz, *The Celebrated Cases of Dick Tracy,* viii.

25. Sheridan, *Comics and Their Creators,* 75.

26. Jerry Robinson, *The Comics: An Illustrated History of Comic Strip Art* (New York: Putnam, 1974), 85.

27. Smith, *The History of Little Orphan Annie,* 17.

28. Zack "Smilin' Jack" Mosley, *Brave Coward Zack* (St. Petersburg, FL: Valkyrie Press, 1976); on pages 22–26, Mosley recounts the birth of his comic strip.

29. Mosley, *Brave Coward Zack,* 29.

30. Mosley, *Brave Coward Zack*, 42–44.

31. Sheridan, *Comics and Their Creators*, 220. This section is also based on my conversations with Caniff.

32. Caniff always credited Patterson with suggesting the basic formula for *Terry*, but it is clear that *Terry* was but another incarnation of *Dickie Dare*. Originally, *Dickie Dare* was about a young boy who dreams himself into adventures with his favorite literary and historical heroes—Robin Hood, Aladdin, Robinson Crusoe, General Custer, Captain Kidd. In May 1934, Caniff wrote the dreams out of Dickie's life by teaming him up with a vagabond adventurer and freelance writer named Dan Flynn, and the duo went off to have "real" adventures. Caniff thought his innovation so promising that he wrote to a Sigma Chi fraternity brother, John McCutcheon at the *Chicago Tribune*, asking for a letter of introduction to Patterson. With that in hand, Caniff visited the Tribune-News Syndicate offices and met Arthur Crawford and Mollie Slott. Nothing came of his visits, though, until that fall, when, as we see, Patterson summoned him to his office. In creating Terry and Pat Ryan, Caniff merely changed Dickie's black hair to blond and Flynn's blond hair to black. Caniff had even introduced the unrequited love theme in the AP strip at the conclusion of the first adventure with Dan Flynn.

33. The other interview took place in the fall of 1941, when isolationist Patterson told Caniff to stop depicting Japanese soldiers as villains in the strip. But Patterson's objection to this practice quickly evaporated when Pearl Harbor was bombed a couple of months later.

34. Al Posen's *Sweeney & Son* and Ed Leffingwell's *Little Joe* were solid efforts and ran at least half as long as Mosley's strip, but neither strip was particularly distinctive. Garrett Price abandoned *White Boy* after three years to concentrate on magazine illustration and *New Yorker* cartoons (a sure indication that *White Boy*'s circulation was not remunerative enough). Gaar Williams's *A Strain on the Family Tie* and Gus Edson's *Streaky* both sank without a ripple (the latter when Edson took over *The Gumps* at Sidney Smith's death in an auto accident in 1935, just after he had signed a new contract for $150,000 per year for three more years). And, as we've seen, the revamped *Teenie Weenies* was not satisfactory either.

35. It was revived in 1948 and ran for another eighteen years until Johnson took over *Moon Mullins* at Willard's death.

36. Waldrop, *McCormick of Chicago*, 181.

The "Monumental" Lincoln as an American Cartoon Convention

ROGER A. FISCHER

A GENERATION OF AMERICANS will carry the image to their graves: Bill Mauldin's Lincoln Memorial likeness, head in hands, mourning the assassination of John Fitzgerald Kennedy. Mauldin had finished his daily cartoon that gray November day when he was told of the shooting in Dallas. Returning to his drawing board at the *Chicago Sun-Times,* he pondered how to render his comment on such a "monumental" tragedy, and from the word "monumental," he derived his inspiration. Racing a looming deadline, he finished it in two hours. In stark simplicity, Mauldin's masterpiece captured precisely the national mood of wrenching grief seasoned with a pinch of shame. According to a *Sun-Times* promotional blurb, more than 150,000 copies were requested in the eight months following the assassination.[1] Another key to the greatness of this cartoon was the appropriateness of its analogy. Both Lincoln and Kennedy had served as uncommonly strong presidents much maligned in turbulent times, in part for their commitments to human rights for black Americans, and both had been gunned down in their political primes by mentally unstable ideologues, JFK just three days after the centennial of the Gettysburg Address.

To judge from an anthology of 1963 assassination cartoons, in which Mauldin's effort was not included, several other American editorial cartoonists utilized the Lincoln/Kennedy parallel, including such worthies as Don Wright and Jim Berryman. Especially successful was the tribute by *Dayton Journal-Herald* artist (and noted Lincoln enthusiast) Lloyd Ostendorf, exploiting the theme of JFK's Pulitzer Prize-winning volume *Profiles in Courage.* In the anthology, Lincoln was represented in profile, bust, and full-figure, as well as the agent of apotheosis in the clouds; but only once is he shown in "monumental" form, in clouds above the Kennedy casket, as drawn by John Milton Morris for The Associated Press.[2] If the cartoons by Morris and Mauldin were uncommon at the time, they did reflect faithfully a tradition of more than a century of cartooning Lincoln more often as a monument, an inanimate representation of the American nation and an icon of American political ideals, than as a man. The inspiration for this flowed neither from Lincoln the prairie rail splitter nor from the savior of the Union martyred on the altar of sectional discord and racial strife, but instead from the august white marble figure by Daniel Chester French that graces Henry Bacon's shrine at the foot of the National Mall in Washington. For two generations before its 1922 dedication and three since, American editorial cartoonists have tended to favor drawing Lincoln not as flesh-and-blood caricature, but as a bronze or marble representational sculpture.

It was not always so. The living Lincoln, during the course of his 1860 candidacy and a troubled presidency, served as a very human foil in many cartoons, ranging from whimsical Currier & Ives lithographs to the caustic satire of John Tenniel and his *Punch* compatriots and the venomous characterizations of Baltimore Confederate artist Adalbert Volck. As mean-spirited and scabrous as many of these creations seem in retrospect, they did suggest in the lean, craggy beanpole with a wicked wit, a ripe figure for creative caricature. One student of American national symbolism has suggested that Lincoln served cartoon artists here and in London as a prototype for Uncle Sam.[3] But then, on the morning of 15 April 1865, he passed on to the ages, and as David Donald has noted, grieving countrymen "suddenly discovered that the President had been the greatest man in the world."[4] To portray a Lincoln of foibles and flaws became for American cartoonists not just what we would term today "politically incorrect" but out and out sacrilege. I am aware of no posthumous Lincoln cartoon that mocks or disparages him and, until recently, few even subjected him to the gentlest of humor. Since political cartooning is an inherently negative medium thriving upon barbed satire, this universal reverence accorded the martyred Lincoln has rendered him of rather limited use to cartoonists.

An inventory of the cartoons in *Puck* and *Judge* yields no more than two dozen Lincoln cartoons from 1877 through 1900, barely one per year. Thomas Nast, despite Lincoln's immense potential as the ultimate Union icon and his own penchant for scourging the Democracy and the South with the graphic art of the "bloody shirt," rarely drew him at all during his heyday at *Harper's Weekly*. An exception, and a somewhat "nasty" one at that, was "Wilkes Booth the Second," featuring Democratic vice presidential nominee Francis "Frank" Blair and *New York Democrat* editor "Brick" Pomeroy sneaking up with sword to assassinate Ulysses Grant, as beneath a portrait of Lincoln he pondered a scroll, reading, "With malice toward none and charity for all . . . Let us have peace."[5] Only in the sunset years of Nast's career, during the 1892 and 1896 campaigns, did he utilize Lincoln along with Grant as stereotypical cartoon conventions to measure (and find wanting) the stature of Democratic nominees Grover Cleveland and William Jennings Bryan.

In his 1947 essay "The Folklore Lincoln," David Donald described Lincoln's posthumous evolution into an American folk icon in terms of a lengthy struggle over essential definition as grateful freedmen sought to define him as a New World Moses; New England clergymen as a blend of Washington and Jesus ("somewhat like a Gilbert Stuart painting with a halo dubbed in by later, less skillful hands"); and westerners as a Bunyanesque but lazy practical joker, "teller of tall and lusty tales."[6] Gilded Age cartoons attest instead to an apotheosis more sudden and less complicated, an almost instantaneous transformation into a national civic deity as suggested by Mark Neely Jr., Gabor Boritt, and Harold Holzer in *The Lincoln Image* and in greater detail recently by Merrill Peterson in *Lincoln in American Memory*.[7]

It should be remembered that in its infancy political cartooning was primarily a New York phenomenon, owing more to the urban centers of the Atlantic seaboard and Europe than to American regional folklore. Thus, the martyr slain on Good Friday for the sins of sectionalism was never a theme in Lincoln cartooning and not till the later emergence of such native midwestern editorial artists as John T. McCutcheon and Jay N. "Ding" Darling would Lincoln be drawn, and uncommonly at that, as a frontier folk figure. More indicative of the thematic exploitation of Lincoln as a cartoon convention is Peterson's thesis that his place in our national memory has hinged on five salient facets: "Lincoln as Savior of the Union, Great Emancipator, Man of the People, the First American, and the Self-Made Man. Nationality, Humanity, Democracy, Americanism, and the individual opportunity which is its essence; these are the building blocks of the Lincoln image."[8]

A revealing parallel to the genesis of Lincoln as a folk icon of the American nation and generations of cartoonists was the earlier apotheosis of George

Washington. In his essay "The Flawless American," Lawrence J. Friedman analyzed perceptively the invention of Washington by eulogists as the ultimate American deity, lauded by historian John Kingston in 1813 as "the statesman's polar star; the hero's destiny; the boast of age; the companion of maturity; and the goal of youth."[9] The pillar of probity, compassionate conqueror, exemplar of republican virtue and common sense, and even in death an immortal mortal, the mythic Washington became to Americans a measure of human perfectibility by which future generations of our would-be statesmen were to be judged. In 1822 the *Richmond Enquirer* exulted, "His character is the scale by which the people will graduate the measures and conduct of his successors."[10] In explaining away or simply ignoring Washington's human failings, his eulogists rendered him, as Donald has noted, "so dignified and remote that it was hard to think of him as a man, much less as a boy; he was a portrait by Peale or a Houdon bust."[11] Cartoon portrayals of Lincoln during the generation after his death followed suit almost identically by casting him as less man than monument, the ultimate yardstick or scale by which a later generation of public men could be measured.

The first victim of such cartoon appraisal was Lincoln's Confederate counterpart, Jefferson Davis, whose 1881 autobiography inspired the acid James A. Wales *Puck* front cover cartoon "A Dead Hero and a Live Jackass," contrasting a monumental "Malice Toward None" Lincoln with Davis (clad in a bonnet, shawl, and hoopskirt to recall his humiliating escape from Fortress Monroe), hawking his *History of Treason* outside a "Secession Cemetery."[12] When Davis died eight years later, a *Judge* front cover cartoon drawn by Bernhard Gillam featured Miss South mourning the rebel chieftain as a "patriot and statesman" as the shade of Lincoln mused, "If he was a PATRIOT, what was I?"[13]

Although such cartoons demonstrate the potential utility of Lincoln for disparaging the South and the Democracy, such was not the case in the ferocious 1884 Cleveland–Blaine contest, although the Blaine forces resorted in speeches and print to strident appeals to wartime passions. The single Lincoln bloody shirt cartoon that year in either *Puck* or *Judge* was an anti-Republican *Puck* centerfold by Gillam savaging James G. Blaine's running mate, John Logan, for his antebellum zeal for hunting down fugitive slaves.[14] *Judge* exploited Lincoln only once that year as well, among a quartet of tattooed figures (with Washington, Blaine, and James A. Garfield) in a rather lame Grant Hamilton attempt to rebut the celebrated *Puck* series lampooning Blaine as the "tattooed man" of political sleaze and scandal.[15]

Why *Judge* artists neglected to exploit Lincoln as a bloody shirt icon until after the election defies logic, but Cleveland's selection of ex-Confederates for key administration positions and other purported outrages against the Lincoln

FIGURE 29. James A. Wales, "A Dead Hero and a Live Jackass," *Puck,* June 22, 1881, 267.

VOL. 17 NO. 427   DECEMBER 21, 1889.   PRICE 10 CENTS.

Judge

ENTERED AT THE POST OFFICE AT NEW YORK AS SECOND-CLASS MATTER.   COPYRIGHT 1889 BY THE JUDGE PUBLISHING CO.

THE TRUTH OF 1861 IS THE TRUTH OF TO-DAY!

SHADE OF LINCOLN—"If he was a PATRIOT what was I?"

FIGURE 30. Bernhard Gillam, "The Truth of 1861 is the Truth of To-day," *Judge*, December 21, 1889, 169.

legacy guaranteed him steady work as a cartoon convention beginning in 1885. Cleveland's pilgrimage to Gettysburg that May, reported by *The New York Sun* as an orgy of gluttony and beer guzzling, prompted the Daniel McCarthy Memorial Day cartoon "Two Presidents at Gettysburg," portraying Cleveland ordering up more beer as he feasts with secretary Daniel Lamont on "Solid South" beef against a backdrop of Lincoln delivering his immortal address.[16]

Even more outrageous as sectional demagogy was Gillam's 1887 Independence Day cartoon, "Halt!," fueled by the return of some rebel battle flags as a conciliatory gesture. Protesting the surrender of flags from Antietam, Gettysburg, Vicksburg, and Appomattox to Lucius Lamar and a scruffy Solid South representation, Lincoln's specter ("Spirit of the War for the Union") declares, "Had you *fought* for those flags, you would not be so quick to give them away!" This reminder of Cleveland's purchase of a substitute to avoid donning Union blue is met with a protest, "They're rubbish anyhow." Other "rubbish" in the room includes Redcoat flags and muskets; a Mexican cannon; a whip for slaves; the bonnet, shawl, and hoopskirt of Jefferson Davis; and—*piece de résistance*—the pistol of John Wilkes Booth.[17] Both vicious and patently dishonest, the cartoon illustrates an irony in Lincoln cartooning, then and since, the exploitation of "Honest Abe" as a device for wholesale deception. This was Lincoln, after all, author of "malice toward none, charity for all," a man who on the evening of Lee's surrender had graciously requested the Marine band to play "Dixie."

Other *Judge* cartoons deploying Lincoln as a weapon against the Democracy include an 1890 Hamilton Memorial Day centerfold and the 11 October 1890 F. Victor Gillam centerfold, "The Same Old Sneaking Deserter."[18] When in 1890 a measure to provide federal protection to African American voters in the South fell victim to Democratic Senate opposition, Victor Gillam adorned a centerfold of Miss Columbia facing down a motley array of Democratic ward heelers and Dixie bigots with a Lincoln portrait inscribed, "My work was not in vain."[19] Just months earlier, a *Judge* editorial by publisher William J. Arkell had mocked black political participation as "the gift of a jewel to a barbarian unaware of the difference between a bead and a diamond" and had urged instead strict literacy tests to weed out most black and immigrant voters.[20] As late as 1896, Lincoln was used as a bloody shirt device against William Jennings Bryan in *Puck* and *Judge* alike. Victor Gillam's September *Judge* centerfold "Forbear!" portrayed Lincoln's ghost demanding of Bryan, "Halt! How dare you try to revive a war of sections?" while Louis Dalrymple's October *Puck* centerfold "History Repeats Itself" featured a vignette of Jefferson Davis defying Lincoln and the Union at Fort Sumter as a parallel to Bryan and his scruffy Dixie and radical minions denouncing federal interference in local affairs.[21]

Lincoln's image as the Great Emancipator was occasionally used more benignly by turn-of-the-century cartoonists. A bookmark bearing his bust adorned Grant Hamilton's *Judge* centerfold "Two Pages in History," a tribute to the 1885 New Orleans Exposition, which contrasted slaves toiling in a cotton field under the whip with freedmen casting votes in Ohio.[22] A Joseph Keppler Jr. *Puck* centerfold, "The New South—The Triumph of Free Labor," a salute to the 1895 Atlanta Exposition, featured whites and blacks paying respects to a statue of Lincoln.[23] Hamilton's "1863–1898, History Repeats Itself," a *Judge* tribute to Cuban liberation, paired a marble monument of William McKinley freeing Miss Cuba with similar background statuary of Lincoln with his proclamation freeing a slave.[24] Hamilton's January 1899 accolade to McKinley for extending federal care to Confederate parts of Civil War cemeteries, "Great Men Make Great Nations," linked McKinley ("Fraternity—Care for Confederate Dead") and Grant ("Let Us Have Peace") with Lincoln ("Liberty—Emancipation").[25] As did the Mauldin assassination cartoon, these efforts utilized Lincoln as a symbolic expression of the fundamental ideals of the American experiment, above party or faction. The vast majority of Lincoln cartoons then and since, however, have been both partisan and pejorative. Yet even at a time when memories of the war and concomitant party battles were yet undimmed, the cartoon Lincoln was never exclusively a device used by Republicans to denigrate Democrats, thus reinforcing the notion of Lincoln as icon and yardstick.

In his 1951 essay "Getting Right With Lincoln," David Donald noted that the tug-of-war over the martyr's shroud began almost at once and, despite the manifest advantages enjoyed by the GOP in laying claim to the Lincoln legacy, rarely did it do so by default.[26] Four *Puck* centerfolds published between 1885 and 1891 co-opted the image of Lincoln to bash his party heirs. Bernhard Gillam's 1885 "A Great Past and a Pitiful Present" utilized a background monument to David Farragut, Grant accepting Lee's sword, and Lincoln freeing the slaves to counterpoint the current GOP slough of scandal and fraud, while Uncle Sam protested in subtext below, "It's no use lifting me up to look at your Monumental Record, gentlemen; what can you give me to stand on *Now?*"[27] Joseph Keppler's 1887 "The Lesson of the Past" summoned the ghost of Lincoln to comfort a beleaguered Cleveland, "They call me martyr, chief among the dead, and speak my name with reverence. In my life no curse too vile, no word of spite too wild they found to cast up on me."[28] Keppler's 1887 "The Ideals of 1863 and the Idol of 1887—The Decadence of a Great Party" utilized marble statues of Lincoln and Charles Sumner in the background as reminders of a noble tradition debased by a current GOP party idol representing the politics of the bloody shirt, pension fraud, and patronage spoils.[29] In "The Old Leaders and the New" four years later, Keppler exploited this same formula to debase Republican chieftains George Frisbie Hoar, "Czar" Reed, Matthew Quay, and Benjamin Harrison as unworthy of party patriarchs Sumner, William Seward, Salmon Chase, and Lincoln.[30]

Like their pro-Republican *Judge* counterparts, these *Puck* centerfolds suggest the evolution of a pat formula for Lincoln cartooning, the gross unworthiness of one or more contemporary politicos in comparison to the legacy of Lincoln (more often than not accentuated by casting Lincoln as a larger-than-life marble or bronze monument). In some instances, the specific issues or character traits informing the invidious comparisons might make sense— Union, civil rights, integrity—in others they were strained or downright silly. It mattered little. If no analogy came to mind, the cartoonist could simply portray his target as woefully deficient in stature, a midget in the shadow of the giant. Thus, after poet-reformer James Russell Lowell saluted Cleveland as "the best representation of the highest type of Americanism that we have seen since Lincoln," *Judge* ran the Bernhard Gillam cartoon, "An Aggravated Case of Big-Head," portraying the president as a puffed-up, froglike gnome dwarfed by bronze statues of Lincoln and Grant.[31] Later that year a Hamilton election-eve *Judge* front-cover cartoon presented an even tinier Cleveland casting by candlelight a huge shadow over a bust of Grant, a statue of Jefferson, and portraits of Washington, Benjamin Franklin, John Quincy Adams, and Lincoln.[32] Victor Gillam's October 1896 *Judge* centerfold "The Sliding Scale" portrayed a linear regression in size from Washington and Lincoln through Cleveland and Bryan.[33] Hamilton's September 1900 *Judge* cartoon "Bryan is Entitled to Another 'Think,'" prompted by Bryan's affinity for quoting Lincoln, provides a textbook example of the formula, with wee Bryan preening on tiptoes alongside a massive marble bust of Lincoln.[34]

Despite his many demonstrated uses, Lincoln's popularity as a cartoon convention did not soar appreciably after the decline of the humor weeklies and the advent of daily newspaper editorial cartoons. Transitions in technology, artistic styles, individual autonomy, and daily deadline pressures did help, however, to bring about greater flexibility in Lincoln's graphic exploitation by twentieth-century cartoonists. Pioneer editorial cartoonists effectuated a partial liberation of Lincoln from his monumental bronze and marble confines, even at a time when Americans were increasingly tending to associate him with the magnificent Daniel Chester French figure at the base of the Mall in Washington, dedicated in 1922 and destined to become, as Merrill Peterson has described it, "the nation's foremost sculptured icon."[35] In his lethal 1924

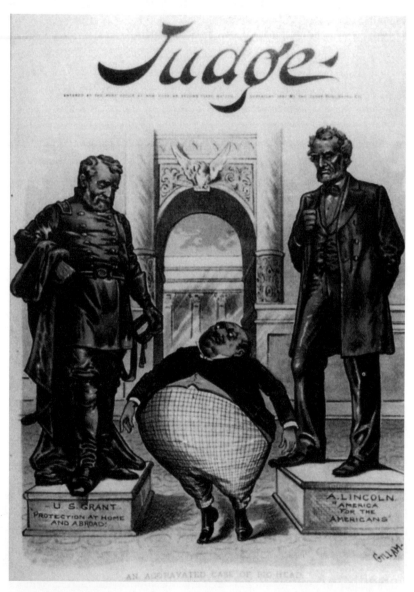

FIGURE 31. Bernhard Gillam, "An Aggravated Case of Big-Head," *Judge*, January 28, 1888, 1.

FIGURE 32. Grant Hamilton, "Bryan is Entitled to Another 'Think,'" *Judge,* September 22, 1900, 1.

cartoon "The Republican Party Down to Date," Art Young utilized imagery identical to that of Hamilton on Lincoln and Bryan by portraying a miniscule Calvin Coolidge dwarfed by a massive marble bust of his party's progenitor.[36] Throughout the course of the twentieth century, daily editorial cartoonists spread their efforts rather evenly between the monumental motif (increasingly French's seated figure) and anthropomorphic forms when they exploited Lincoln as a convention.

The genesis in 1892 of a national holiday on 12 February to honor Lincoln's birthday gave rise to the phenomenon of the birthday cartoon. Predictably, most of these efforts were cartoons the world would (and should) little note nor long remember, disappointing as art and commentary alike—short on incisive irony and long on noble sentiment. Since these cartoons were inspired not by timely events but by the calendar, appropriate counterpoints rarely obliged. When Lincoln was trotted out as a yardstick, then, it was to deplore the likes of pettifogging politicos, immigrant extremism, and laziness. This annual rite was the forte of such native midwesterners as *Chicago Tribune* artist John T. McCutcheon and *Des Moines Register* mainstay Jay N. "Ding" Darling, exemplars of a folksy, somewhat benign style of cartooning. Representative of such birthday offerings were Darling's 1921 *Collier's* opus featuring Lincoln (an agnostic with three months of formal schooling) prescribing "the little red schoolhouse and the white church" as antidotes to radical agitation and McCutcheon's contemporary *Tribune* cartoon of the young rail splitter deliberating between upward mobility and sloth.[37]

Another midwesterner, Daniel Fitzpatrick of the *St. Louis Post-Dispatch*, executed in 1943 one of the few Lincoln birthday cartoons that transcended such banality both as art and as political expression, "That These Dead Shall Not Have Died in Vain." His distinctive rendering of the Lincoln visage in the smoke of a smoldering planet evokes not a simplistic yearning for peace in the midst of war but rather a gritty resolve that this peace be worth preserving and worth its horrible cost, much like Mr. Lincoln's challenge to the nation at Gettysburg.[38] Unrivaled during his generation as a master of the medium, this fiery progressive was also capable of using Lincoln's image with wry drollery. In 1935 the Republican party, hitting rock bottom in public approval at the nadir of the Great Depression, staged a "grass-roots" conclave in Lincoln's Springfield to affirm its origins. Fitzpatrick's burlesque of bloated GOP plutocrats masquerading in Lincoln masks, "At the Grass-Roots Convention," surgically conveyed Fitzpatrick's impression that "nothing important came out of this show and they fooled no one but themselves."[39] In a similar vein, *Baltimore Sun* cartoonist Richard Q. Yardley exploited Lincoln in 1949 and 1951 birthday drawings to lampoon a Republican Party mired in defeat and caught in the crossroads between its conservative and moderate camps.[40]

Use of Lincoln in American political cartooning has remained somewhat selective, despite cogent parallels that seemed to beg for his presence. Although several cartoonists utilized him to render commentary on John Kennedy's assassination, apparently none did so in the wake of the 1968 slayings of his brother Robert or of Martin Luther King Jr., or the attempted handgun assassinations of Gerald Ford and Ronald Reagan, occasions ripe for "John Wilkes——" analogies. Cartoon linkages of the Great Emancipator to black American struggles against Jim Crow were few, an exception being Richard Q. Yardley's 1964 *Baltimore Sun* drawing "His Soul Goes Marching

"THAT THESE DEAD SHALL NOT HAVE DIED IN VAIN"

FIGURE 33. Daniel R. Fitzpatrick, "At the Grass-Roots Convention," *St. Louis Post-Dispatch,* June 11, 1935. Used by permission of The State Historical Society of Missouri, Columbia Research Center.

On," portraying a smiling Lincoln seated with the new civil rights legislation in hand.[41] Two weeks later, Yardley lampooned Senate Republican kingpin Everett Dirksen as "Abe Lincoln Dirksen in Illinois" for his capitulation to the Barry Goldwater insurgency.[42] The abrupt departure from the GOP's Lincolnian pedigree prompted Louisville *Courier-Journal* artist Hugh Haynie to reprise Tenniel's immortal 1890 Bismarck-Kaiser Wilhelm masterpiece with a malevolent Goldwater supplanting Lincoln on the deck of "S. S. Grand Olde

AT THE GRASS-ROOTS CONVENTION

FIGURE 34. Daniel A. Fitzpatrick, "That These Dead Shall Not Have Died in Vain," *St. Louis Post-Dispatch,* February 12, 1943. Used by permission of The State Historical Society of Missouri, Columbia Research Center.

Party" and Herb Block to portray a Goldwaterite trampling with muddy boots a glassed Lincoln portrait under the wry caption "We Stand upon our Historic Principles—."[43]

Watergate inspired very few Lincoln cartoons, despite the compelling contrast provided by "Tricky Dick" Nixon and "Honest Abe." Ray Osrin did just that in a 1974 Cleveland *Plain Dealer* cartoon portraying the two men seated next to one another in the pantheon of history, with Lincoln inquiring, "They

called me 'Honest Abe.' What do they call you?"[44] Vic Roschkov exploited
Gerald Ford's self-deprecating "I am a Ford, not a Lincoln" in a *Windsor Star*
(Ontario) cartoon of the two worthies, plus Nixon as "Edsel!"[45]

Perhaps Lincoln has been used so sparingly through the years because,
with few exceptions, cartoons that did exploit him did so in such a reverent
way. Cartoonists must draw to earn paychecks, but they take pride in creative
subtlety and find enjoyment in using symbols with which they can have fun.
Unlike the actual Lincoln, a man of deadly one-liners and risqué humor, the
somber, monumental Lincoln can scarcely be considered a "fun" fellow. For
more than a century cartoonists have used him to have fun with foils, but they
have not had much fun with him. Many of these cartoonists had memorized
by heart as school children the Gettysburg Address and the 1865 inaugural.
Thus, Lincoln's symbolic stature has tended to limit his use to those causes
and events of proper magnitude. Mauldin's 1963 classic, for example, made
perfect sense to grieve a martyred sitting president but would have been silly
to lament a Chicago alderman slain during a shakedown, just as Fitzpatrick's
Lincoln in the smoke of a burning planet required World War II, not a Gre-
nada or a Panama. Moreover, those qualities of character for which the mythic
Lincoln has become a symbol—rigid integrity, compassion for the disadvan-
taged, lofty national idealism—provide contrasts lacking in subtlety. His use
as an icon of integrity requires as a foil a Richard Nixon, just as his use as an
exemplar of Union needed a Jefferson Davis. Foils so inviting come along less
frequently than cartoonists might wish. Finally, cartoonists seem to have been
intimidated, and understandably so, by a pervasive sense of sadness evoked by
the Lincoln mystique, causing what Charles Press has aptly described as the
casting of a "certain blackish pall over the proceedings."[46] The wonder may not
be that he has been cartooned so seldom but that he has been cartooned at all.

Press describes the troubles cartoonists have encountered in attempting
to exploit as dynamic symbols inanimate national monuments, for they "suggest solemn dignity and gravity, but they are always at rest and this limits
somewhat the range of emotions they can express."[47] A useful parallel to the
monumental Lincoln might be the Statue of Liberty. As I noted in a similar
essay on Liberty as a cartoon convention, the statue served our cartoonists
superbly during a generation when it was popularly regarded as a French
engineering oddity or a New York tourism boondoggle, then it evolved into
a sacred national symbol drawn primarily for purposes of eagle-screaming
patriotism.[48] Only recently, as a new generation of cartoonists has downplayed
high moral dudgeon for zany iconoclasm, has Liberty cartooning recaptured
an element of irreverent wit, epitomized by Paul Conrad's 1976 portrayal of the
statue as a voluptuous nude in a prurient Jimmy Carter fantasy.[49]

If a cartoon of Lincoln sitting jaybird naked in his memorial seems a trifle far-fetched, a fine 1990 cartoon by Steve Benson suggests that it need not be an impossibility. His portrayal of a stricken monumental Lincoln stripped down to polka-dot briefs over the legend "Four Score and Several Hundred Billion Dollars Ago" underscored at once a decade of American fiscal irresponsibility as well as a crisis in banking.[50] It epitomizes two recent trends in political cartooning, a movement even further away from the art of moral indignation to that of irreverent humor and an increasing use of flexibility in the use of national symbols for wry commentary. As a result, Lincoln has emerged as a cartoon symbol either emancipated from his monumental straitjacket or, as in Benson's piece, given a wide latitude of burlesque within it.

In 1980, for example, Carter's labored apologia for refusing to debate third-party candidate John Anderson prompted Mike Peters to evoke the Lincoln–Douglas debates in a *Dayton Daily News* cartoon featuring a TV producer dictating to a bemused Lincoln the Carter conditions on behalf of Douglas.[51] When in 1982 Reagan indicated his support of tax breaks for racially segregated private academies, Pat Oliphant drew him as an actor playing Lincoln, but balking over emancipation ("I free the WHAT???").[52] Geraldine Ferraro's 1984 waffling on the abortion issue prompted the wry Benson riposte "What if Geraldine Ferraro had been Abraham Lincoln's Speech Writer?" with Lincoln fudging on emancipation.[53] The tenor of modern politics and a soured American electorate was captured well in Jack Ohman's 1985 Portland *Oregonian* effort "If Abe Lincoln were President Today."[54] Reagan's opposition to sanctions against the Union of South Africa for racial apartheid inspired the 1986 Ed Stein *Rocky Mountain News* cartoon "The Great Emancipator Meets the Great Communicator," featuring Reagan perched on the arm of a disgusted monumental Lincoln as he prattles on about quiet diplomacy.[55] Scott Stantis lampooned the George H. W. Bush–Michael Dukakis debates in a 1988 *Memphis Commercial Appeal* cartoon depicting Lincoln and Douglas viewing via television with looks of chagrin.[56] After Bush vetoed a civil rights bill in 1990 for its affinity for racial preference quotes, Ohman responded with side-by-side statues of Lincoln ("Freed the Slaves 1863") and Bush ("Freed the Owners 1990").[57] Evoking shades of Nast, Benson drew him as "John Wilkes Bush" lurking outside Lincoln's theatre box.[58]

As contemporary cartoonists have begun to "lighten up" on him, they have helped transform Lincoln from a monumental icon of limited utility into a much more flexible cartoon convention. For example, when genetic research advances prompted speculation in 1991 that human life (including Lincoln, expressly) could be cloned through DNA reconstruction, M. G. Lord (*Newsday*) and Ohman both responded with cartoons, Lord to mock Democratic desperation for a savior and Ohman to lampoon Republican anxieties over another run with Dan Quayle.[59] Also in 1991, Ohman chided Mario Cuomo and other Democrats wavering between candidacies and bleacher seats in "If These People Had Been Democratic Presidential Hopefuls," with Paul Revere cancelling his midnight ride as too dangerous, Martin Luther King Jr. abandoning his dream because of high negatives; and Lincoln forsaking his 1860 quest for the presidency because polls showed the cause of Union less popular than he had believed.[60] During the 1992 campaign, while Bush vacillated over committing American forces to beleaguered Bosnia, an *Akron Beacon Journal* cartoon by Chip Bok portrayed Lincoln learning that a party focus group opposed committing ground troops to a civil war.[61] When following his inauguration Bill Clinton sought to run his presidency as he had his campaign, relying heavily on media town meetings and talk shows to ensure that the winds of transient popular acclaim blew steadily at his back, Don Wright drew a caustic critique featuring Lincoln scanning printouts and opting not to free the slaves after all.[62]

Although the editorial cartoonists of today have largely liberated the mythic Lincoln from the rigid confines of inanimate bronze and marble, they continue in the long tradition of their medium by using him as a measure, perhaps the ultimate yardstick, of public figures and of qualities that transcend the mundane banalities of TV "talking heads," sound bites, daily headlines, and the ubiquitous spin doctors. A splendid example of this came in June 1993 as Clinton was reeling from popular disapproval, unique so early in a modern presidency. Seeking to ameliorate his poisonous relations with the White House press corps, he admired a reporter's Mickey Mouse necktie then put it on and mugged for the cameras. Impressed little by such patently phony Disneyland populism, *Detroit News* cartoonist Draper Hill executed "With Malice Toward None, With Charity for All," featuring a nonplussed monumental Lincoln sporting a garish Mickey Mouse tie to suggest a gentle but deadly contrast in stature between Lincoln and the latest of his successors. This cartoon, like Benson's savings and loan effort exploiting the memorial Lincoln while wryly lampooning its limits, conveys both the enduring power of Lincoln as a cartoon convention and myriad possibilities for future exploitation.[63]

ENDNOTES

1. *Newsweek*, July 20, 1964, 5A–5B. Interestingly, Mauldin was neither a fan of the cartoon nor of John Kennedy. He thought the drawing a failure because he had botched the Lincoln hairline. On JFK, he confided to a *Rolling Stone* reporter in 1976: "You know, I never was

one of those Kennedy suckers. . . . I went to Berlin with Kennedy in 1963. That was when he stood in the square and said 'Ich bin ein Berliner.' I puked. Soured on Kennedy right after that speech. . . . The fucker was inciting them and he knew it." See *Rolling Stone* (November 4, 1976): 58.

2. Raymond B. Rajski, ed., *A Nation Grieved: The Kennedy Assassination in Editorial Cartoons* (Rutland, VT: Charles E. Tuttle, 1967), 37 41, 107.

3. See Stephen Hess and Milton Kaplan, *The Ungentlemanly Art: A History of American Political Cartoons* (New York: MacMillan, 1968), 85–91; Albert Shaw, *Abraham Lincoln* (New York: Review of Reviews, 1930), 37–270; and Alton Ketchum, *Uncle Sam: The Man and the Legend* (New York: Hill and Wang, 1959), 80–86. I find Ketchum's hypothesis improbable. Uncle Sam's predecessor Brother Jonathan had been portrayed as bearded in *Punch* cartoons long before Lincoln sprouted chin whiskers. Moreover, Lincoln was much less favored in physiognomy than the quintessential Yankee trader Uncle Sam and, in *Punch* and other hostile British publications, much less worthy of humane virtues than characterizations befitting a generic representation of the American nation.

4. David Donald, *Lincoln Reconsidered: Essays on the Civil War Era*, rev. ed. (New York: Vintage Books, 1961), 60.

5. Thomas Nast, "Wilkes Booth the Second," *Harper's Weekly* (November 7, 1868): front cover. For a cogent analysis of this cartoon, see Mark E. Neely Jr., "Wilkes Booth the Second," *Lincoln Lore* 1752 (February 1984): 1–2. Ironically, Nast had not always been an admirer of the living Lincoln, drawing him on occasion as more simian than human, before victory was nearly inevitable and Lincoln stoked the ego of the young *Harper's* cartoonist by proclaiming him the Union's premier recruiting sergeant.

6. Donald, *Lincoln Reconsidered,* 144–66.

7. See Harold Holzer, Gabor S. Boritt, and Bark E. Neely Jr., *The Lincoln Image: Abraham Lincoln and the Popular Print* (New York: Charles Scribner's Sons, 1984), 149–216; and Peterson, *Lincoln in American Memory,* 3–35.

8. Peterson, *Lincoln in American Memory,* 27.

9. Lawrence J. Friedman, *Inventors of the Promised Land* (New York: Alfred A. Knopf, 1975), 71.

10. Friedman, *Inventors of the Promised Land,* 71.

11. Donald, *Lincoln Reconsidered,* 14.

12. James A. Wales, "A Dead Hero and a Live Jackass," *Puck* (June 22, 1881): 267.

13. Bernhard Gillam, "The Truth of 1861 is the Truth of To-Day," *Judge* (December 21, 1889): 169.

14. Bernhard Gillam, "John A. Logan in 1859," *Puck* (July 9, 1884): 296–97.

15. Grant Hamilton, "Men Whom the American People have Learned to Admire have been Tattooed," *Judge* (June 28, 1884): 16.

16. Daniel McCarthy, "Two Presidents at Gettysburg," *Judge* (May 30, 1885): 16.

17. Bernhard Gillam, "Halt!" *Judge* (July 2, 1887): 8–9.

18. Grant Hamilton, "Remember the Dead, but Forget Not the Living," *Judge* (May 31, 1890): 122–23; F. Victor Gillam, "The Same Old Sneaking Deserter," *Judge* (October 11, 1890): 8–9.

19. F. Victor Gillam, "Acknowledging the Truth," *Judge* (July 19, 1890): 236–37.

20. *Judge* (October 5, 1889): 410.

21. F. Victor Gillam, "Forbear!" *Judge* (September 19, 1896): 184–85; Louis Dalrymple, "History Repeats Itself," *Puck* (October 28, 1896): 8–9.

22. Grant Hamilton, "Two Pages in History," *Puck* (October 23, 1895): 152–53.

23. Joseph Keppler Jr., "The New South—The Triumph of Free Labor," *Puck* (October 23, 1895): 152–53.

24. Grant Hamilton, "1863–1898, History Repeats Itself," *Judge* (April 2, 1898): 211.

25. Grant Hamilton, "Great Men Make Great Nations," *Judge* (January 14, 1899): 17.

26. David Donald, "Getting Right with Lincoln," *Harper's Magazine* 102 (April 1951): 74–80; reprinted in *Lincoln Reconsidered*, 3–18.

27. Bernhard Gillam, "A Great Past and a Pitiful Present," *Puck* (October 28, 1885): 136–137.

28. Joseph Keppler, "The Lesson of the Past," *Puck* (July 20, 1887): 340–41.

29. Joseph Keppler, "The Ideals of 1863 and the Idol of 1887—The Decadence of a Great Party," *Puck* (October 19, 1887): 124–25.

30. Joseph Keppler, "The Old Leaders and the New," *Puck* (January 14, 1891): 356–57.

31. Bernhard Gillam, "An Aggravated Case of Big-Head," *Judge* (January 28, 1888): 1.

32. Grant Hamilton, "The 'Man of Destiny' Overshadows the Fathers of his Country," *Judge* (October 27, 1888): 50.

33. F. Victor Gillam, "The Sliding Scale," *Judge* (October 3, 1896): 216–17.

34. Grant Hamilton, "Bryan Is Entitled to Another 'Think,'" *Judge* (September 22, 1900): 1.

35. Peterson, *Lincoln in American Memory*, 216.

36. Art Young, *The Best of Art Young* (New York: Vanguard Press, 1936), 154.

37. Jay N. "Ding" Darling, "From One Who's Familiar with the Roads," *Collier's Weekly* (February 12, 1921): 17; and John T. McCutcheon, "When Lincoln Made His Choice Between Mediocrity and Immortality," reprinted in *John McCutcheon's Book* (Chicago: Caxton Club, 1948), 267.

38. Daniel R. Fitzpatrick, "That These Dead Shall Not Have Died in Vain," *St. Louis Post-Dispatch*, February 12, 1943; reprinted in Fitzpatrick, *As I Saw It* (New York: Simon and Schuster, 1953), 90.

39. Daniel R. Fitzpatrick, "At the Grass-Roots Convention," *St. Louis Post-Dispatch*, June 11, 1935; reprinted in *As I Saw It*, 5.

40. Richard Q. Yardley, "An Elephant Should Really Learn to Forget . . . ," *Baltimore Sun*, February 19, 1949; Richard Q. Yardley, "The Democrats' Trouble is That They Don't Know Where They're Going," *Baltimore Sun*, February 13, 1951.

41. Richard Q. Yardley, "His Soul Goes Marching On," *Baltimore Sun*, June 20, 1964.

42. Richard Q. Yardley, "Abe Lincoln Dirksen in Illinois," *Baltimore Sun*, July 2, 1964.

43. Hugh Haynie, *Hugh Haynie: Perspective* (Louisville, KY: Courier-Journal, 1974), 96; Herbert L. Block, "We Stand Upon Our Historic Principles—" *Washington Post*, July 14, 1964.

44. Ray Osrin, "They Call Me 'Honest Abe.' What Do They Call You?" in Charles Brooks, ed., *Best Editorial Cartoons: 1975 Edition* (Gretna, LA: Pelican Press, 1975), 24.

45. Vic Roschkov, "Lincoln/Ford/Edsel," in Brooks, *Best Editorial Cartoons: 1975*, 17.

46. Charles Press, *The Political Cartoon* (Rutherford, NJ: Associated University Presses, 1981), 212.

47. Press, *The Political Cartoon*, 210.

48. Roger A. Fischer, "Oddity, Icon, Challenge: The Statue of Liberty in American Cartoon Art, 1879–1986," *Journal of American Culture* 9 (Winter 1986): 63–82.

49. Paul Conrad, *Pro and Conrad* (San Rafael, CA: Neff-Kane, 1979), 9.

50. Steve Benson, "Four Score and Several Hundred Billion Dollars Ago," repr., *Duluth News-Tribune*, April 18, 1990, 80.

51. Reprinted in *Providence Evening Bulletin*, September 10, 1980.

52. Pat Oliphant, *Ban This Book!* (Kansas City, MO: Andrews and McMeel, 1982), 102.

53. Steve Benson, *Fencin' with Benson* (Phoenix: Arizona Republic, 1984), 68.

54. Jack Ohman, "If Abe Lincoln were President today . . . ," *Portland Oregonian*, February 24, 1985.

55. Ed Stein, "The Great Emancipator Meets the Great Communicator," *Rocky Mountain News*, July 8, 1986.

56. Charles Brooks, ed., *Best Editorial Cartoons: 1989 Edition* (Gretna, LA: Pelican Press, 1989), 48.

57. *Portland Oregonian,* February 24, 1985.

58. Reprinted in *Duluth News-Tribune,* November 3, 1990.

59. M. G. Lord, untitled cartoon of Democrat asking if biologist can clone Lincoln, *New York Newsday,* May 4, 1991; Jack Ohman, untitled cartoon of Bush-Lincoln 1992 Republican ticket, *Gannett Westchester Newspapers,* April 3, 1991.

60. Jack Ohman, "If These People had been Democratic Presidential Hopefuls . . . ," *Portland Oregonian,* September 5, 1991.

61. Chip Bok, untitled cartoon of advisor warning Lincoln against committing ground troops against the Confederates, repr., *Providence Journal-Bulletin,* September 12, 1992, A-12.

62. Don Wright, untitled cartoon of Lincoln junking emancipation because of talk show call-ins repr., *Dallas Morning News,* February 20, 1993.

63. This cartoon was drawn 20 June 1993 but never published because more pressing events decreed a substitute.

Easy-Going Daddy, Kaptayn Barbell, and Unmad

American Influences Upon Asian Comics

JOHN A. LENT

AFTER A VISIT to the *New York World* in 1922, Japanese cartoonist Ippei Oka-moto expressed his enthusiasm for American funnies in a report to the daily *Asahi*. He wrote, "American comics have become an entertainment equal to baseball, motion pictures, and the presidential elections. Some observers say that comics have replaced alcohol as a solace for workers since Prohibition began."[1] In other dispatches to the newspaper, Okamoto described *Bringing Up Father* and *Mutt and Jeff*, resulting in the serialization of George McMa-nus's strip in *Asahi Graph*, beginning 14 November 1923. Subsequently, *Mutt and Jeff, Polly and Her Pals, Felix the Cat*, and *Happy Hooligan* were translated and serialized in Japanese newspapers. Okamoto's encounter with American newspaper comic strips demonstrated their pervasive influence, creating as they did a worldwide medium by the mid-twentieth century. Many Asian car-toonists received their inspiration from American comics, reacting to them in different ways as this overview of cartooning in five East Asian, six Southeast Asian, and four South Asian countries shows. Some Asian cartoonists encour-aged the importation and publication of American comics; others drew Asian clones of U.S. characters; still others sought to replace foreign with indigenous comics.

FIGURE 35. *Nonki na Tosan* (*Easy-Going Daddy*), a Japanese clone of *Bringing Up Father,* was created by Yutaka Aso in 1924.

In Japan, all three trends were evident early on. By 1902, famous pioneer cartoonist Rakuten Kitazawa had learned enough (especially about serialization, while working on an American magazine in Yokohama) to create the first Japanese serialized strip with a regular character, *Tagosaku to Mokube no Tokyo Kenbutsu* (*Tagosaku and Mokube Sightseeing in Tokyo*). It ran in *Jiji Manga*, a Sunday color supplement not unlike those in the United States. As other cartoonists, in addition to Okamoto and Kitazawa, returned from visits to the U.S., they too adapted American comics. In 1924, Yutaka Aso created for *Hochi* a four-panel strip, *Nonki na Tosan* (*Easy-Going Daddy*), which was a direct spinoff of *Bringing Up Father,* with Japanese characteristics, and in 1930, Sako Shishido did *Spido Taro* (*Speedy*) in *Yomiuri Sunday Manga*. Shishido's strip was influenced in layout, pacing, and sound-words by his nine-year stay in the U.S. where he studied cartooning through a correspondence course.[2]

Throughout the 1920s and 1930s, the U.S. impact upon Japanese comics came through in the *ero-guro-nansensu* (erotic, grotesque, and nonsensical) genre, which echoed aspects of the American Jazz Era. One cartoonist of that period, Yukio Sugiura, said these comics were especially favored in 1931 and 1932, when the "mood was gloomy and desperate." A proponent of American-style cartooning, Sugiura and others, including Okamoto and Ryuichi Yokoyama, started Shin Mangaha Shu-dan (New Cartoonists Faction Group) in 1932. Its main purpose was the adoption of foreign (mainly US) styles of cartooning. Sugiura himself was greatly influenced by *Bringing Up Father*, admitting that he was "still under the influence of that cartoon."[3]

Later, the U.S. occupation (1945–1951) left its mark upon Japanese comics. Strips that reflected feudal values or criticized Americans were censored, while those that showed "average families making the best of hard times, and loved little children" were touted.[4] Standing out was *Sazae-san*, created by Machiko Hasegawa in 1946. The newspaper strip lasted more than four decades, inspiring many imitations as well as *Sazae-San* songs, a TV series, film, and books. One researcher likened it to *Blondie*, claiming that the humor derived from the contradiction between the ideology and the actual life of the middle-class family.[5]

As elsewhere, Japanese strips soon found their way into comic books (*manga*), which, since World War II, have eclipsed the importance of the newspaper funnies. Today, mainstream dailies have only one strip each, while sports and sex newspapers carry more.

Prominent strip cartoonist Sanpei Sato, who with his salaryman (white-collar worker) themes, created some of the most successful strips in *The Asahi Shimbun*, commented that Japanese cartoonists suffer from the stiff competition offered by manga and the unenviable task of making their strips understood in a fast-changing society.[6] Agreeing with Sato, longtime cartoonist and president of the Japan Cartoonists Association, Yoshiro Kato, attributed the loss of audiences for strips to a change of public taste and the lack of sophistication on the part of visually-oriented readers to find the "essence of comic strips."[7] Kato has bucked this trend with his *Mappira-kun* (*Mr. Mappira*), Japan's oldest continuous strip started in 1954. Among his other works was *Onboro Jinsei* (*Miserable Life*) in *Mainichi* weekly magazine for eight years. Kato folded this strip in 1961 when the prime minister announced that all Japanese salaries would be doubled and, according to Kato, the "people did not have such a miserable life any longer."[8]

Early Chinese comic art was influenced by both foreign and domestic factors. After World War I, foreign comic strips were translated into Chinese and circulated among families with foreign contacts. Western influences were also obvious in the names of cartoon magazines (for example, *Shanghai Puck*, the first by that name in 1918) and the major locale for cartooning—Shanghai, known for its cosmopolitan lifestyle.

From the liberalizing 4 May 1919 movement through the 1930s,[9] China had its golden age of comic art as the number of cartoonists mushroomed and cartoon and humor periodicals and newspaper supplements with children's pages developed.[10] By 1934, Shanghai sported seventeen periodicals devoted mainly to cartoons, described as having "necessarily a certain amount of eroticism, influenced to a great extent by such journals as the American *Esquire,* but with an element of quite Chinese abandon."[11] Writer/cartoonist Jack Chen said of 1930s comics: "Western influence was of course very strongly evident, but it was expressed as adaptation rather than imitation."[12]

Probably fitting Chen's description were the two most important strips of 1930s China, *Wang xiansheng* (*Mr. Wang*) and *Sanmao* (*Three Hairs*). *Wang xiansheng* was started in 1928 by a twenty-one-year-old cartoonist, Ye Qianyu, and it appeared first in *Shanghai Cartoons.* The four to eight panels were built around a "triangular-headed, middle-class philistine, proud possessor of all the typical Chinese vices,"[13] a character similar to David Low's Colonel Blimp. The strip dealt with the sensations of modern urban life—luxury, gluttony, deceit, and pleasure-seeking.[14] *Sanmao* was a serialized strip drawn by Zhang Leping that initially was published in Shanghai's *Xiaochenbao* in 1935. The strip went through different renditions that corresponded with the political climate. In pre-war China, *Sanmao* was mainly a humor strip based on the mischievous life of a street urchin. A second version appeared in *Shen Bao* after Zhang participated in anti-Japanese propaganda during the war, while the post-1947 strip in *Dagong Bao* had strong social overtones, depicting official greed, the widening poverty gap, and Sanmao's own unfortunate life.[15] After 1949, *Sanmao* promoted the tenets of Maoism.[16]

Chinese cartooning is declining today, according to cartoonists interviewed by the author. Quality of work has decreased,[17] fewer cartoons are submitted to periodicals,[18] and there is increased commercialization,[19] the latter a reflection of modern-day U.S. influences.

Outside forces played roles in the development of newspaper comics in other parts of East Asia. In Hong Kong, British, French, Australian, and American cartoonists stopped off at various times and contributed strips. The *South China Morning Post* (hereafter *Post*) had *Buzzy the Bee* in the 1950s, a strip that eavesdropped on Hong Kong society, and *Hong Kong Sweet and Sour* in the 1960s, relating the antics of a bachelor tourist in pursuit of local women. The latter was drawn by a Frenchman known as Daniel Zabo, who was in Hong Kong to paint a bar mural.[20] *Jackson Road,* published in the *Post* in 1980, was the first regular four-panel strip in an English-language daily. The illustrations never changed, showing the backs of patrons at a bar as they commented on Hong Kong's problems. Another strip, *Basher,* was started by

FIGURE 36. *The World of Lily Wong,* 13 July 1992. This Hong Kong daily strip by Larry Feign was pulled from the *South China Morning Post* in May 1995 for political reasons.

a lawyer, Christopher Young, in 1984. As the colony's longest-running comic, it gives a clue to the recentness and tenuousness of strips in Hong Kong. Other titles appeared in the 1980s, such as Larry Feign's *Kowloon Kats*; Hope Barrett's *Spray,* featuring cockroaches; Zunzi (Wong Kee-kwan)'s *Through the Tiger's Eye*; Stuart Allen's *Twigg*; and Tung Pui-sun's *The Boss*.[21]

The strip that has been most successful—surviving eight years in the newspapers—is *The World of Lily Wong*. Appearing in the *Post* most of its life (although it was carried by the *Hong Kong Standard* for a time), *Lily Wong* is drawn by Larry Feign, a native of Buffalo who worked in California animation studios briefly before venturing to Hong Kong in 1985. The strip features a strong-willed Chinese woman and her *gweilo* (foreign) husband, Stuart. One writer said that Feign "alternately highlights the gaffes of one culture according to the standards of the other, underlining the absurdity of racial prejudice and the shared humanity of Asians and Westerners."[22] In Feign's depictions,

> Hong Kong Chinese are shameless racists who love to gamble, toss garbage out their apartment windows and make money. A greedy, materialistic lot, they prefer stability and prosperity to democratic freedoms. His Hong Kong Westerners are also shameless racists who love the luxurious colonial life they lead here but complain that the Chinese who make it possible spit and jump taxi lines. A hypocritical bunch, they say they have Hong Kong's best interests at heart, even as they sell out the colony and its people to the Communist Chinese.[23]

Feign's own description of what he does is this: "The humour is in the irony, the different ways people act around food, children, etc. Both are right in their own way, and yet they will never agree."[24] Originally, Feign tried to balance equally political and non-political themes but eventually 70 percent became political.[25] The latter landed him in trouble in late May 1995, at which time the *Post* dropped his strip.

The foreign connections to Taiwanese and Korean cartooning are mainly in animation, where Dae Won in Seoul and Wang Film Productions in Taipei handle a large proportion of U.S. and European film and television cartoons, and in comic books, where both countries have tried to ward off the impact of Japanese manga.

Taiwanese strips can be traced to the 1949 publication of Chen Kuan-hsi's *Hsiao Pa Yeh* in a student monthly.[26] Two years later, the first newspaper strip, Lee Fei-meng's (Niu Ko) *Uncle Niu Struggles as a Guerrilla,* came out. Unique among those early strip artists was elementary school teacher Liu Hsing-ching, who drew a serial strip imploring students not to read comics of which he disapproved. His campaign backfired as the strip itself became a smash hit. By 1956, Liu had four successful strips, one of which, *Robot,* resulted in another career as an inventor with more than 138 patents.

A revitalization of comic strips occurred in 1984–1985, spurred mainly by the China Times Publishing Company. Throughout the following decade, many strips were created, a few of which became runaway successes. Chu Teh-yung's (he is also known as Ronald Chu) *Shuang Hsiang Pao (The Couple)* in *China Times Express* was the most popular. Slapstick in nature, Chu's strip revolves around a couple in their sixties and reminds one of Reg Smythe's *Andy Capp* in meanness and defensiveness. Seven or eight of the famous Taiwanese cartoonists are women, the first of whom was Lao Chung, creator of *Tamen,* a story about gender differences.[27] Taiwanese strip artists have attempted to broaden their audiences, publishing books of their strips for sale in Asia and elsewhere and seeking affiliations with American syndicates.

Korean strips were developed rather early, with a four-panel children's cartoon, *Daeum Eotchi (What's Next?)* appearing in a 1914 magazine (it was probably a translated foreign comic). In 1920 Kim Dong-Seang, who had studied journalism in the United States, did the four-panel *Geurim Yiyagi (Pictured Story),* and in the 1920s, his plotted cartoons similar to those in the United States were published in newspapers and magazines. Particularly in the 1950s, a number of significant four-panel socio-political strips were born that survived at least until the 1990s. Chief among them is *Kobau,* drawn by Kim Song Hwan since 1955. These extremely popular strips are unique as political cartoons in that they carry a regular title with a symbolic meaning, feature the same character every day, and are numbered consecutively. Funnies are expected to become a more important staple of Korean dailies as the public "gets its fill" of political cartoons[28] and sheds its traditional belief that comics are for youngsters only[29] and as Korea moves even closer to democratization and economic stability.[30]

For obvious reasons, the impact of U.S. comics was most profound in the former American colony of the Philippines. All aspects were affected—from naming of characters and writing of plots to developing comic books (*komiks*) and setting up codes for them.

The first Philippine comic strip, Antonio Velasquez's *Kenkoy* in 1929, contained American traits as the main character mouthed English terms such as "okedokey," "wait a minute," or "nothing doing." A contemporary cartoonist, Nonoy Marcelo, attributed the strip to a trend of satirizing the rapidly Americanized Philippines, saying, "*Kenkoy*, with his ukulele, Valentino hair, bell bottoms was a ludicrous portrait of the Filipino of the time pathetically trying but barely succeeding in keeping up with his American mentors."[31]

There have been suggestions that *Mickey Mouse* was the inspiration for *Kenkoy* because of some similarity in appearance. Velasquez emphatically dismissed this assertion:

> It's not patterned after anyone. In fact, I had not seen his [Disney's] *Mickey Mouse* when I created my *Kenkoy*. Because *Mickey Mouse* was born also in the 1920s by Walt Disney and *Kenkoy* was born in the 1920s. He was in the United States; I was in the Philippines.[32]

Velasquez conceived *Kenkoy* after a senior cartoonist for the vernacular magazine, *Liwayway,* reneged on the assignment. Originally, the four-panel strip was used as *Liwayway* filler. The public response was so favorable that it was translated into five dialects, made the basis for a poem and a lively march, and it inspired other strips. By the 1930s *Kenkoy* had rivals in the Philippine comic strip world, including *Huapelo,* a Chinese owner of a corner store; *Saryong Albularyo,* a village quack doctor; *Goyo at Kikay,* dead-ringers for *Maggie & Jiggs*; Francisco and Pedrito Reyes' *Kulafu,* a character like *Tarzan,* who was raised by the apes and roamed the jungle; Francisco Coching's *Hagibis,* another jungle character inspired by *Kulafu* and *Tarzan; Lucas Malakas,* a local version of *Popeye,* and so on. *Lucas Malakas* was one of the early strips of Jose Zabala Santos; among his others were *Titina, Sianong Sano,* and *Popoy,* all published in *Sampaguita* magazine.[33]

The post–World War II period saw the further nurturing of strips, as well as the launching of the *komiks* industry for which Velasquez takes credit, but a couple of other individuals played a part. In 1946, while still in short pants, according to his account, the sixteen-year-old Larry Alcala was hired by *Liwayway* to draw strips. Three years later, Mars Ravelo, after drifting from one menial job to another, was able to get someone to read his *Rita Kasinghat,* a strip unlike most others in that it was Filipino, not American, in settings, concepts, and stories. Although Velasquez and Alcala both called the 1950s the golden years when cartoonists did their best work, not many of those cartoons found their way into dailies, which favored the less expensive American strips. Also, cartoonists liked the new *komiks,* patterned after comic books left behind by the GIs, because they paid better.[34] Nevertheless, some strips prospered in the postwar generation. By 1968 one of the local strips, *Tisoy* by Nonoy Marcelo, outpolled all foreign and domestic strips combined. *Tisoy* depicted the dilemma of urbanized Filipino youth caught between generations.

Newspaper strips fared much better after 1970, partly because of the existence of more tabloids and because of demands by the national cartoonists' group for "chances to do our own strips."[35] Marcos-owned and -operated dailies published many strips, leading one to suspect they were diversions from the Filipinos' daily misery. One of the most popular has been *Ikabod,* started in 1979 by Marcelo and described by him as a "balance to the heavy repression during the Marcos years as it was against the big fat cats."[36] Other popular and long-surviving (since the 1970s) strips are *Siopawman* by Alcala, *Baltic and Co.* by Roni Santiago, and *Kusyo at Buyok* by Tito Milambiling. By the 1990s all Philippine dailies contained a total of fifteen to twenty local strips. U.S. strips, however, still present a formidable challenge: in 1986 the *Manila Chronicle* dropped all local strips because it could obtain foreign ones for fifty cents each.[37]

Americanisms continue to show up in strips and *komiks,* as indicated by titles and storylines: *D. I. Trece (Dick Tracy), Flash Ter (Flash Gordon), Lastikman (Plastic Man), Kaptayn Barbell (Captain Marvel), Bulko (The Hulk), Cha Lee's Angels (Charlie's Angels), Farrah Garbo* (a cross between two famous American actresses), *Dama* (a female do-gooder in the mold of *Wonder Woman*), *Og* (another *Tarzan* clone), and Larry Alcala's *Kalabog en Bosyo* (loosely adapted from *Batman and Robin*). Marcelo said Alcala, like Velasquez much earlier, incorporated a baleful look at a Westernized Philippines in *Kalabog en Bosyo,* ridiculing "his countrymen's clumsy handling of the new-found language with clever word-play."[38]

There were other influences from the United States. When the American comic book industry set up its code in the mid-1950s, Ace Publications in Manila drew up a similar set of self-censorship guidelines. The Association of Publishers and Editors of Philippine Comic Magazines was established to promote "the moral welfare of *komiks* reading public by publishing 'only clean, wholesome, entertaining and educational strips.'" Its Golden Code encouraged self-censorship. Conversely, Philippine cartooning has left its mark in the United States. In the early 1970s, American comics publisher James Warren, while visiting Manila, took an interest in Fred Alcala's artwork, much of which copied the styles of Hal Foster and Alex Raymond. Alcala led a troupe of Filipino cartoonists, including Nestor Redondo, Jesse Santos, Alex Niño, and Edgar Soller, who began work for DC, Marvel, Filmation, and other American publishers and studios. Some migrated while others worked from the Philippines.

Heavy dependence upon U.S. strips is endemic to Thailand and Malaysia as well. A check of the three main Sunday newspapers in Thailand in August 1993 found eight-page color supplements, made up entirely of American strips and in Malaysia, each major English-language daily has twelve strips, all emanating from the United States except for one each in *New Straits Times* and *Star.* The Sunday *Times's* eight-page color comics supplement is made up of seventeen U.S. strips.

For decades the most popular Thai cartoonist has been Chai Rachawat, who draws *Pooyai Ma and Ah Joy* for the daily *Thai Rath.* The sixteen-year-old strip features a village headman and a villager who symbolically represent the government and the people.[39] Chai self-exiled to the United States during the mid-1970s, when he feared government reprisals for his cartoons.

Pioneer cartoonist Prayoon Chanyawongse, the only Magsaysay (often called the Pulitzer Prize of Asia) awardee for cartoon arts, also stayed in the United States for a while. He trained at Disney Studios in Burbank after being introduced to Walt Disney by King Bhumibol.[40] Prayoon's fame resulted from his serialized folk strip *Chantha Korope* and verse editorials. The latter were one-panel creations mixing poetry and comic illustration on a current topic. Another prominent early cartoonist was Sawas Jutharop, credited with introducing serialized strips to Thailand with his *Popeye* imitation, *Kbun Muen.*

In Malaysia, local comic strips have had a richer tradition in the Bahasa Malaysia and Chinese dailies than in the English ones. In the 1930s Ali Sanat did *Wak Ketok* and *Wak Keledek* for *Utusan Zaman,* while Salleh bin Ally produced nationalist strips for *Warta Jenaka.* Salleh's major character was Sa-Hari Balun, a highly emancipated village belle who wore outrageously daring costumes and got entangled in difficult situations from which she emerged triumphant.[41] The most successful Malaysian cartoonist has been Lat (Mohammad Nor Khalid), whose *Scenes of Malaysian Life* has appeared in the *New Straits Times* for about twenty years and his *Si Mamat* in *Berita Minggu* even longer.[42] Describing the world reflected in comics read by Malaysians when he started, Lat said, "Before that, there was nothing. They only printed foreign comics, and they didn't draw us. It was not Malaysian. It always had something to do with something Western."[43]

FIGURE 37. *Djon Domino* by Johnny Hidajat of Indonesia contained numbers readers used to play the lottery, similar to Bud Fisher—including tips for horse race bettors in *Mutt and Jeff.*

The most important contribution American comic art has made to Malaysia involves the plethora of humor magazines that have appeared since 1978. The first, *Gila-Gila (Crazy about Mad),* was patterned after *Mad Magazine,* with much imitation of stories and artistic styles.

American strips have stimulated other cartoonists: in Myanmar, U Aung Shein has famous characters imitative of Tarzan and Sherlock Holmes,[44] while in Singapore, Lee Hon Kit's adventure story has touches of *Flash Gordon.* Unique as Johnny Hidajat's *Djon Domino* strip is to Indonesia, it has, perhaps by coincidence, a trait found in *Mutt and Jeff*—tips for the gambler. In *Djon Domino,* Hidajat includes numbers that readers use in playing the national lottery.[45]

Indigenous newspaper strips are not very common in any part of the subcontinent and certainly not in the dominant English-language press. For decades, when editors decided to use strips, they invariably imported them from the United States or England. King Features provided the very popular *Phantom* and *Mandrake the Magician,* as well as *Flash Gordon, Archie,* and *Beetle Bailey*; Asia Features, *Garth* and *Kerry Drake*; and Famous Features, *James Bond, Modesty Blaise,* and *Mutt and Jeff.* Publishers such a Chandamama Classics and Dolton Comics brought out comic books based on Disney characters or adopted *Asterix* and *Archie.*[46]

It was as a reaction to these types of behavior that some early Indian comics appeared. One was *Daabu,* the tale of a teenage boy and a science professor, started by Pran (Pran Kumar Sharma) in 1960. Pran incorporated Indian themes, customs, and settings, so that "Indians thought these strips were their own."[47] By the 1990s Pran's stable of strip titles had increased to seven, distributed to twenty newspapers and magazines nationwide through a syndicate

(Pran's Features) he operated out of the third floor of his home. Additionally, Pran collaborated with Diamond Comics, which compiled the seven series into more than 225 comic book titles.

In January 1969, Pran launched his most famous strip, *Chacha Chaudhary,* a "not very sophisticated wise man" who, joined later by a giant, Jupiter-born sidekick, Sahu, solves people's problems. Pran said his characters differ from American prototype heroes in that they do not possess supernatural powers, such as the ability to fly and perform miracles.[48]

A chemical engineer, Anant Pai was also distressed by the preponderance of American and British strips in India in the 1960s. Believing that Indian children were ignorant of their country's history and culture, Pai started the educational *Amar Chitra Katha* comic book series of 436 titles, which eventually sold seventy-nine million copies.[49] Earlier in 1963, he had launched *Indrajal Comics* with the publication of a sixteen-page *Phantom* story. In 1969, along with cartoonist Abid Surti, he established a features syndicate, Rang Rekha,[50] which has about seventy newspaper subscribers for its eight comic stories provided in eleven languages. India is unique among Asian countries in having feature syndicates, another concept borrowed from the United States. At least five syndicates have existed, according to cartoonists interviewed by the author.

The market for strips is very competitive, according to one syndicate's comics editor, Luis Fernandes of Amrita Bharat. U.S. strips sell for 70 to 80 rupees each and are preferred by smaller papers because of their low rates and high prestige value, but the twenty or more local strips have been gaining respect and clientele because of their culture specificity.[51] Despite this, the long tenure of U.S. strips in India has not been offset by the production of local comics, for many of the latter are rather Americanized. The *Nootan Chitra Katha* series, for example, features the character, Bhoot Nath, described as a "fantastic hero with a stout physique who puts on a mask almost identical to that of *Phantom* and is able to travel far and wide in the universe in different planets like *Flash Gordon*."[52]

One scholar portrayed the Indian comics scene as one where

> the publishers have benefitted from the experience of Western comic producers. . . . The producers working at the international level also adopted fantasy characters from Indian soil and Indian atmosphere such as *Bahadur, Secret Agent Vikram, Inspector Garud, Shaikh Chilly, Manka Jascos, Babloo, Mia Manju, Inspector Azad, Chacha Chaudhary,* etc. The creators of these comics seek motivation and ideas from international comics but they transform and improvise them to suit the Indian atmosphere and background.[53]

FIGURE 38. *Chacha Chaudhary* is Pran's comedy-adventure strip published in India.

Strips in Bangladeshi newspapers have been around since their introduction by the *Morning News* in the 1950s, but they have not been in abundance and almost all have been done by Americans and Europeans.[54] The exception is Tokai, Ranabi's character started in 1977. It took Ranabi (Rafiqun Nabi) two years to conceptualize *Tokai*. Initially, he looked to Charles Schulz's *Peanuts* for a model but decided instead to dwell on a street-wise, poverty-stricken child, witty and insightful in depicting Bangladeshi society.[55] The very name, "Tokai," has come to represent extreme poverty and has been added to the Bengali dictionary. Other strips are very rare in Dhaka dailies, attributable to factors such as newspaper disinterest and the low payment and degree of respect given strip cartoonists.[56] From the late 1970s until recently, Bangladesh was served by two humor magazines, *Cartoon* (defunct after 1993) and *Unmad*, the latter patterned after *Mad* magazine.[57]

Strip cartooning is dismal in Pakistan. Ali Anwar projected the antics of a single character, Nanna, a lovable boy in the spirit of *Dennis the Menace*, and Sadaquat did a daily strip on a typical Pakistani family. The female cartoonist Nigar Nazar "assimilated the work of many European and American masters" in *Gogi Giggles*, which ran in the daily *Muslim* of Islamabad.[58] Gogi was described as a timeless, transportable character who in one sequence might be shown as a harried victim of the system and in another as an instrument of bureaucratic corruption.[59]

Strip cartooning in Sri Lanka dates to at least the mid-1950s. Some of the early ones were done by Henry Tennekoon, W. R. Wijesoma, G. S. Fernando, W. P. Wickramanayake, and Camillus Perera.[60] A few have survived twenty to thirty years;[61] those of Perera have lived on in his "comics papers." The oldest is *Camillusge Don Sethan*, started by Camillus in 1966 for the daily *Janatha*, and moved to the "comics paper" *Sathsiri*.[62]

Sinhalese dailies carry local comic strips, which borrow heavily from Western material,[63] while English-language papers use mostly U.S. and British comics. The three Sinhalese dailies have a total of six strips, usually of three panels, and English-language newspapers have three to six U.S. strips. In the Sunday editions, *Silumina* and *Divaina* each have two, and *Lankadipa*, one local strip. The English Sunday *Times*, *The Island*, and *The Sunday Observer* carry from two strips to a full page of U.S. and British material. Popular stories revolve around romance, adventure, ghosts, and household problems. Amid these strips are *Pelanthiya* and *Attakaka Pipi* (a ghost story), both by W. P. Wickamanayake, and S. C. Opatha's *Silva*, about a problem-plagued family man. Mainly a political cartoonist, Opatha gets double use out of *Silva*, bringing the character into his political cartoons as a bystander.[64]

Identifying problems associated with strip cartooning, Wickamanayake singled out a deterioration of ideas, drawings, and dialogue due to social changes, many brought about by television.[65] Another cartoonist said the void in English-language strips results because of a lack of cartoonists able to work in that language.[66]

Almost from their earliest days, American comic strips have influenced the development of cartooning in Asia. In some cases, Asians learned about the U.S. strips from returning cartoonists who sang their praise or from English-language newspapers and magazines established in Asia. Many of these periodicals carried American strips provided by the syndicates. Gradually, local artists created their own versions of the strips, oftentimes copied closely from U.S. and British ones. Particularly in the last twenty years, there has been some negative reaction to the dominance of American strips, with Asian cartoonists doing strips with more indigenous stories, characters, and styles and launching local syndicates and humor magazines for their distribution and exhibition.

ENDNOTES

1. Frederik Schodt, *Manga! Manga! The World of Japanese Comics* (Tokyo: Kodansha, 1983), 43.
2. Schodt, *Manga! Manga!*, 51.
3. Interview by the author with cartoonist Yukio Sugiura in Tokyo, Japan, 6 November 1993.
4. Schodt, *Manga! Manga!*, 63.
5. Taihei Imamura, "Comparative Study of Comics: American and Japanese—*Sazae-san* and *Blondie*," in *Japanese Popular Culture*, ed. Hidetoshi Kato (Rutland, VT: Tuttle, 1959), 96.
6. Interview by the author with cartoonist Sampei Sato in Tokyo, Japan, 8 November 1993.
7. Interview by the author with Yoshiro Kato, president, Japan Cartoonists Association, in Tokyo, Japan, 6 November 1993.
8. Kato, interview, 1993
9. On 4 May 1919, students of Peking National University rioted against the venal Chinese government. The date was considered a landmark in the Chinese revolution and is celebrated as such by the communist government. The May Fourth Movement challenged traditional norms and "sought to free the people's will from the confinement of the past." Hung Chang-tai, *War and Popular Culture: Resistance in Modern China, 1937–1945* (Berkeley: University of California Press, 1994), 23.
10. John A. Lent, "Comic Art," in *Handbook of Chinese Popular Culture*, ed. Wu Dingbo and Patrick D. Murphy (Westport, CT: Greenwood, 1994), 279–305.
11. Jack Chen, "China's Militant Cartoons," *Asia* (May 1938): 311.
12. Chen, "China's Militant Cartoons," 311.
13. Chen, "China's Militant Cartoons," 312.
14. "55 Years of Innovation," *Asiaweek* (24–31 December 1982): 26–27.
15. Hung Chang-tai, "The Fuming Image: Cartoons and Public Opinion in Late Republican China, 1945 to 1949," *Comparative Studies in Society and History* 36, no.1 (1994): 129.

16. Mary Ann Farquhar, "Sanmao: Classic Cartoons and Chinese Popular Culture," in *Asian Popular Culture*, ed. John A. Lent (Boulder, CO: Westview, 1995).

17. Interview by the author with cartoonist Zhan Tong in Shanghai, China, 15–16 August 1993.

18. Interview by the author with cartoonist/editor Sun Shao Bo, *World of Cartoons*, in Shanghai, China, 16 August 1993.

19. Zhan, interview, 1993; interview by the author with Zheng Xin Yao, managing editor, *World of Cartoons*, in Shanghai, China, 16 August 1993.

20. Jack Moore, "Cartooning Characters," *Hong Kong Sunday Post-Herald*, 25 May 1969, 5.

21. Interview by the author with cartoonist Larry Feign, *South China Morning Post*, in Hong Kong, 11 July 1992; Interview by the author with Zunzi (Wong Kee-kwan), in Drexel Hill, Pennsylvania, 30 July 1991 and in Hong Kong, 12 July 1992.

22. James L. Tyson, "It's a Hard Place to Raise Hackles," *Christian Science Monitor*, 11 August 1989, 6.

23. Barbara Basler, "Help! Wicked Satirist is Loose. Colony Skewered," *New York Times*, 12 January 1990.

24. Tony Allison, et. al., "Figure It Out," *Asia Magazine*, 7–9 January 1994, 10–11.

25. Feign, interview, 1992.

26. Chen Yueh-yun, "Thirty Years of Cartoon's Vicissitude," *Commercial Times* (Taipei), 9 September 1981, 10.

27. Interview by the author with cartoonist Lao Chung in Taipei, Taiwan, 10 July 1992.

28. Interview by the author with cartoonist Yoon Young-Ok, *Seoul Shinmun*, in Seoul, Korea, 3 July 1992.

29. Interview by the author with cartoonist Park Soo Dong in Seoul, Korea, 7 July 1992.

30. Interview by the author with cartoonist Park Jae Dong, *Hankyoreh Shinmun*, Seoul, Korea, 7 July 1992, and 5 July 1994.

31. Nonoy Marcelo, "Komiks: The Filipino National Literature?" *Asian Culture*, January 1980, 18.

32. Interview by the author with cartoonist Antonio Velasquez in Manila, Philippines, 26 September 1988; see also, John A. Lent, "Antonio Velasquez, Father of Philippine Komiks," *Philippines Communication Journal* (March 1993): 47–50.

33. Cynthia Roxas and Joaquin Arevalo Jr., *A History of Komiks in the Philippines and Other Countries* (Quezon City: Filipinas Publishing, 1985), 67, 73.

34. Interview by the author with Antonio Velasquez in Manila, Philippines, 26 September 1988; Interview by the author with cartoonist Larry Alcala in Manila, Philippines, 26 September 1988.

35. Alcala, interview, 1988.

36. Interview by the author with cartoonist Nonoy Marcelo of the *Manila Chronicle*, in Manila, Philippines, 29 September 1988.

37. Marcelo, interview, 1988.

38. Marcelo, "Komiks: The Filipino National Literature?," 20.

39. Interview by the author with cartoonist Chai Rachawat of *Thai Rath*, in Bangkok, Thailand, 1 August 1993.

40. Pairote Gesmankit and Kullasap Gesmankit, "Cartoon Techniques Widely Applied in Thailand," *Asian Culture*, January 1980, 22.

41. John A. Lent, "Comic Books, Funnies and Political Cartoons: The Asian Experience," *International Popular Culture* 2, no. 2 (1982): 40; Redza, "Enlightening Cartoon Shows," *Sunday Times* (Kuala Lumpur), October 28, 1973; John A. Lent, "Few Laughs Left for Asia's Cartoonists," *Leader: Malaysian Journalism Review* 2 (1973): 10.

42. Interview by the author with cartoonist Lat in Kuala Lumpur, Malaysia, November 1986; E. J. Dunfee, "The Joker's Wild," *Asia*, 19 March 1989, 8–13.

43. Lat, interview, 1986.

44. Interview by the author with cartoonist U Aung Shein in Rangoon, Myanmar, 30 July 1993.

45. Interview by the author with cartoonist Johnny Hidajat in Jakarta, Indonesia, 29 July 1992. Hidajat has been a prolific cartoonist; from 1970 to 1975 he did sixty to seventy-five strips of three- to four-frames every day.

46. O. P. Joshi, "Contents, Consumers and Creators of Comics in India," in *Comics and Visual Culture,* ed. Alphons Silbermann (Munich: K. G. Saur, 1986), 213, 215.

47. Interview by the author with cartoonist Pran, in New Delhi, India, 5 July 1993.

48. Pran, interview, 1993.

49. Interview by the author with Anant Pai, editor, *Amar Chitra Katha,* in Bombay, India, 9 July 1993.

50. Interview by the author with cartoonist Abid Surti in Bombay, India, 10 July 1993.

51. Interview by the author with Luis Fernandes, comics editor, *Amrita Bharat,* in Bombay, India, 9 July 1993.

52. Joshi, "Contents, Consumers and Creators," 219.

53. Joshi, "Contents, Consumers, and Creators," 215.

54. Mahmud Shah Qureshi, "Cartoons: Mirror of Bangladesh Society," *Asian Culture* (January 1980): 27.

55. Interview by the author with cartoonist Ranabi in Dhaka, Bangladesh, 26 July 1993.

56. Ranabi, interview, 1993; Interview by the author with Nazrul Islam in Dhaka, Bangladesh, 25 July 1993; Interview by the author with Asiful Huda in Dhaka, Bangladesh, 27 July 1993.

57. Interview by the author with Ahsan Habib, editor, *Unmad,* in Dhaka, Bangladesh, 25 July 1993.

58. Anwar Enayetullah, "Many Young Cartoonists Appearing: Pakistan," *Asian Culture* (January 1980): 24–25.

59. Roxas and Arevalo, *A History of Komiks,* 265.

60. Interview by the author with cartoonist W. R. Wijesoma, Upali Group, in Colombo, Sri Lanka, 15 July 1993.

61. "Comics papers" appear weekly as a form of comic book. The first was *Sathuta* in 1972, followed by *Sittara* three years later. By the 1980s, ten to fifteen appeared weekly. A typical "comics paper" has sixteen pages, made up of fourteen stories by almost as many artists. A strip usually lasts about two years, and one has been serialized since 1986. All stories are done by freelance story writers and artists. The number of titles has decreased in recent years because of a saturated market, lack of experienced cartoonists, competition from TV and children's magazines, and discouragement by school officials. Interview by the author with cartoonist W. P. Wickamanayake in Colombo, Sri Lanka, 17 July 1993; Interview by the author with cartoonist Janaka Ratnayake, Upali Group, in Colombo, Sri Lanka, 15 July 1993; Interview by the author with artist Paliyagoda Dayananda, *Bindu,* in Colombo, Sri Lanka, 15 July 1993; Interview by the author with Camillus Perera, chairman, Camillus Publications, in Colombo, Sri Lanka, 19 July 1993.

62. Camillus, interview, 1993.

63. "Asia's Factories of Fantasy," *Asiaweek* (4 December 1981): 51.

64. Interview by the author with cartoonist S. C. Opatha of the *Observer,* in Colombo, Sri Lanka, 17 and 20 July 1993.

65. Wickamanayake, interview, 1993.

66. Interview by the author with cartoonist Wasantha Siriwardena, *Lankadipa,* in Colombo, Sri Lanka, 16 July 1993.

Literature in Line

Picture Stories in the People's Republic of China

JULIA F. ANDREWS

THE TERM *LIANHUANHUA*, literally "linked pictures," was coined in Shanghai in the 1920s to describe a form of illustrated story that had been developing in urban China since the introduction of Western printing technology in the late nineteenth century.[1] *Lianhuanhua* books are usually only about three by five inches in size, with one picture to a page, and serve a market similar to that for comic books in the West.

It has been argued that because China has a long tradition of illustration in religious, ethical, historical, dramatic, and fictional texts, *lianhuanhua* should be viewed as an ancient Chinese genre. In particular, ink outline (the basic technique of classical Chinese figure painting) and sequential reading (which is required by the traditional handscroll format) provide ancient parallels to modern comics. China, where printing was invented, indeed has a significant history of illustration in painted, carved, and, finally, woodcut form that goes back almost two millennia.[2]

Lianhuanhua, however, developed in China's modern cities, particularly Shanghai, in a period when Western publications were easily available and were themselves published using imported printing technology.[3] Thus, although different in format and theme from most Western comic books, the appearance of *lianhuanhua* was part of the Chinese response to and adoption of new forms of publishing from the West. As such, it was a new urban entertainment, one that joined novel imported elements with traditional Chinese tastes. The thorough integration of modern Western idioms with popular Chinese concerns make neither name particularly relevant. Intended during the Republican period for the profit of the producers and the transitory pleasure of the consumers, *lianhuanhua*'s hybrid qualities, with links to both China's past and the modern world, capture the flavor of their place and moment of creation.

Major changes in the purpose and production procedures for *lianhuanhua* took place following the establishment of the People's Republic of China in 1949. *Lianhuanhua* books of the Republican period (1911–1949) often took their stories from popular dramas, traditional fiction, or contemporary film. Publishers made use of the speed and cheapness of Western printing technology to satisfy the urban market for inexpensive entertainment literature. The little books circulated not only through sales but also in rental stalls that were set up on the Shanghai streets to tempt passersby. Those documenting current runs of successful dramatic productions, as well as those based on movies, were generally rushed to press (sometimes drawn and printed the night of the opening performance for sale the following morning) and were generally sold at prices lower than the cost of a theater ticket.

Before 1949, *lianhuanhua* were published both by large publishers and by small fly-by-night printing shops. Artists were usually self-taught or had come into the business as apprentices in a master artist's workshop. Drawings done partially or even completely by apprentices were published under the master's name, and the incomes of master and disciples alike could be uncertain.

A typical example of this genre is Shen Manyun's *Arrest of the Orchid*, a two-booklet set. Published in August of 1949, well after Shanghai came under control of communist troops but about six weeks before establishment of the People's Republic of China, it continues the format, style, and content typical of pre-communist *lianhuanhua*. Characteristic of the appeal of *lianhuanhua* in the period is that the story, which focuses on crime and punishment, is filled with lively action. Further, and typical of good marketing in the period, is that it is billed as one episode of a continuing series entitled "The Cases of Judge Shi."

Shen Manyun, one of the four most famous cartoonists of the 1940s (along with Zhao Hongben, Qian Xiaodai, and Chen Guangyi), was best known for his *lianhuanhua* based on traditional operatic performances, and the characters in this book are dressed in the stylized headgear and flowing robes of actual stage performers. At the same time, some effort was made to situate the

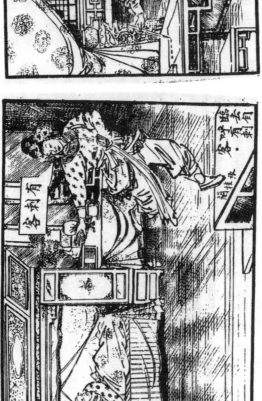

FIGURE 39. Zhang Guilan signs a note for the sleeping Judge Shi and then awakens him by shouting, "Assassin!" as she escapes. From *Arrest of the Orchid* (*Cases of Magistrate Shi*) by Shen Manyun, 1949.

FIGURE 40. Zhang Guilan returns home by her original route; Judge Shi, startled out of sleep, assembles his staff. From *Arrest of the Orchid*.

characters in a three-dimensional setting, for which interior scenes are drawn with elements of Western perspective and shading. One particularly amusing example of the artist's interplay of theater and narration occurs when attempts are made to break down the formulaic appearance of the characters through realistic details. The hero, Judge Shi, is awakened in the night with news of the crime. Not yet dressed, he stands near his bed in his bloomers but is surrounded by his staff, dressed in full operatic regalia.

Lianhuanhua of the 1940s may have balloons for dialogue in the Western manner, but the majority rely on captions written in panels above, below, or inside the pictures. In *Arrest of the Orchid*, Shen Manyun uses several kinds of text: dialogue balloons, identifying labels for the characters, and short passages of text in cartouches at the bottom of the page that describe the action. The books read from right to left, with the spine at right, and the text cartouches, even those that are arranged in horizontal panels, also read as traditional vertical columns.

As early as the 1930s, both the intrinsic interest and the didactic potential of this immensely popular form of entertainment had been recognized by leftist intellectuals, including the influential writer and editor Lu Xun, who lamented the decline of China's age-old art of woodblock printing. Among his efforts to revive illustration was his involvement in publishing Chinese reprints of European modernist woodcut illustrations, including narrative series by Käthe Kollwitz and Frans Masereel. Although these European prints had little in common with Chinese *lianhuanhua* beyond using monochromatic images to tell a story, Lu Xun called them *lianhuan tuhua*. He presumably sought to expand the potential connections between a cosmopolitan modern art and China's own popular culture. Young artists inspired by Lu Xun's work began making woodblock print series that were conceived in an essentially European avant-garde manner but told Chinese stories. These have also been called *lianhuanhua*.

There is little evidence that commercial *lianhuanhua*, which had a large audience, was affected by the avant-garde *lianhuanhua* woodcuts of the leftists, which were printed in small editions and received relatively little exposure. During the Anti-Japanese War, which began in 1937, many of the urban artists went to work as propagandists among the north Chinese peasantry, and some remained in the countryside for a full decade. At the communist base in Yan'an, particularly following Mao Zedong's 1942 talks on art and literary policy, it was decided to largely abandon the European manner favored in the previous decade. Instead of making pictures that were often bleak and dark, leftist artists now pursued a clearly readable and relatively upbeat manner of presentation that would appeal to illiterate peasants.[4] The result was an emphasis on outline drawing and simple settings and an image that often appears somewhat naive.

The programmatic reform of popular culture represented by the *lianhuanhua* artists and publishers, especially in the 1950s and early 1960s, is a complicated phenomenon.[5] On the one side is a set of circumstances that seem largely negative. The Shanghai art world, China's artistic hub during the first half of the twentieth century, was all but decimated by the communist takeover. Efforts to transform the economy destroyed the domestic art market, which was predicated upon a financially secure class of private art patrons. With the disappearance of their clients, many professional painters were left unable to make a living. Next, a policy of reforming Shanghai's decadent culture and centralizing administration on the Soviet model led to transfer of Shanghai's art schools, which historically were among the most influential in the nation, out of the city. The alternative of teaching art as a livelihood was thus closed to Shanghai artists. Artists were left with the options of relocating or retraining.

The publishing industry, which even in Republican Shanghai supported many artists with its need for various kinds of commercial art, stepped in to fill the void. From the early 1950s until today, a huge segment of Shanghai's art world has been employed in publishing. This concentration of talent was one precondition for the rapid development of *lianhuanhua* in the 1950s and 1960s. In 1950, cadres from the New Fourth Army were sent to work as supervisors in the Shanghai publishing industry, with *lianhuanhua* as a particular focus of their attention. Some of the new communist art authorities came from the working-class Shanghai families who were *lianhuanhua*'s primary consumers. Others were admirers of Lu Xun. As part of the communist effort to wipe out vice, most notably drugs, prostitution, and organized crime, the new cultural leaders tried to eradicate the supply of violent, pornographic, or superstitious comics that were said to have dominated the pre-liberation market. At first, effort was put primarily into censorship of new publications and regulating the stock of older books still on the market. Following the Yan'an model, the new regime sought to establish a positive alternative, one that would inculcate the values of new China while continuing to entertain the readership of *lianhuanhua*.

In spite of the many practical difficulties presented by the implementation of communism, many artists and intellectuals greeted the reunification of China under a seemingly incorrupt government with enthusiasm in 1949 and devoted serious and idealistically motivated efforts to achieving the new society promised by the revolution. The new socialist art, even at its most turgidly didactic, was not produced by faceless cogs in the communist machinery, but,

FIGURE 41. From the 1950 *lianhuanhua* by Mi Gu, *Young Blacky Gets Married* (*Xiao erhei jie-hun*), in which Blacky suggests to his girlfriend that they announce their engagement despite opposition from their parents.

for the most part, by enthusiastic young artists. Some *lianhuanhua* artists who came out of workshop apprenticeships viewed themselves as the exploited workers the communists aimed to assist. And, like all citizens of the People's Republic of China, these artists underwent thought reform and ideological indoctrination, a process from which many emerged with sincere intentions and the idea of improving society through art.

An early revolutionary work, Mi Gu's *Young Blacky Gets Married* (*Xiaoer-hei jiehun*), is the product of such an effort.[6] The pictures and the text adaptation, based on a novel written in the communist base area during the war, are by the artist himself.[7] Mi Gu, who had attended but not graduated from two of China's most prestigious art schools, the Hangzhou National Art Academy and the Shanghai Art Academy, was an aspiring cartoonist in Shanghai when the Japanese invaded. In 1938, at the age of twenty, he moved to the communist base in Yan'an, where he did propaganda drawing for the war effort and received training in the new arts policies. In 1942 he transferred to the New

Fourth Army, active in his native Jiangsu-Zhejiang area, and he subsequently published a number of anti-Nationalist party cartoons in Shanghai periodicals. After 1949, still in his early thirties, he became an editor and Communist party art official in Shanghai. The year he drew *Young Blacky,* he became founding editor of *Cartoon Magazine.*[8]

A notable feature of *Young Blacky Gets Married,* which promotes love marriages rather than parental arrangements, is the artist's adherence to the principles established under Mao Zedong's direction in Yan'an. Mi Gu thus avoided the Western-style drawing with shading and chiaroscuro that appealed to urban readers and worked instead in ink outline with a minimum of shadow. From an aesthetic viewpoint, Mi Gu's folky naiveté may not be entirely successful, but its weaknesses were undoubtedly instructive to other *lianhuanhua* artists. In Shanghai at least, the relatively crude Yan'an manner was soon abandoned in favor of greater professionalism.

One important change that was soon institutionalized was to relieve artists of responsibility for writing the texts. The result was that the artist was sometimes simply presented with a set of captions for which pictures were to be supplied. This was an attempt to professionalize both writing and drawing, potentially raising the qualitative level of each. At the same time, it may have made state control of the textual content more efficient.

The communist cultural and economic program required a complete reorganization of the Shanghai art world, including absorbing *lianhuanhua* artists from the old workshops and private publishers into studios run by major publishing houses. The government's commitment to developing *lianhuanhua,* which was seen as an art for and by the people, is of particular importance in this context. With the restructuring of the publishing industry, unprecedented resources were dedicated to developing talent among *lianhuanhua* artists.

The administrators of the fledgling art bureaucracy considered most *lianhuanhua* artists poorly trained in drawing techniques. The Shanghai Cultural Bureau sponsored special classes for artists in 1951 and 1952 to retrain them to produce higher quality *lianhuanhua.* Two or three hundred artists, including old comic book artists, young art enthusiasts, and painters in other media who found themselves unable to market their art, were recruited for retraining in drawing and communist ideology. The addition of art school graduates and other professional painters to the ranks of the cartoon artists substantially strengthened the talent pool. In 1952, the Shanghai publishers were reorganized into two large presses, the state-run East China People's Art Press (renamed Shanghai People's Art Publishing House in 1954) and the New Art Press, which absorbed the artists of many private *lianhuanhua* publishers. The *lianhuanhua* section of the former was headed by Gu Bingxin, an instructor

FIGURE 42. From Ding Bingzeng and Han Heping's *Railroad Guerillas* (*Tiedao youjidui*), published 1954–1962.

in the 1952 art classes, and Cheng Shifa, a Shanghai Art Academy graduate who was retrained there. Well-trained art school graduates, including Ding Bingzeng and Han Heping, as well as some workshop-trained or self-taught cartoonists such as He Youzhi, were assigned to the state press; many older artists worked for the quasi-private New Art Press, where the famous Zhao Hongben directed the *lianhuanhua* section. Zhao, it turned out, was not only an excellent illustrator but also an underground party member.

The fruits of the re-education and reorganization efforts began to appear in the mid-1950s. One of the most beautifully drafted of the new *lianhuanhua*, *Railroad Guerillas* (*Tiedao youjidui*), was the creation of Ding Bingzeng and Han Heping, both 1952 graduates of the East China campus of the Central Academy of Fine Arts in Hangzhou. Based on the novel by Liu Zhixia, the ten-volume work with more than a thousand drawings was completed between 1954 and 1962. The refined drawing and lively postures make clear that the artists were masters of academic drawing.

Set in southern Shandong during the Anti-Japanese War (between 1938 and 1945), the work tells the story of coal miners and railway workers who joined forces under the direction of the Communist Party to fight a guerrilla war against the Japanese along the Lin-Zao railway line. Work on this influential *lianhuanhua* began less than a decade after the Japanese surrender, during the highly nationalistic first five years of the People's Republic of China. It creates heroic working-class Chinese characters while at the same time demonizing the Japanese enemy of the occupation years.

The dramatic drawing and action-filled story was immensely popular in the decades following its first release. As of 1997, it had been reprinted at least thirty-seven times with almost four million copies in print. Its popularity may have to do with its military subject matter, in particular its vivid action and violence. From a purely artistic and technical point of view, *Railroad Guerrillas* was admired as a watershed in the development of Shanghai *lianhuanhua*. Beautifully drawn in outline, it brings the best of academic figure drawing and, to some extent, heroic socialist realist imagery into the cartoon genre.

The artists effectively limit any use of shading or chiaroscuro, thus creating a more Chinese flavor as well as a very clean image. Furthermore, they adopt conventions of traditional illustration, but combine them remarkably effectively with realistic drawing. These include a sharply tilted ground plane; broad expanses of white paper, which contrast with heavily patterned areas; interior scenes in which all but essential details of the walls and floors are left blank; screen-like use of foreground rocks to define an outdoor setting; and a broad but varied brush rendering of rocks and grasses that have the feel of a traditional woodcut.

Some of these elements, particularly those for rendering landscape, may be found in commercial *lianhuanhua* of the 1940s. A similar clean, linear quality, particularly in the settings, may be found in some propaganda art from Yan'an. Nevertheless, the combination of extremely fine drawing and realistic figure rendering displays an unprecedented mastery and synthesis of several aesthetic standards. A comparison of this work with Mi Gu's cruder attempt of half a decade earlier makes clear the remarkable innovations of these young artists.

At the beginning of 1956, nationalization of Shanghai's publishing industry was complete. New Art Press was merged into Shanghai People's Art Publishing House, which over the years commissioned many of China's most successful *lianhuanhua*. Artists Zhao Hongben and Gu Bingxin then became co-directors of the expanded *lianhuanhua* studio. One could argue that the decade between 1956 and 1966 was the heyday of Shanghai's new *lianhuanhua*.

Zhao Hongben, one of the four most famous Shanghai *lianhuahua* artists of the pre-1949 period, was known for his "modern costume" *lianhuanhua*. Artists in the pre-1949 era and, to a lesser extent in the 1950s, tended

FIGURE 43. From Zhao Hongben and Qian Xiaodai's 1962 work, *Monkey Beats the White-boned Demon* (*San da baiguijing*), in which the Tang monk, deluded by the White-boned Demon's disguise, tries to protect the demon from Monkey's attack.

FIGURE 44. The white-boned demon, disguised as an old lady, scolds Pigsy.

to specialize in "modern costume stories" or, like Shen Manyun, "antique costume stories." His most famous post-1949 work, a collaboration with the equally famous Qian Xiaodai, was completed in 1962. *Monkey Beats the White-boned Demon* is typical of the revival of traditional Chinese subject matter that characterized the nationalistic cultural policies of the period between the Anti-Rightist Campaign of 1957 and the Cultural Revolution of 1966, a period that included a diplomatic break with the Soviet Union. This work, with its simplified settings, linear rock and tree contours, and stylized drapery folds, evokes traditional prints. But the characters are three-dimensional and heroic, betokening a knowledge of both socialist realism and Western superhero comics. *Monkey Beats the White-boned Demon,* with its convincing characterizations, voluminous quality, and marvelous contrasts of blank paper and complex linear details, fully modernizes the "ancient costume" manner of drawing *lianhuanhua.*

Both Zhao Hongben and his colleague Gu Bingxin became extremely interested in seventeenth-century woodblock prints in the course of their efforts to raise the quality of Shanghai *lianhuanhua.* They particularly admired the work of the mid-seventeenth-century eccentric painter Chen Hongshou, whose elegant sense of pattern, expressive use of exaggerated draperies, and exquisite manipulation of setting clearly inspired many illustrators of the period.

These virtues, as well as traditional ways of rendering trees and rocks, may be seen in the masterpiece by Zhao and Qian, which nevertheless is a completely modern work. Almost no shading is used, in a self-consciously archaistic manner. Instead, volumes and textures are described by lines of various widths, shapes, and densities. Some of them may be identified with techniques from classical Chinese painting, such as the "nail-head rat-tail" stroke for drapery folds or the "trembling brush" outline found on some rocks.

The repeating drapery folds that delineate the gown of the White-boned Demon (disguised here as an old lady) is a convention probably taken from Chen Hongshou's prints. They serve not only to model her form, but also to intensify her act of aggression against Pigsy with their sense of motion and sheer density. This ominous quality is accentuated by the gnarled cypress tree across the front of the picture. While the appearance of the tree comes from traditional sources, the dramatic composition, and especially the radical diminution in scale of the Tang monk, are almost cinematic.

Adapting elements from an antique manner to render the mythological Monkey as a superhero was an extremely influential achievement in its time. The characterizations that Zhao and Qian developed for Monkey and his friends have assumed almost iconic status in Chinese popular culture, cropping up like a Chinese Mickey Mouse on all forms of consumer items even today.

A pair of *lianhuanhua* produced in the same studios in 1962 explore some of the same technical and aesthetic possibilities from a completely different point of view. *Great Change in a Mountain Village* and *Li Shuangshuang* are both based on modern stories of somewhat propagandistic themes. He Youzhi, one of the talented self-taught artists to emerge from the *lianhuanhua* classes

FIGURE 45. Mid-seventeenth century woodcut drinking card, from Chen Hongshou's *Comprehending Antiquity* (*Bogu Yezi*).

FIGURES 46–47. From He Youzhi's *Great Change in a Mountain Village* (*Shanxiang jubian*), published in 1962.

FIGURE 48. From He Youzhi's *Li Shuangshuang,* 1962.

of the early 1950s, is a keen observer of human nature with a remarkable flair for characterization.

Great Change, based on a novel by Zhou Libo, ostensibly describes the success of China's collectivization movement in the early 1950s. The story takes place in an isolated village in the southern province of Hunan in 1955, during the height of China's movement to collectivize agriculture. It recounts the experiences of its peasant characters in the midst of the tidal wave of change required by the movement. The Communist Party swept into every aspect of life, transforming not only the foundations of the rural economy but also social customs, family life, attitudes toward romantic love, relationships between people, and the very nature of the village itself. The text itself is somewhat turgid, but this *lianhuanhua* owes its high reputation in the Chinese art world to the five hundred poignant drawings that more than compensate for the weakness of the story's plot. The psychological insights the artist He Youzhi has conveyed by the appearances and interactions of his characters make completely plausible the struggles undergone by people required to suddenly change their entire way of life.

The artist was sent by the Shanghai People's Art Publishing House to study village life in the area in which the story takes place. The authentic flavor he conveys by his details of gesture, facial expression, dress, architecture, furniture, and so forth are presumably the result of his careful fieldwork.

He Youzhi's drawings are remarkable in integrating the same clean overall appearance and textural contrasts that we have traced to antique woodcuts into a realistically rendered modern story. His colleagues at the press marveled at the extraordinary variety with which he managed to imbue the endless party meetings required by the plot. One of the most telling is a study of the rustic floor and varied footwear of the meeting's somewhat bored participants.

The same style of drawing and composition may be found in *Li Shuang-shuang,* a feminist story about the life and changing relationship of a young peasant couple in the period following the communization of the countryside. The wife, Li Shuangshuang, is hard working, bold, and opinionated. Her husband, Sun Xiwang, is depicted as clever in small ways but short sighted. When Li Shuangshuang becomes active in party affairs, spending time helping improve her village, her husband first quarrels with her and then leaves her and their small daughter. In the end, he sees the error of his ways and returns.

As in *Great Change in a Mountain Village,* He Youzhi's brilliant characterizations make up for the rigidly propagandistic text. This *lianhuanhua* is based on a film of the same title, and its characters are dressed in essentially the same fashion as the film actors. If anything, however, the artist's freedom from the practical constraints of filmmaking allowed him to explore human relations in a way not completely possible in the movie studio. He Youzhi is particularly gifted at selecting a minor element of the scene, such as the arguing couple's small child or the departing husband's bundle of clothes, and using it as a focus for the intense emotion of the scene.

In 1963, the Chinese Ministry of Culture somewhat belatedly took note of the accomplishments of *lianhuanhua* artists by awarding six first-class prizes to work made between 1949 and 1963. Three of the prizes went to *Railroad Guerillas, Monkey Beats the White-boned Demon,* and *Great Change in a Mountain Village. Li Shuangshuang* was awarded a third-class prize.

The linear style of *lianhuanhua* typified by the preceding examples became standard for the period. Hua Sanchuan's 1963 rendering of *White-haired Girl,* another *lianhuanhua* based on a film of the same title, is a technically refined example of the same manner.[9] Truly innovative, combining the best of old and new, this linear *lianhuanhua* style had other qualities suitable to its time. Elegant and complete with no need for color, the low cost of printing linear *lianhuanhua* was a great advantage, both ideologically and practically, during the economic collapse following the disastrous Great Leap Forward of 1958.

The closing of most publishing houses during the Cultural Revolution, beginning in late 1966 or early 1967, radically reduced the number of *lianhuanhua* that were produced. After the death of Mao Zedong a decade later, the publishing industry began reorganizing. In addition to returning the exiled

FIGURE 49. From Hua Sanchuan's *White-haired Girl* (*Baimaonü*), 1963.

older artists to work, young draftsmen were added to the *lianhuanhua* studios. By the end of the decade, they were meeting a seemingly insatiable demand for popular entertainment. Although one may identify didactic or moral messages in many of these publications, such content was extremely subtle compared to the bludgeoning propaganda that dominated reading matter of the previous decade.

Lianhuanhua production following the death of Mao was dominated by a new generation of artists, one born at about the time the new regime was founded in 1949, largely educated before the Cultural Revolution, and reaching maturity during the tumultuous years of the Cultural Revolution. They brought to their art very different qualities than their elders. Most were self-taught under extremely difficult circumstances, and the styles they developed following 1976 tended to be more diverse than the well-established manner of their elders. Some artists, such as Shi Dawei, excelled at Western drawing and had no compunction about using heavy black ink. Others, like Lu Fusheng, mastered traditional outline and color painting and produced elegant archaistic works that emulated Song dynasty court painting.

上海人民美术出版社连环画专用稿纸

FIGURE 50. From *Qing Troops Enter the Pass* (*Qingbing rusai*) by Shi Dawei, Luo Xixian, Wang Yiqiu, Xu Youwu, and Cui Junpei, published in 1978.

During the Cultural Revolution, attempts were made to stamp out the supposedly selfish notion of seeking recognition for artistic achievement. Many works were published anonymously. In other cases, collaboration was required so that any credit might go to the team and any individualistic excesses might be stamped out. *Qing Troops Enter the Pass* of 1978 is a typical late example of the practice of collaboration, but in a transitional form, whereby innovation is emphasized, but credit is shared. After the rise to power in 1979 of Deng Xiaoping, who generally downplayed the importance of art to the nation, such rigid controls on the artistic process were gradually abandoned.

Many of the best *lianhuanhua* of this period were designed by young men who had spent their adolescences laboring on collective farms or in factories. In spite of the xenophobic rhetoric of the Cultural Revolution period, the emphasis on propaganda painting led to a generation of young people who were thoroughly trained in Western drawing. Shanghai People's Art Publishing House, for example, hired a group of young *lianhuanhua* artists who had established their reputations during the Cultural Revolution as factory worker–artists. In the case of *Qing Troops Enter the Pass,* the twenty-eight-year-old

Shi Dawei collaborated with three fellows recently transferred from Shanghai factories and with the well-known older staff artist Wang Yiqiu. This dramatic work, based on a novel about the collapse of the Ming dynasty, is one of the best examples of the period.

Lu Fusheng, the creator of *Phoenix Hairpin*, represents a different kind of artist to emerge during the early post-Mao period. *Lianhuanhua* were so profitable that Shanghai People's Art Publishing House, like other art presses, actively recruited submissions from artists not on staff. Lu Fusheng was a recent graduate of the Chinese painting department of the Zhejiang Academy of Fine Arts in Hangzhou, the same institution that had trained Ding Bingzeng and Han Heping thirty years earlier. He completed this series two years after receiving his graduate degree. The 1984 publication won first prize in the National Art Exhibition of the same year. Painted in ink and color on silk, this set of illustrations clearly required much more sophisticated and expensive printing than the line drawings that dominated the 1950s and 1960s.

The period between *Qing Troops* and *Phoenix Hairpin*, roughly 1978 to 1984, marked a second qualitative high point in People's Republic of China (PRC) *lianhuanhua*. The little booklets were so popular with readers that they became extraordinarily profitable for the publishing houses, which in turn attracted first-rate artistic talent with the high fees and instant fame they could offer their artists. For reasons that were not understood in the publishing world at the time, but may be related to the sudden and widespread availability of television sets and video cassette recorders in China, the market for *lianhuanhua* crashed in 1986 and 1987, and it has never regained its previous level. Most artists have consequently moved on to other work, either making fine art paintings, teaching art, or administering newly profitable productions of the publishing house, such as decorative calendars.[10]

The golden age of PRC *lianhuanhua* may be over, but its occurrence at all is a remarkable phenomenon. The field of *lianhuanhua* may serve as an example of the unpredictable results of trying to engineer the art world. In spite of a host of highly destructive art policies, including relocation of artists, closing of art schools, regulation of commerce that effectively abolished the domestic art market, and censorship of contents and styles, *lianhuanhua* drawing reached unprecedented qualitative levels in the 1950s and 1960s. On the positive side, the Shanghai publishers and the Communist Party provided greater support for travel, study, and contemplation than most artists had ever seen before as well as professional and financial rewards for good work. In spite of the institutional constraints on art in China, the conjunction of human talent, motivation, and opportunity in the Shanghai publishing industry in the 1950s and 1960s yielded superbly designed and drafted *lianhuanhua*.

Lu Xun, in a typically flamboyant comment, wrote in the 1930s that there was no reason the field of *lianhuanhua* could not produce a Michelangelo.[11] It is difficult to imagine how the Michelangelo of *lianhuanhua* might look, but I expect that he might be found in this group, which represents the best work of the best period of *lianhuanhua* and whose artists ought to make the dreams of a new culture come true.

ENDNOTES

1. For further background on pre-1949 *lianhuanhua*, see Kuiyi Shen, "Comics, Picture Books, and Cartoonists in Republican China," *INKS* 4.3 (1997): 2-16. Many ideas in the introductory portions of my essay were developed as part of our collaboration on the exhibition *Literature in Line*, co-curated by Professor Shen.

2. This now orthodox interpretation is best exemplified in A Ying, *Zhongguo lianhuan tuhua shihua*, 2nd ed. (Beijing: People's Art Publishing House, 1957, 1984).

3. A Ying dates the first use of the term *lianhuan tuhua* to a 1925 World Book Company publication. See A Ying, *Zbongguo lianhuan tuhua shihua*, 21. Lu Xun wrote in 1933, "The term lianhuan tuhua is now already somewhat familiar, so need not be revised. . . ." Lu Xun, "Yigeren de shounan, xu," preface to *Die Passion eines Manschen*, by Frans Masereel, Chinese repr. (Shanghai: Liangyou Book Company, 1933), reprinted in Jiang Weipu, ed., *Lu Xun lun lianhuanhua*, rev. ed. (1956; repr., Beijing: People's Art Press, 1982), 18.

4. This process has been described by Ellen Johnston Laing in *The Winking Owl* (Berkeley: University of California Press), 15, and Shirley Sun, *Modern Chinese Woodcuts* (San Francisco: Chinese Culture Foundation, 1979).

5. Some aspects of this were described in Julia F. Andrews, *Painters and Politics in the People's Republic of China*, 1949 (Berkeley: University of California Press, 1994): 128–34, 246–51.

6. I am indebted to the Shanghai People's Art Press for plot summaries of the post-1949 *lianhuanhua* discussed in this article. Material presented in lectures at The Ohio State University by Xiaomei Chen (8 May 1997) and Kirk Denton (29 May 1997) was also invaluable.

7. Rustic characters in *lianhuanhua* are often named according to the most prominent feature of their appearance or behavior, such as Dummy, Fatty, or, in this case, the swarthy Blacky.

8. *Zhongguo meishu nianjian*, (Shanghai, 1948), 374.

9. This tale is ostensibly based on a real story that took place in the 1940s. Performed as a play at the communist base in Yan'an and many times thereafter, the story was adapted as a movie in the early 1960s. The *lianhuanhua* was based upon the film script. Later, during the Cultural Revolution, the story was made into one of the eight model operas.

10. Oral communication from Kuiyi Shen, 12 June 1997.

11. Lu Xun, "Lun disanzhong ren (On middle characters)," in *Lu Xun Lun Lianhuanhua* (Lu Xun on Lianhuanhua), ed. Jiang Weipu (Beijing: People's Art Publishers, 1982), 33.

Drawing the Line
An Absolute Defense for Political Cartoons

CHRISTOPHER LAMB

FOR THE FIRST TIME, in *Hustler Magazine v. Jerry Falwell* in 1988, the U.S. Supreme Court made the history of political cartooning central to a decision.[1] While ruling on a magazine parody, the Court said that caricature could not be actionable unless it contained a false statement of fact that was made with actual malice: "Were we to hold otherwise, there can be little doubt that political cartoonists and satirists would be subjected to damages without any showing that their work falsely defamed their subject."[2]

Hustler dealt with an advertisement parody, not with a political cartoon. The two are not synonymous, and the distinction is important. While *Hustler* (and other First Amendment cases) would indeed influence the Supreme Court's decision in any case involving a political cartoon, it does not guarantee the same result. Although state courts have determined that cartoonists have considerable freedom to satirize people and issues, this, too, does not guarantee that the Supreme Court will automatically reach the same conclusion. Lower courts must defer to the Supreme Court, not vice versa. Without direct precedent, one cannot presuppose any decision by the Supreme Court, and, since 1907, the Court has not decided on the matter of the constitutional freedom of cartoonists.

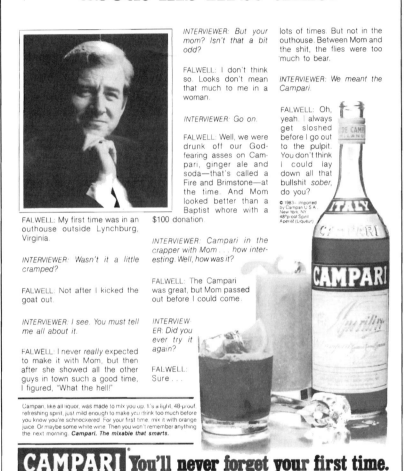

FIGURE 51. Inside front cover of *Hustler,* November 1982.

While not ruling directly on a cartoon, the Court has, nevertheless, fashioned a formidable defense for the cartoonist. The Court has consistently maintained that criticism of public affairs—or political speech—be protected under the First Amendment. Additionally, the Court has emphasized that opinion and rhetorical hyperbole are generally considered protected expression. When a statement of "opinion" on a matter of public concern reasonably implies false and defamatory facts regarding public figures or private figures, the plaintiff in a libel suit must prove the statement was made with "actual malice," or knowledge of the falsity or reckless disregard for the truth.[3] For a political cartoonist, however, one newspaper editor said, "That's not a definition of libel; that's a job description. That's what they're supposed to do."[4]

This article argues that political cartoons, as political speech, should be accorded the highest level of First Amendment protection and outlines a legal framework for the protection of political cartoons in this country. Prominent First Amendment decisions by the Supreme Court, such as *New York Times v. Sullivan* and *Hustler v. Falwell,* are reviewed, then the evolution of lawsuits against cartoonists is described, and the reliance of lower courts on Supreme Court decisions is discussed. The standard expressed here allows cartoonists to contribute to the dialogue of ideas free of the threat of a lawsuit. It does not, however, apply to drawings about private figures not involved in matters of public concern.

In 1964, the U.S. Supreme Court constitutionalized the libel standard. In *New York Times v. Sullivan,* the Court held that a public official could not recover damages in a libel action brought against a critic of his official conduct unless it could be proved, by clear and convincing evidence, "that the statement was made with 'actual malice'—that is, with knowledge that it was false or with reckless disregard of whether it was false or not." The Court said it thought this standard would avoid self-censorship by the press.[5] Writing the opinion in *New York Times,* William Brennan said that our tradition of free press meant there should be a commitment to robust speech and that this might include caustic and free attacks on public officials.[6]

In *Gertz v. Robert Welch* in 1974, the Court defined public figures as either people of widespread fame or people who have injected themselves into the debate of a public issue for the purpose of affecting its outcome. Private people, on the other hand, have fewer opportunities to counter false statements and therefore needed greater protection from the law.[7] The Court also said opinion was protected expression: "Under the First Amendment there is no such thing as a false idea. However, pernicious an opinion may seem, we depend for its correction not on the conscious of judges and juries but on the competition of other ideas."[8]

In *Old Dominion Branch No. 496, National Association of Letter Carriers v. Austin,* which was decided the same day as *Gertz,* the Court said the use of the word "blackmail" was protected expression because "even the most careless reader must have perceived that the word was no more than rhetorical hyperbole."[9] The Court, in *Greenbelt Publishing Association v. Bresler,* had earlier recognized that rhetorical hyperbole, or that which is exaggerated beyond belief, is protected expression and must be considered within its context.[10]

While pure opinion is protected expression, the courts have not permitted the same freedom to "mixed" opinion. The *Restatement (Second) of Torts* defined pure opinion as that which is simply expressed and based on disclosed or assumed non-defamatory facts. Mixed opinion, on the other hand, is defined as those opinions apparently based on facts regarding the plaintiff or their conduct that have not been stated by the defendant or assumed to exist by the parties to the communication.[11]

The Supreme Court expanded First Amendment protection in *Philadelphia Newspapers, Inc. v. Hepps,* where it held that a plaintiff who is a private figure must prove the falsity of a defamatory statement in a matter of public concern.[12] To provide "breathing space" for true speech on matters of public concern, the Court said it was necessary to insulate even demonstrably false speech from liability.[13]

In *Milkovich v. Lorain Journal,* the Court rejected the dicta in *Gertz* that provided absolute protection to opinion. It suggested that editorials, columns, and other expressions of opinion should not be constitutionally protected if they are based on information that is either incorrect or incomplete. The Court emphasized that it would protect statements about public concern that cannot be proven false. While opinions with provably false assertions are not protected, that which is clearly satirical, hyperbolic, or rhetorical is.[14]

For purposes of a defense for cartoonists, the most important case is *Hustler v. Falwell. Hustler* magazine published a parody of a Campari advertisement where celebrities talk about the first time they drank Campari wine. In the magazine parody, Reverend Jerry Falwell said his "first time" involved not only Campari but also included his first sexual experience, which involved incest with his mother in an outhouse. Falwell sued *Hustler* publisher Larry Flynt and the magazine for invasion of privacy, libel, and the intentional infliction of emotional distress. The trial court granted summary judgment for Flynt on the issue of invasion of privacy. The jury, applying the *New York Times* standard, found that there was no libel because the parody "could not reasonably be understood as describing actual facts." However, the jury found that publication of the parody constituted intentional and reckless misconduct and awarded Falwell $200,000 in damages. The Fourth Circuit Court of Appeals upheld the verdict.[15]

The U.S. Supreme Court unanimously overruled the appeals court. The Court said the state's interest in protecting public figures from emotional distress was not sufficient to deny First Amendment protection that is intended to inflict emotional injury when that speech could not reasonably have been interpreted as stating actual facts about the public involved. The Court said Falwell could not collect damages because the ad parody could not be believed.[16] In *Hustler,* the Supreme Court took pains to emphasize that it was dealing with what it termed *political speech,* which is entitled to the highest degree of protection under the First Amendment. Moreover, the Court said it was deciding the issues on the facts of the case, which dealt with a *public figure* claiming injury from political speech, not a company, such as Campari, claiming the parody was a copyright infringement.[17]

In recent years, however, the Supreme Court has clarified the difference between what is copyrighted material and what is fair use of that copyright. For instance, the Court said that a rap group's graphic parody of the song "Oh, Pretty Woman" was a fair use of copyright and thus protected expression. In *Campbell v. Acuff-Rose Music, Inc.,* 2 Live Crew recorded "Pretty Woman" to satirize the original work. In *Campbell,* the Court held that 2 Live Crew's parody was fair use even though it was of a commercial nature. It said that 2 Live Crew took the heart of the original song and created a distinctive new song that was not excessive in light of the song's parodic purpose. If a work targets another for humorous or ironic effect, it is by definition a new work.[18] Well-known products are highly attractive subjects for parodists, who engage in social or humorous commentary, often using common trademarks as the object of their work. For a parody of a trademark to be effective requires it be a well-known trademark.[19] The doctrine of fair use gives protection to the parodist. While "noncommercial" parody receives full First Amendment protection, "commercial" parody does not. If a commercial parody targets a work for creating an effect that is humorous or ironic, the parody is considered an entirely new work and thus receives full protection. Finally, parodies that involve political commentary or matters of public concern also are afforded considerable protection. This applies directly to political cartoons.

In 1808, English chief justice Lord Ellenborough pronounced the doctrine of fair comment, which protected pure opinion and comment on public affairs.[20] Fair comment helped cartooning to thrive in the second half of the nineteenth century in magazines such as *Harper's Weekly* and comic weeklies such as *Puck* and *Judge.*[21] Their impact was so powerful that newspapers hired popular cartoonists during circulation wars.[22] Politicians tried to stifle the cartoonists with legislation.[23] Between 1895 and 1915, five states, New York, California, Pennsylvania, Indiana, and Alabama, considered anti-cartoon legislation. When New York City political boss Thomas Piatt presented an anti-cartoon bill in the Legislature, cartoonist Homer Davenport compared him with the ignominious "Boss" Tweed in the *New York Journal and Advertiser.* The bill was summarily killed.[24] Similar bills also were killed in Indiana and

Alabama. California and Pennsylvania passed laws restricting the expression of cartoons, but neither achieved their intent.[25]

In 1907, the U.S. Supreme Court ruled directly on a political cartoon for the only time in U.S. history. The Court in *Patterson v. Colorado* affirmed the contempt conviction of a newspaper editor for publishing editorials and a cartoon in his newspaper that impugned the reputations of judges on the Colorado State Supreme Court.[26] The cartoon was called "Lord High Executioner" and portrayed the chief justice beheading some public officials. Another cartoon, "The Great Judicial Slaughter-House and Mausoleum," implied that justices were controlled by political bosses.[27] The following year, President Theodore Roosevelt urged that the editors of the *Indianapolis News* be indicted for criminal libel for publishing editorials and cartoons that said that influential Americans profited from the building of the Panama Canal.[28] The charges were dismissed when a federal judge in Indiana refused to extradite the editors to Washington, DC.[29]

In 1911, a cartoon, "City Farm," which implied that a Massachusetts mayor was hostile toward the conditions of the poor, was found to be "plainly defamatory."[30] The cartoon showed emaciated inmates being brought a tray with a little bit of food and a teapot. The tray was labeled, "Poor Food," "Rancid Butter," and "Shadow Tea." It was accompanied by a statement that a mayor had closed a charity board and replaced it with another that was hostile to the needs of the poor. The drawing urged voters to vote against him in the next day's election in the name of "humanity." The Massachusetts Supreme Judicial Court said that the cartoon held the mayor "up to ridicule and contempt" and harmed his reputation.

During World War I, cartoons in the socialist magazine *The Masses* were considered seditious and prohibited from the mail under the Espionage Act.[31] Judge Learned Hand agreed with the magazine. In a decision that foreshadowed the development of greater civil liberties in this country, he said, "To (equate) agitation, legitimate as such, with direct incitement to violent resistance, is to disregard the intolerance of all methods of political agitation which in normal times is a safeguard of free government.[32] Judge Hand's decision, however, was overturned on appeal.[33]

Two cartoonists on *The Masses* were among those personally indicted under the Espionage Act but were ultimately freed after two hung juries. The offending cartoons included a drawing by Henry Glintenkamp of a skeleton measuring an Army recruit and one by Art Young called "Having Their Fling," which showed an editor, capitalist, politician, and minister in a war dance being led by the devil. Two German–American cartoonists, who criticized U.S. participation in the war, were arrested and charged as spies in early 1918.[34]

FIGURE 52. Art Young, "Having their Fling," *The Masses*, September 1917.

Cartoonists found little consistency in the courtroom during the next several decades. In 1921 the *Los Angeles Record* published a cartoon depicting the city's police chief holding a halo over his head with one hand and taking a bribe with the other. The California Supreme Court ruled that while the cartoon obviously accused the police chief of accepting bribes, it was still protected expression.[35]

When a meeting between Boston Mayor James Curley and *Boston Telegraph* publisher Frederick W. Enright in 1926 resulted in a fistfight, Enright published a cartoon showing Curley in prison garb behind bars with the caption, "Sober Up, Jim." Though Curley had once served a prison term for taking a civil service examination for a friend, Enright was prosecuted for criminal libel because it was proven that Curley and Enright had a fight prior to the publication of the cartoon, and thus the cartoon was published out of ill will.[36] In a 1936 case, *Doherty v. Kansas City Star,* the Kansas Supreme Court held that a cartoon that implied that the plaintiff charged exorbitant gas rates was capable of defamatory meaning.[37]

The Supreme Court began its process of creating a more unified and coherent libel law in 1964. Since *New York Times v. Sullivan,* the Court has provided a wide latitude of freedom when criticizing the conduct of public officials. In *Greenbelt Cooperative Publishing Association v. Bresler* and *National Association of Letter Carriers v. Austin,* the Court said rhetorical hyperbole, or an exaggerated statement for effect, was protected expression. Political cartoons are, by their nature, opinions, or rhetorical hyperbole, in other words, an artist's satiric interpretation of a news story.

The rhetorical hyperbole defense has regularly been applied to political cartoons. A California court first applied the rhetorical hyperbole protection to a political cartoon in *Yorty v. Chandler.* After Los Angeles Mayor Sam Yorty expressed an interest in the position of Secretary of Defense in President-elect Richard Nixon's cabinet, *Los Angeles Times* cartoonist Paul Conrad drew Yorty talking on the phone, saying, "I've got to go now. . . . I've been appointed Secretary of Defense and the Secret Service men are here!" while four orderlies prepared to slip a straightjacket on him. Yorty argued that the cartoon said he was suffering from insanity and should be placed in a straightjacket. The court, however, said that even the most careless reader would perceive the cartoon as "no more than rhetorical hyperbole."[38] In *Yorty,* the court said,

> A political cartoon which falsely depicts a public officials selling franchises for personal gain, or a judge taking a bribe, or an attorney altering a public record, or a police officer shooting a defenseless prisoner, will not be exempt from redress under the laws because the charge is depicted graphically in linear form rather than vertically in written statement. . . . On the other hand, a cartoon which depicts a fanciful, allegorical, anthromorphical, or zoomorphical sense will not be considered libelous because it depicts a public person as a flower, a block of wood, a fallen angel, or an animal.[39]

The *Yorty* court did, however, indicate that a cartoon could be libelous if it could reasonably be interpreted as an accusation of criminal activity.[40] This is, however, problematic: satire is not literal truth but rhetoric. If a cartoon is considered opinion by the trial court judge, the case will be dropped, but the question of whether or not an artist knew what he drew was false is a decision for a jury.[41]

"I've got to go now. . . . I've been appointed Secretary of Defense and the Secret Service men are here!"

FIGURE 53. "I've Got to Go Now," Paul Conrad, *Los Angeles Times*, November 19, 1968.

Other courts have since applied the rhetorical hyperbole defense in ruling that cartoons are protected expression. In *Keller v. Miami Herald*, for instance, a Florida court ruled that a cartoon was "pure opinion." The plaintiff sued the *Miami Herald* over a cartoon that exaggerated the conditions of a nursing home, which was closed by the state and its proprietors were investigated for criminal misconduct. The nursing home was identified in the cartoon with a condemnation notice. Also included were three men depicted as gangsters, each carrying a sack with a dollar sign on it, and one of the men was saying, "Don't worry, boss, we can always re open it as a haunted house for the kiddies." The court, in granting a summary judgment for the defendant, said that the facts surrounding the case "had been well-publicized so that the newspaper's readers were aware of the series of events upon which the cartoonist based his opinion."[42]

William Loeb, the publisher of the *Manchester Union Leader,* sued *The Boston Globe* over a cartoon called "The Thoughts of Chairman Loeb," which pictured the publisher, eyes askew with a cuckoo springing from his forehead. While the cartoon was obviously literally incorrect, the court decided it was "an opinion and not a diagnosis."[43] A Massachusetts court used the same rationale in *King v. Globe Newspaper Co.* It said a cartoon depicting the state's governor dressed in gangster attire while being handcuffed to a police officer, who was reading a list of the governor's controversial political appointments to a desk sergeant, could not reasonably be interpreted as saying the governor was criminal or unethical.[44]

Other political cartoons have been similarly protected. An Ohio county administrator sued the Dayton, Ohio, newspapers over a series of news stories, editorials, and cartoons that depicted her as a liar, skunk, rat, and witch, but the court found it protected expression, regardless of their viciousness.[45] In *Palm Beach Newspapers, Inc. v. Early,* a Florida appellate court called a cartoon mean-spirited but said it was rhetorical hyperbole and thus protected expression.[46] In *Russell v. McMillan,* a court ruled that a cartoon was "clearly a symbolic expression of the opinion espoused in the accompanying article and editorial."[47] *Restatement of Torts* said that if all a cartoon does "is to express a harsh judgment upon known or assumed facts, there is no more than an expression of opinion of the pure type."[48]

In granting summary judgment for a newspaper that published a cartoon critical of a ski resort, a Vermont court said the drawing expressed a harsh judgment upon known or assumed facts and was thus protected.[49] The cartoon satirized a ski resort that wanted to make snow using sewer waste. The state Supreme Court of Oklahoma said a cartoon was not libelous in *Miskovsky v. Oklahoma Publishing Co.* The *Oklahoma City Times* published a cartoon that inferred that a candidate for the U.S. Senate influenced another man to ask his opponent if he were a homosexual during a press conference. The court said that the newspaper did not know that the cartoon was false.[50]

While courts have said that cartoons that imply defamatory facts were not protected, they have been reluctant to punish cartoons that do just that. In *La Rocca v. New York News,* the court said that should there be a minor mistake of fact in an allegedly libelous cartoon, a court may still grant a summary judgment in favor of the cartoon. In *La Rocca,* two policemen sued a newspaper for libel, alleging that an article, editorial, and cartoon defamed

FIGURE 54. "Eau de Cover-up," Bob Englehart, *Dayton Journal-Herald,* 13 March 1979.

them. The police officers had arrested a teacher for assault and escorted him from the school. In a cartoon the next day, the officers, who were drawn wearing dunce caps, were shown handcuffing the teacher in the classroom. The arrest did not occur in the classroom, yet the court said the mistake was minor and unrelated to the gist of the alleged libel.[51]

But in *Buller v. Pulitzer Publishing Company,* a cartoon, which was based on an article, portrayed a psychic as lacking integrity. The Missouri Court of Appeals determined that the article and cartoon that injured the reputation of the psychic, a private figure, were libelous per se. The court said that if the psychic's business were a matter of public concern, there would be no libel.[52] There is an important distinction between *Buller* and other suits against cartoonists. It involved a private figure, not a public figure or public official, who was not involved in a matter of public concern.

Despite repeated assurances from the courts that cartoons are protected expression, lawsuits against cartoonists proliferated during the 1980s.[53] As lawsuits increased, so did the cost of defending them. Libel suits do not have to be effective in court to chill expression. Factors such as the high cost of both libel insurance and litigation can be a greater deterrent for cartoonists than a jury verdict.

While *Hustler v. Falwell* did not directly concern a political cartoon, but rather a magazine parody, the decision had ramifications for cartoonists. If "the emotional distress" claim had been accepted by the Supreme Court, it would have been "tantamount to the end of commentary in this country," one cartoonist said.[54] In an *amicus curiae* brief to the Supreme Court, the Association of American Editorial Cartoonists said that political satire was uniquely vulnerable to this tort "because satire's instrument is the direct, often crude and tasteless, ad hominem attack." The Court said that the *Hustler* caricature was at best a distant cousin to the political cartoon, that if it were possible to separate one from the other, public discourse would not suffer by penalizing Flynt, "but we doubt that there is any such standard." In rejecting the tort of intentional infliction of emotional distress, the Court said that a contrary decision would subject political cartoonists and satirists to damages without showing that their work falsely defamed their subject.[55] *Hustler* affirmed the freedom of cartoonists and must be credited, in some part, with ending the trend of lawsuits against cartoonists.[56]

Another issue that may eventually have to be addressed is the protection that cartoonists have when dealing with copyrights and registered trademarks. The fact pattern in *Campbell v. Acuff-Rose* differs from that of a political cartoon that may spoof the president's health care reform package by using a parody of a slogan used by an aspirin manufacturer. In *Campbell,* the Court dealt with a commercial parody, which has partial First Amendment protection in matters of copyright infringement, while noncommercial parody has full First Amendment protection in matters of copyright infringement. A political cartoon is noncommercial speech and should have First Amendment protection. It also has been argued that companies that promote their trademarks widely can be analogized to public figures in a defamation case. By the nature of their activities, the owners of such trademarks have injected themselves into the public eye and should not therefore complain if their efforts are so successful that a parody of their protect is well understood by the public.[57]

It is doubtful that any type of political cartooning about public officials, public figures, or genuine matters of public concern lacks constitutional protection under the First Amendment, given decisions by the U.S. Supreme Court over the last thirty years. This standard allows cartoonists to contribute to the dialogue of ideas free of nuisance lawsuits, which may be brought merely to intimidate the cartoonist and his or her newspaper from publishing further drawings and thus infringe on the value of dialogue regarding matters of social concern.

In *Hustler,* the Supreme Court took pains to emphasize that it was dealing with what is termed *political speech,* which is entitled to the highest degree of protection under the First Amendment.[58] Political cartoons, by their nature, deal with controversial issues on sensitive topics and involve public officials and public figures. They criticize the conduct of politicians and other public officials, and therefore are accorded broad protection under the *New York Times* standard, which requires "actual malice," or that a statement is intentionally false.[59]

But proving that cartoons contain factual statements that are false is a formidable task. A political cartoon—like any satire—misrepresents facts. All satire involves a departure from literal truth, a reliance on what might be called "satiric fiction."[60] Unlike a photograph, which is a literal representation of an actual event, a political cartoon exaggerates an actual event by using hyperbole. Cartoons appear in a setting that makes it obvious that they are intended to be humorous, fantastic, or allegorical, and that they should not be taken literally and thus cannot be considered libelous because they are rhetorical hyperbole, and this, according to the Supreme Court, is protected expression.[61]

ENDNOTES

1. Robert Spellman, "Pricking the Mighty: The Law and Editorial Cartooning," *Communications and the Law* 10 (December 1988): 44.
2. *Hustler Magazine v. Falwell*, 485 U.S. 51 (1986).
3. *Milkovich v. Lorain Journal*, 497 U.S. 19 (1992).
4. Chris Lamb, "With Malicious Intent," *Target: The Political Cartoon Quarterly* 17 (August 1985): 15.
5. *New York Times v. Sullivan*, 376 U.S. 279–80 (1964).
6. *New York Times v. Sullivan*, 376 U.S. at 270.
7. *Gertz v. Robert Welch*, 418 U.S. 346–50 (1974).
8. *Gertz v. Robert Welch*, 418 U.S. at 339–40.
9. *Old Dominion Branch No. 496, National Association of Letter Carriers v. Austin*, 418 U.S. 264 (1974).
10. *Greenbelt Publishing Association v. Bresler*, 398 U.S. 6 (1970).
11. *Restatement of the Law of Torts*, 2nd ed. (St. Paul, MN: St. Paul American Law Institute, 1977), 566.
12. *Hepps v. Philadelphia Newspapers, Inc.*, 475 U.S. 767 (1986).
13. *Hepps v. Philadelphia Newspapers, Inc.*, 475 U.S at 794.
14. *Milkovich v. Lorain Journal*, 497 U.S. at 1, 19.
15. *Hustler Magazine v. Falwell*, 485 U.S. at 46.
16. *Hustler Magazine v. Falwell*, 485 U.S. at 46.
17. David Welkowitz, "Trademark Parody After *Hustler Magazine v. Falwell*," *Communications and the Law* 11 (December 1989): 69.
18. *Campbell v. Acuff Rose Music, Inc.*, 127 L. Ed 2d 500, 524, 525 (1994).
19. Welkowitz, "Trademark Policy after Hustler," 72.
20. Spellman, "Pricking the Mighty," 46.
21. Spellman, "Pricking the Mighty," 46.
22. Stephen Hess and Milton Kaplan, *The Ungentlemanly Art* (New York: Macmillan and Co., 1968), 100.

23. Richard Samuel West, "Cartoonists and the Law," *Target: The Political Cartoon Quarterly* 17 (Autumn 1985): 17.

24. Hess and Kaplan, *The Ungentlemanly Act*, 25.

25. See Statutes of California, 1899, Chapter XXLX, and Laws of Pennsylvania, Session of 1903, 353.

26. *Patterson v. Colorado,* 205 U.S. 454 (1907).

27. *Patterson v. Colorado,* 205 U.S. at 463.

28. Spellman, "Pricking the Mighty," 48.

29. *United States v. Smith,* 173 Fed. 227 (D.Ind. 1909).

30. *Brown v. Harrington,* 208 Mass. 600, 95 N. E. (1911).

31. Title XII of the Espionage Art forbade mailing any matter violating the Act or advocating treason, insurrection, or forcible resistance to any law of the United States. See The Espionage Act, Stat. 217 (1917).

32. *Masses Publishing Company v. Patten,* 244 Fed. 535 (S. D. N. Y. 1917).

33. *Masses Publishing Company v. Patten,* 246 Fed. 26 (S. D. N. Y. 1917).

34. "Two Cartoonists Jailed as Spies," *Cartoons Magazine* (February 1918): 288.

35. *Snively v. Record,* 185 Cal. 565 (1921).

36. Robert Phelps, *Libel: Rights, Risks, and Responsibilities* (New York: Macmillan, 1966), 108.

37. *Doherty v. Kansas City Star,* 144 Kan. 206, 59 P2d 30 (1936).

38. *Yorty v. Chandler,* 13 Cal. App. 3d 467 (1970).

39. *Yorty v. Chandler,* 13 Cal. App. 3d at 472.

40. *Yorty v. Chandler,* 13 Cal. App. 3d at 472.

41. Spellman, "Pricking the Mighty," 53.

42. *Keller v. Miami Herald Publishing Co.,* 778 F2d 711 (11th Cir. 1985).

43. *Loeb v. Globe Newspaper Co.,* 489 Fed. 481 (D.Mass. 1980).

44. *King v. Globe Newspaper Co.,* 512 2d 241 (Mass. 1987).

45. *Ferguson v. Dayton Newspapers,* 7 Med. L. Rptr. 2506 (Ohio App. 1981).

46. *Palm Beach Newspapers, Inc., v. Early,* 334 So. 2d 50 (Fla. Dist. Ct. App. 1976).

47. *Russell v. McMillan,* 685 P2d 259 (Colo. Ct. App. 1984).

48. *Restatement,* 556.

49. *Killington Ltd. v. Times Argus,* 14 Med. L. Rptr., 1316.

50. *Miskovsky v. Tulsa Tribune Co.,* 678 P2d 242 (Okla. 1983).

51. *La Rocca v. New York News,* 383 A2d 451 (1978).

52. *Buller v. Pulitzer Publishing Co.,* 684 S. W. 2d 473 (1984).

53. Rosalyn Maser, an attorney who represents several cartoonists, recorded nineteen suits that advanced in state and federal courts in the years between 1981 and 1987. See George Garneau, "Libel Panel," *Editor and Publisher* (13 February 1988): 28.

54. Lamb, "With Malicious Intent," 15.

55. *Hustler Magazine v. Falwell,* 485 U.S. at 51–52.

56. As of January 1993, I could find no new lawsuits against cartoonists since *Hustler Magazine v. Falwell.*

57. Welkowitz, "Trademark Parody After Hustler," 72.

58. Welkowitz, "Trademark Parody After Hustler," 69.

59. *New York Times v. Sullivan,* 376 U.S. at 254.

60. David Rosenheim, *Swift and the Satirist's Art* (Chicago: University of Chicago Press, 1963), 12.

61. *Milkovich v. Lorain Journal,* 497 U.S. at 19.

Black is the Color of My Comic Book Character

An Examination of Ethnic Stereotypes

CHRISTIAN DAVENPORT

PART OF THE HISTORIC AGENDA for civil rights and Black power movements was a change in the portrayal of African Americans within the mass media. This agenda developed because representations of this minority group produced and distributed throughout the culture were frequently seen as offensive and unrepresentative. Another factor for change was the institution of the comics code in the 1950s that forbade "ridicule or attack on any religious or racial group." Over time, the acceptance of this standard became clearly manifest within comics.[1] The improved economic status of blacks was a third factor that necessitated greater sensitivity by companies concerned with the sale of their products to this group. By examining the image of black characters in comic books, we can gauge whether or not the effort to portray more accurately African Americans as a diverse group of individuals was successful. This particular issue is important not only because it provides a way to identify changes in ethnic stereotypes over time but also because it allows us to examine systematically one way of communicating attitudes and opinions about race.

Within comic books a precarious balance has always been maintained between fantasy and reality. At the same time, another component to the story provided something to which readers could relate. Often this occurs through familiar physical settings like a school or an office. Generally, however, this "grounding" is most often found within the characters themselves. A way of speaking, a look, a personality trait, an emotion is given to a character that allows readers to label, recognize, and identify them. As a consequence of this process, individuals from Brooklyn would speak with an accent and make gestures with their hands; intergalactic pirates would drink some alcohol-like substance and plunder unsuspecting vessels; bikers (from any planet or microverse) would wear tattoos and dark glasses; and black characters (whether they appeared on a street corner or on Mars) would be represented by characteristics that were/are usually associated with African Americans, such as threatening demeanor, high levels of athletic prowess, low intellectual capabilities, exotic and mysterious backgrounds, residence within an inner city, and menial employment or unemployment. This characterization was (and is) particularly harmful to blacks, for, even within a medium usually associated with fantasy and escape, they were not allowed to get away from American racism and ethnic stereotypes. As a result, the characterization is harmful for everyone else for the same reasons.

Over time there have been numerous studies of black stereotypes.[2] Many were conducted by asking university students from around the country to identify particular traits on a list that they felt represented blacks as well as other racial/ethnic groups. Although there are several limitations with this approach, such as nonrandom sample selection and forced categorization, this process does give an indication of how individuals perceive African Americans, since they are compelled to describe this group with regard to certain characteristics.

The characteristics selected by respondents in these studies have been generally negative, with the only variable being the extent of this negativity. Within a study conducted by Braly and Katz in 1933, black people were characterized as "superstitious," "lazy," "ignorant," "ostentatious," and "physically dirty."[3] Indeed, the only redeeming characteristics identified were those of being "musical," "happy-go-lucky," and "very religious," which are traits that can still be viewed as somewhat negative (especially if placed in context). In a 1971 study, several negative characteristics are still present with black individuals still categorized as "argumentative," "ostentatious," "emotional," "aggressive," "defiant," and "hostile." These characteristics are countered by several positive attributes, like "open," "intelligent," and "straightforward."[4] This significantly improves the stereotype by increasing the diversity of characteristics used to describe African Americans, but the overall impression is still negative. In other words, some factors about blacks are deemed positive, but most are still those that would be considered negative.

A similar investigation conducted in 1993 found the same pattern of characteristics to describe black people that were identified within the earlier studies.[5] Black individuals are still generally characterized as "argumentative," "emotional," "ostentatious," "aggressive," "boastful," "noisy," and "loud." Equally important is the fact that some of the more positive attributes no longer appear. No longer are blacks described as "intelligent," "critical," or "sensitive." Although they are described as "witty" and "friendly," these two phrases might be considered negative within the context of African American stereotypes. Thus, the image appears to be relatively static over time.

Reconfirming the results of this work, many of the same characteristics are found within different aspects of American media across the same time periods. Similar themes are found within film,[6] television,[7] and advertising.[8] Most relevant to this analysis are two studies of ethnicity that examine cartoon art: the first investigating ethnic images in all comics (books as well as strips) in the twentieth century and the second investigating cartoons in *The New Yorker* magazine from 1946 to 1987. The first study observed portrayals of black characters from 1900 to the 1980s, with two distinct periods identified.[9] In the earlier period (1900 to 1960), blacks tended to be represented as one-dimensional characters closely associated with the stereotypes identified above, often being portrayed as superstitious savages (in the *Phantom, Tarzan,* and *Little Nemo in Slumberland*) or dim-witted servants (in *Abie the Agent* and *Bringing Up Father*). Within the latter time period (1960 to the 1980s), black characters were found in numerous roles with varied levels of significance to the storyline and a corresponding alteration in the representation of African Americans.

The second examination of black stereotypes was undertaken by Thibodeau, who conducted a content analysis of each cartoon published by *The New Yorker* from 1946 to 1987. This study complements the findings of the previous one rather well.[10] Throughout the pre-1960 time period, black characters are portrayed as mentally inferior, and their image is directly race-related with the portrayals intended to represent African Americans as a group. From 1960 to 1987, black characters were found to be passive, cast in roles where they do not speak or where they were of secondary importance to the strip, and their image is "token" in nature, where the character appears in a crowd, group or some other integrated setting. While not obviously characterizing black people negatively, this representation does treat them as marginal in importance, reinforcing the conception that black individuals are second-class citizens while simultaneously obscuring the exact standing of that citizenship.

To investigate stereotypes of African American characters in comic books, a content analysis of forty-two black superhero comic book series was conducted.[11] (See the Appendix for a complete list of the works studied.) Sixty-five issues were randomly selected to investigate three factors: the general characteristics of the superheroes, their relationships with other characters, and their use of superpowers. As general characteristics, all of the black characters' superpowers (flight, strength, impenetrability, telekinesis, etc.) were itemized. Based upon existing stereotypes of African Americans being physically and athletically endowed, the characters might be expected to possess superpowers involving brute strength and/or athleticism. The underlying premise here is that these powers are not distributed randomly but are given to superheroes to correspond with racial stereotypes of black people. Since superheroes often lead double lives (their superhero life and their "normal" life where they perform everyday roles), it might be expected that the lives of the characters would be somewhat similar to those generally believed to be held by African Americans. This stereotype might include unemployment, reflecting the widely held belief that most black people are unemployed and/or on welfare.

Interaction between black superheroes and other characters within the comic books was examined next. As many of the stereotypes identified in previous studies portray African Americans as being "aggressive" or "hostile," these character traits might be expected within comic book panels. To explore this possibility, the threatening nature of actions depicted by the superheroes was observed. The use of black English was also examined in order to gauge the degree to which the character is portrayed as being unable to speak so-called standard English, thus maintaining the stereotype of the poorly educated or ignorant black individual.

The third issue addressed concerned the application of the characters' superpowers: the relative balance between uses of brute force, athleticism, and intelligence; the problems they confront (i.e., racism, crime and drugs, world domination, violence); and the target of the threat identified within a particular storyline, such as the character's neighborhood, country, region, world, or universe. The expectation was that black superheroes would use brute force and athleticism over intellect; that they would confront crime and violence on earth more than intergalactic conflict or some other form of threat; and that they would generally be concerned with their own neighborhoods over the city, planet, or universe. This expectation was based on the perception that African Americans are overly physical, involved with specific forms of drug-related or violent criminal behavior, and are usually involved in things that do not effect (or have limited implications for) the greater society.

The most notable feature of this analysis was the relatively small number of black superheroes that have appeared in comic books since 1970.[12] From the first appearance of Luke Cage in 1972 as the first black superhero to be the primary character in a comic book, only forty-two black superheroes have been

FIGURE 55. From *Strange Tales* #171 (Marvel, 1973). Len Wein, script; Gene Colan, pencils.

featured, thirty-two of which appeared in the last years surveyed. The identification of African American superheroes is not completely straightforward because many wear costumes, which makes it difficult to determine their race. In addition, thirteen appeared briefly and then disappeared when the comic book featuring them was discontinued. Three appeared with teammates for the better part of their careers. Three others took over roles initially created for white characters. Twelve appear only in the context of a large team where they are featured as members.[13] Two initially start in superteams before going out on their own.

There appear to be three distinct periods of black superheroes. From 1973 to 1978, seven black superheroes existed (Black Goliath, Black Lightning, the Black Panther, Brother Voodoo, the Falcon, Luke Cage, and Storm). In the second period, from 1983 to 1987, there are several carryovers from the previous wave (Luke Cage teams up with Iron Fist, the Black Panther and the Falcon join the Avengers superteam, and Storm stays with the X-Men), plus several newcomers, like Cloak, Strike, Megaton, Jim Rhodes as Iron Man, and John Stewart as the Green Lantern.[14] The later surge of black characters is, however, by far the largest. Starting in 1991 and extending until this study ended in 1994, there were still several carryovers. More important, however, during this time period a significant number of black superheroes was introduced, including Bishop, Brotherman, Captain Marvel, Ebony Warrior, Flatbush Native, Hardware, Horus, Icon and Rocket, Meteor Man, Night Thrasher, Nightwatch, Numidian Force, Original Man, Purge, Shadowhawk, Sustah-Girl, Tribe, and Zwanna.

FIGURE 56. From *Hardware* #1 (Milestone, 1993). Dwayne McDuffie, script; Denys Cowan, pencils.

The powers held by African American superheroes are complex. Six characters surveyed use strength and two use agility in the performance of their "superdoings," and seven use armor. Most, however, display significant variety. For example, three employ the absorption of other's powers; two use creation; two use lasers; one uses the weather; one uses speed; one uses invisibility, and one can do anything that he wants. Black superheroes are capable of doing anything that their white counterparts are, a significant challenge to the expected stereotype of limited superpowers.

This situation changes, however, if publication date is factored in, since diversity in powers is revealed only within the latter two time periods. During the first wave of black superheroes, powers range from strength (Luke Cage, Black Goliath) to agility/athleticism (Black Panther) to weather control (Storm) to magic (Brother Voodoo); all clearly fall within the realm of black stereotypes, as the characters are portrayed as virile, naturally athletic, and mystical. During the second period, additional superpowers are identified, including armor (Iron Man), the power of darkness (Cloak), and the power to create anything (Green Lantern). The roles of black superheroes are altered, introducing more narrative possibilities. During the third period, powers expanded even further through lasers (Captain Marvel and Meteor Man), absorption (Bishop, Flatbush Native, and Rocket), a Thor-like hammer (Horus), speed (Franklyn of Tribe), invisibility (Murdock of Tribe), and absolutely anything the character wanted (Original Man).

In no other portrayal of American life have blacks done as well economically as they have in comic books. Thirty-one of the characters surveyed have jobs. In the earliest period surveyed are several somewhat stereotypical positions (the Falcon was a social worker, Black Lighting was a high school teacher, while Luke Cage and the Black Panther were private detectives [also leader of a country in the case of the latter which is far from stereotypical]), but the jobs depicted change dramatically in the latter two periods. Although two characters teach in high schools (Black Lightning and Sustah-Girl) and two teach at the college level (Captain Marvel and Nightwatch), three are lawyers (Brotherman, Icon, and Shadowhawk), one runs a bookstore (Ebony Warrior), and six characters have major corporate positions where they are the best in their respective fields (Black Goliath, Hardware, Jim Rhodes as Iron Man, Night Thrasher, Purge, and Steel).

The first few black superheroes appearing from 1973 to 1978 (Black Goliath, Black Lightning, Black Panther, Brother Voodoo, Luke Cage, and the Falcon) exhibited a strong tendency toward threatening imagery. Nearly three-fourths of the panels in these comics were identified as being threatening, and the depiction of black characters is consistent with existing stereotypes.

By contrast, between 1983 and 1987, the content of the panels changed considerably. Half of the panels during this period were identified as threatening, the storylines develop more fully, and the time spent in active combat decreases. This change allowed more time for reflection, conversations with other characters, and general character development, as exemplified by John Stewart as Green Lantern. The final time period is also interesting as 57 percent of the panels were identified as threatening. Black superheroes became more threatening than the previous time period, but less threatening than the earliest one. A wide range of behaviors was depicted from the stereotypical image of the blacks-as-savages perspective (in *Power Man* with Luke Cage, *Meteor Man, Nightwatch, Purge,* and selected issues of *Flatbush Native, Original Man, Night Thrasher, Tribe,* or *Zwanna*) to nonthreatening representations (in *Brotherman, Ebony Warrior, Horus, Icon,* John Stewart episodes in *Green Lantern,* and *Static*) to balanced representations where threatening and nonthreatening imagery is about even (*Hardware, Steel, Shadowhawk,* and *War Machine*).

Almost all of the comic books surveyed use black English to some extent, perhaps explicitly identifying the race of the character in the eyes of the audience. At the same time, the stereotype that blacks can only speak black English is not supported. At one extreme is Luke Cage and all of the other characters within *Power Man* who use black English almost exclusively. Many of the comic books examined (including *The Falcon, Hardware, Meteor Man, Shadowhawk, Static, Steel,* and *Zwanna*) mix black and standard/mainstream/white English. This practice tends to make and break the stereotype. On the one hand, it shows that black people retain certain stereotypical behavior patterns, and, on the other hand, it reveals that blacks have a complex language structure combining certain aspects of African dialects as well as American English.

It is interesting to note that most nonsuperhero black characters within the comics sampled used black English, while the superheroes themselves spoke standard English (Black Goliath, Brotherman, Captain Marvel, Icon, Night Thrasher, Nightwatch, and Storm). While depicting diversity within the black community, this finding twists the stereotype issue. The stereotype predicts that most black people would speak in the vernacular, and this is validated because more black characters in the comic books studied continue to use it. At the same time, since the superhero speaks standard English and this is established as the desirable trait, the reader is left with the message that standard English is the one to be emulated.

Only four black superheroes in this study make no use of black English at all (Bishop and Storm from the *X-Men,* Horus, and John Stewart as Green Lantern). In the case of Bishop and Storm, the explanation is straightforward:

Bishop is from the future, so he does not speak as black people do presently. Because Storm is from Africa, she does not speak the black American vernacular either. Since Horus was born in ancient Egypt (before black English existed), he does not use it. The explanation for John Stewart's not using black English as Green Lantern is somewhat complicated. This character emerged from the streets of an inner city and initially spoke like most of the black people in residence there. When the character goes into outer space for an assignment on another planet, he is empowered with certain capabilities. He develops an extensive vocabulary and alters his speech pattern. This may be due to his lack of association with African Americans in space; or, alternatively, it may be that the writers of this comic book are suggesting that a black person who is empowered does not speak black English.

More than either athleticism or intelligence, black superheroes are likely to use a significant amount of force in the performance of their "superduties." Once more, however, it is important to note the differences that exist over time. In the first time period, there are on average more than seven acts of brute force per comic book while fewer than two acts of athleticism or intelligence are shown. *Black Lightning* is the most brutal series of the period with fourteen acts of brute force issue. The second most brutal comic is *Power Man* (*Luke Cage: Hero for Hire*), with twelve acts of brute force. On the low end of the spectrum is the *Black Panther* with three acts of brutality. Overall, in the early days of black superheroes, the image of the brutal savage was well represented.

By the second period a more balanced use of superpowers emerges with the average number of brute force acts dropping slightly to about five per comic book, the average number for acts of athleticism increasing to around two, and the average number of acts of intelligence increasing to more than three per comic book. These averages veil other significant factors, however. For example, if one eliminated the particularly brutal *Power Man and Iron Fist* issue #123 of 1986 (which included nineteen acts of brute force), the overall average would be markedly lower than the previous time period. Acts of athleticism would be notably lower if *Falcon* #2, where there are numerous instances of aero-acrobatics, were eliminated. The highest use of intelligence exhibited by a black character was by Jim Rhodes in *Iron Man* #171, with seven acts where the character displays a deliberative and reflective approach to the superhero business.

From 1989 to 1994 extreme uses of brute force are observed in *Power Man, War Machine, Tribe,* and *Zwanna,* each with nine acts per comic book. Other black superheroes in titles such as *Brotherman*; *Green Lantern: Mosaic*; *Hardware*; *Icon*; *Shadowhawk*; and *Static* are relatively nonviolent. Characters like John Stewart (in *Green Lantern: Mosaic*) and Static use significant amounts of intelligence, each with more than eight acts apiece in certain issues. *Brotherman, Cage, Hardware, Icon,* and *Night Thrasher* use little intelligence, with a single act apiece for specific issues. *Shadowhawk* and *Tribe* display no intelligence whatsoever, as defined in this study. As a consequence, once again the existence of the stereotype is significantly challenged.

Earlier it was suggested that black superheroes would concern themselves exclusively with threats having relatively narrow consequences and that African American superheroes would concern themselves with threats targeted against themselves, their family, friends, and neighborhoods. The findings of this study support the first part of the stereotype, but the second tends to change over time. The data indicate that forty-eight out of the sixty-five problems confronted by the characters encompass the categories identified above. Consequently, black superheroes usually have a relatively narrow focus with regard to the problems they address. Rarely is it the case (like it is with Superman, for example) that the citizens of the universe will owe their safety to the acts of an African American hero. It is more likely that a neighborhood would owe its well-being to the black character, thus reinforcing the view that black individuals are somewhat inconsequential to anyone but themselves. In the seventeen exceptions to this trend are wide variations. Eight involve kidnaping/hostage crises; six concern moral dilemmas; one involves getting home from another planet; one involves keeping a diverse group of beings together on another planet; and one concerns an international arms dealer.

With regard to the target of these threats, the situation changes dramatically. In the beginning, African American superheroes were generally the primary targets, along with their family, friends, and neighborhoods. As time progressed, however, the targets became more varied. In the second period identified, the targets move from a more personal and neighborhood focus to address those on a citywide level (e.g., *Power Man and Iron Fist* #53 and #123, *Falcon* #4, *Iron Man* #171, and *Green Lantern* #183). Black characters take part in saving a planet with John Stewart in *Green Lantern* issues #197 and #14 and in *Green Lantern: Mosaic* #1. In the more recent comic books examined, the largest array of targets emerged. Not only is the number more diverse, but individual characters also vary their focus from issue to issue. For example, in some comic titles the characters will protect themselves or their friends in one issue (such as *Shadowhawk* #9, *Icon* #14, *Static* #1, *Steel* #1, and *War Machine* #1) only to turn in another issue to protecting the city or the globe (*Shadowhawk* #1, *Icon* #1, *Static* #7, *Steel* #4, and *War Machine* #3). The most recent African American superheroes studied confront more problems in more areas, again seriously challenging the stereotype of the narrowly focused black individual.

When black superheroes first emerged, readers were easily able to cat-
egorize them by referring to a few commonly held stereotypes. These characters relied on strength and natural athletic ability rather than intelligence,
and they tended to fight violent crime in their own neighborhoods. They protected only themselves or their families and friends from wrongdoing. They
held low-status jobs commonly believed to be occupied by African Americans.
Ordinary, black characters within the same comic books tended to use black
English. Over time, black superheroes have become more complex with a
greater variety of superpowers; better employment; more articulate characters;
a greater balance between acts of brute force, athleticism, and intelligence;
and an increased concern for threats to individuals not directed toward the
character's family, small circle of friends, or neighborhood. It appears that a
more representative view of the black community as a whole has been captured within this medium of popular culture.

It is no surprise that African American superheroes began to emerge
during the early 1970s, since in the 1950s and 1960s black people received
important recognition through the passage and common acceptance of
civil rights legislation, and many became more active in numerous aspects
of American political, cultural, and economic life through the Black Power
movement. Perhaps inspired by images of the Black Power movement and
by the successful lobbying of the civil rights organizations, the comic book
industry created several black superheroes. Although these characters were
not uniformly positive, some representation was obtained.

From 1983 to 1987, representation significantly improved, capturing
examples of the diversity within the African American community. During
the more recent period examined, several independent companies released
numerous comic books with African American superheroes that sold well.
The market had been identified. As a result of the awareness of black consumers, the larger comic book companies published similar titles, the number
and diversity of black superheroes increased dramatically, and the representation of the characters improved. During this time, more intellectual acts are
shown and there is greater variety in superpowers, types of threats, targets of
threats, and jobs held by the superhero themselves. Although there was also
an increase in the number of threatening panels, athletic acts, and brute force,
the general trend could still be viewed as rather positive.

As of late 1994 to the early 2000s (the point at which my observation of the
relevant phenomenon stopped), the situation for improving black representations within comics has come to a somewhat depressing stage. Of the comic
books in the last period studied, the *Black Panther, Power Man, Captain Marvel, Ebony Warrior, Flatbush Native, Green Lantern: Mosaic* with John Stewart,

Horus, Meteor Man, Numidian Force, Original Man, Purge, Sustah-Girl, Tribe, and *Zwanna* are gone. Most of the independent black companies that initiated black characters had either been bought out, lost valuable personnel, or gone bankrupt.[15] From these developments, one can only conclude that the commitment of comic book publishers to diversity was and is of secondary importance to economic concerns. While several African American characters still remain in current comic books, the diversity observable just a year or so ago is gone, and old characterizations are returning. Ironically, the future of black superheroes and diverse representations may be determined not by their color but by the content of their character, the quality of the drawing style, the development of the storyline, and the popularity the superhero has with a wider audience.

APPENDIX: COMICS SURVEYED (TITLE, ISSUE, YEAR OF PUBLICATION, PUBLISHER)

Black Goliath #2 (1976), #5 (1976), Marvel.
Black Lightning #2 (1977), #6 (1978), DC.
Black Panther #21 (1976), #24 (1976), Marvel.
Brotherman #1 (1991), #5 (1992), Big City.
Brother Voodoo #170 (1973), #171 (1973), Marvel.
Cage #1 (1992), #14 (1993), Marvel.
Captain America and the Falcon #177 (1974), #191 (1975), Marvel.
Captain Marvel #1 (1994), Marvel.
Cloak and Dagger #3 (1989), #14 (1990), Marvel.
Ebony Warrior #1 (1993), ANIA.
Flatbush Native #2 (1993), #3 (1993), Flatline Comicbook Company.
Green Lantern #183 (1984), #197 (1985), #14, 3rd series (1991), DC.
Green Lantern: Mosaic #1 (1992), DC.
Hardware #1 (1993), #11 (1993), Milestone.
Hero for Hire #9 (1973), #16 (1973), Marvel.
Horus #1 (1991), ACME.
Icon #1 (1993), #14 (1994), Milestone.
Iron Man #171 (1983), #190 (1985), Marvel.
Meteor Man #2 (1993), #5 (1993), Marvel.
Night Thrasher #5 (1993), #12 (1994), Marvel.
Nightwatch #1 (1994), #3 (1994), Marvel.
Original Man #0 (1992), #1 (1992), Omega 7.
Power Man #21 (1974), #34 (1976), Marvel.

Power Man and Iron Fist #53 (1978), #123 (1986), Marvel.

Purge #0 (1993), #1 (1993), ANIA.

Shadowhawk #1 (1993), #9 (1993), Image.

Static #1 (1993), #7 (1993), Milestone.

Steel #1 (1994), #4 (1994), DC.

Strike #4 (1987), #5 (1987), Eclipse.

Sustah-Girl #1 (1993), Onli Studios.

The Falcon #2 (1984), #4 (1984), Marvel.

Tribe #1 (1993), Image Comics, #3 (1994), Axis.

War Machine #1 (1994), #3 (1994), Marvel.

X-Men #198 (1985), #220 (1987), Marvel.

Zwanna #1(1993), ANIA.

ENDNOTES

1. Charles Hardy and Gail Stern, *Ethnic Images in the Comics* (Philadelphia: Balch Institute for Ethnic Studies, 1986), 13.

2. To stereotype is not simply to classify some individual by certain traits attributed to a larger group, as is most often suggested. As defined by Walter Lippman, *Public Opinion* (New York: MacMillan, 1965), 63–64:

> A pattern of stereotypes is not neutral. It is not merely a way of substituting order for the great blooming, buzzing confusion of reality. It is not merely a short cut. It is all of these things and something more. It is the guarantee of our self-respect; it is the projection upon the world of our own sense of our own value, our own position and our own rights. The stereotypes are, there fore, highly charged with the feelings that are attached to them. They are the fortress of our tradition, and behind its defenses we can continue to feel ourselves safe in the position we occupy.

3. Kenneth Braly and David Katz, "Stereotypes of 100 College Students," *Journal of Abnormal and Social Psychology* 28 (1933): 120–49.

4. Dennis Ogawa, "Small-group Communication Stereotypes of Black Americans," *Journal of Black Studies* 1 (1971): 273–81.

5. Rebecca Leonard and Don Locke, "Communication Stereotypes: Is Interracial Communication Possible?" *Journal of Black Studies* (1993): 332–43.

6. See, for example, Lawrence Reddick "Educational Program for the Improvement of Race Relations in Films, Radio, Press and Libraries," *Journal of Negro Education* 13 (Summer 1944): 9–17; Allen Woll and Randall Miller, *Ethnic and Racial Images in American Film and Television Since 1948* (New York: Garland, 1988).

7. See, for example, Fred Macdonald, *Blacks and White TV: Afro-Americans in Television Since 1948* (Chicago: Nelson-Hall, 1983); Bishetta Merritt and Carolyn Stroman, "Black Family Imagery and Interactions on Television," *Journal of Black Studies* 23 (1993): 492–99.

8. See, for example, J. David Colfax and Susan Sternberg, "The Persuasion of Racial Stereotypes: Blacks in Mass Circulation Magazine Advertisements," *Public Opinion Quarterly* 36 (Spring 1972): 8–18; Robert Douglas, "Black Males and Television: New Images Versus Old Stereotypes," *The Western Journal of Black Studies* 11 (Summer 1987): 69–73; Jane Dates, *Split Image: African-Americans in the Mass Media* (Washington, DC: Howard University Press, 1990).

9. Hardy and Stern, *Ethnic Images in the Comics.*

10. Ruth Thibodeau, "From Racism to Tokenism: The Changing Face of Blacks in New Yorker Cartoons," *Public Opinion Quarterly* 53 (1989): 482–94.

11. An alternative would have been to identify black characters within white comics but given the relatively infrequent presence that black characters had there, this was not considered. The superhero genre is particularly important for two reasons: (1) the amount of money they make each year clearly establishes the popularity of this form of comic book and (2) given the exaggerated nature of superheroes (i.e., their physical form, abilities, and the situations that they are put within), the genre most clearly presents an opportunity for abusing stereotypical characterizations.

12. Comparatively, it is very difficult to identify how many white characters there are.

13. There are also black members in *Armorines, Harbinger, Stormwatch, Psi-Force,* the *Suicide Squad, New Mutants, New Teen Titans, Avengers, Batman and the Outsiders, Shadow Cabinet, Nightstalkers, Youngblood, Harlem Heroes,* and *Bloodstrike.* I have not included these, however, for the black characters are not featured often enough to provide sufficient information about them.

14. Most notable about the last two characters is the fact that they replace important white characters amid some controversy. Jim Rhodes steps into the iron armor because Tony Stark is an alcoholic and can no longer take the pressure. John Stewart becomes ring bearer after the Guardians decide that he is more worthy than Hal Jordan. In both cases, the white characters do not go away. In fact, one of the primary elements of these stories is the struggle between the white and black characters to determine who is in charge, in addition to the inner struggle of the black characters to deal with their inferiority complexes. Both of these battles are fought as they are trying to save people and defend truth, justice, and one another.

15. See *Comics Journal* 160 (June 1993) for a good discussion of this phenomenon. Interestingly, the trend mirrored the demographics of black television shows and films during the same time.

Heartbreak Soup

The Interdependence of Theme and Form

CHARLES HATFIELD

AUTHOR'S NOTE (2016)

Rereading this twenty-year-old article, which was written in the midst of—or, frankly, helped kick-start—my dissertation, has inspired a bemusing mix of pride toward my younger self and embarrassment over the things I neglected, shortchanged, misunderstood, or got plain wrong. The thesis argued here, which struck me with the force of revelation in the mid-1990s, now strikes me as a bit obvious, and the assumed distinction between "content" and "form" now seems naïve, though there's a moment of jujutsu in the second-to-last paragraph that seems to test the distinction (I'm proud of that). Of course, I'm flat-out wrong when I say that graphic technique "does not lend itself" to analysis; clearly I hadn't read enough yet, or my horizons were too narrowly literary. Also, the article's approach to the cinema/comics analogy strikes me as tentative or muddled, though the question continues to be important. Finally, the prose gives off such an anxious, starchy sense of trying to be serious: all that talk about "transcending" genre and so on. I am happy to see comics studies get past fretting over status that way.

So, I'm proud of this article, but also a bit abashed to see it going out into the world again. Overall, I see it as demonstrating, in spite of itself, the limitations of an unalloyed formalism. The argument leans toward issues of politics, self-representation, and the vexed cultural status of comics but doesn't pursue them. At the same time, the argument implies a yearning for a more comics-specific kind of formalism that actually talks about drawing, something I could only take up later, in my work on Jack Kirby. Formalism continues to be my obsession when it comes to comics, but I now see limitations in the way I practiced it here and can't help but see this article as trying to take off in several directions, in effect prophesying the mix of perspectives I've tried to work with since. Still, it's been bracing to be reminded again of just what Gilbert Hernandez achieved in the 1980s. Going through this piece once more has renewed my sense of awe at his early masterpieces. I still remember why I wanted to write about these works—and I'm still proud that I did.

This article began as a paper I presented at the Popular Culture Association conference in Las Vegas in March 1996. That was only the second paper on comics I had given at a national conference. It also marked my first experience with organizing conference events; thanks to co-panelists Wendy Goldberg, William Nericcio, and Joseph Witek, I had the pleasure of assembling what I believe was the first academic panel devoted to *Love & Rockets*. That was a memorable day, and a confidence booster. It led to working up this article for *INKS*. From there, the article became the seed of the Hernandez chapter in my dissertation (2000), which then became my first book, *Alternative Comics* (2005). In fact, what you see here became the oldest, earliest stuff in *Alternative Comics,* and by the time that book went to press I had revised, tweaked, and proofread certain passages for the better part of a decade—which is enough to drive anyone crazy!

I should point out that some of the sources cited here can now be found more easily in other places. For instance, Gilbert Hernandez's classic stories of the eighties can more readily be found in the series of *Love & Rockets* paperbacks launched by Fantagraphics in 2007, particularly in the volumes *Heartbreak Soup* and *Human Diastrophism* (both 2007). The 1989 edition of *Blood of Palomar* is now out of print and rare. Also, to find the indispensable *Comics Journal* interview of 1989, go to Marc Sobel and Kristy Valenti's *The Love and Rockets Companion* (2013).

To this day, having published in the original *INKS* gives me a shivery sort of pride, and I can't thank Lucy Caswell enough for guiding the work of this raw but enthusiastic young scholar into print. *INKS* set the bar; it was an elegant, smart, rigorous, diverse, and loving model for the infant field of comics studies to follow. How can we not be grateful for that? I'm looking back at this article and realizing that it changed my life.

BETWEEN ITS LAUNCH IN 1981 and its fissuring into separate projects in 1996, the comics anthology *Love & Rockets,* created by brothers Gilbert, Jaime, and (occasionally) Mario Hernandez, broke new ground for comic books in terms of both content and form.[1] Fusing underground and mainstream traditions, *Love & Rockets* at first built on such shopworn genres as science fiction, super-heroics, and romance. It quickly transcended these conventions, revitalizing the comic book not only with new themes and character types but also with new approaches to narrative technique. Indeed, the formal and thematic innovations of *Love & Rockets* are of a piece: *what* the series has to say and *how* it goes about saying it are necessarily, inextricably, bound together. In particular, Gilbert's story cycle *Heartbreak Soup* epitomizes this interpenetration of theme and form—and thus reveals the comic book's potential to evoke complex settings and confront challenging social issues.

From the outset, *Love & Rockets* tackled themes and characters hitherto unknown in U.S. comics. Jaime and Gilbert invoked the looks and attitudes of Southern California's punk rock scene, capturing its rough-and-tumble ethos with humor and passion while applying its do-it-yourself aesthetic to the comic itself.[2] At the same time, Los Bros Hernandez (as they became known) exploded the cultural horizons of U.S. comics by portraying Hispanic culture—their own culture—with candor and affection, thus bringing to comic books a new sense of intercultural exchange and volatility. Social and political life in California's barrios, and in the provincial villages of Latin America, became their abiding concerns and, indeed, the wellsprings of most of their work. In addition, Los Bros defied the long-standing masculine bias of comic books by focusing on complex, clearly individuated female characters. In mature form, these characters (evolved from the exotic, frankly clichéd femmes of the Brothers' unpublished juvenilia)[3] were neither glamorized nor caricatured and as such broke with the fetishism of both mainstream comics, with their feverish romanticism, and underground comix, with their corrosive satire. These refreshing thematic innovations—the punk milieu, the Brothers' willingness to explore their cultural roots, and their regard for women characters—inspired steadfast loyalty among the magazine's readership.[4]

At times this loyalty was sorely tested by the Brothers' innovative approach to narrative structure. *Love & Rockets* demanded much of its audience, as its storylines were often serialized over many issues, creating long, sometimes novel-length, narratives of unprecedented depth and scope. In fact, the stories grew in length and complexity throughout the 1980s, climaxing between 1990 and 1993 as *Love & Rockets* ran no fewer than three serialized graphic novels at once (a period Gilbert has described in hindsight as "crazy").[5] Such extended stories added new layers of meaning and complication to the Brothers' respective fictional cycles: Jaime's open-ended series *Locas*, based on the lives of several young women in "Hoppers 13" (a barrio implicitly modeled on the Brothers' own hometown of Oxnard, California), and Gilbert's epic *Heartbreak Soup*, based in the fictional Central American village of Palomar but including various locales in Latin America and California. These vast, densely populated cycles, built up over the fifty issues of *Love & Rockets*, represent the comics form at its most ambitious.

This ambition is a matter not simply of scale but of formal daring. For if *Love & Rockets* has extended the thematic range of comics, it has also, necessarily, pioneered new approaches to the comic book's most basic units of meaning: the panel and the page. Comics scholarship, newly armed with the formalist vocabulary of such critics as Robert C. Harvey, Scott McCloud and Will Eisner,[6] has just begun to pay attention to such formal developments, and the work of Los Bros suggests a new horizon, or new problem, for inquiry: the intrinsic relation between form and content. If both Gilbert and Jaime have used the tools of comics (e.g., style, composition, and panel-to-panel continuity) to pack as much meaning as possible into their work, it is because the thematic content of the work encourages, even demands, such formal sophistication. The thematic and formal riches of *Love & Rockets* are inseparable—particularly in *Heartbreak Soup*, which, in its emphasis on the town of Palomar as a distinct entity, demands much from both creator and reader.

Heartbreak Soup is about a place as well as the people who inhabit it. As such, it focuses on the development of the community as well as the individual, in contrast to the agonistic individualism that has traditionally dominated comic book fantasy. Whereas most comic books favor lone heroes who have been clearly set apart from society, Gilbert's stories acknowledge, even depend upon, the energy and variety of social life. More specifically, they emphasize the always-complex relationship between personal anxieties and desires and social constraints, opportunities, and frictions. For Gilbert, individual psychology and communal interaction go hand in hand: insofar as *Heartbreak Soup* is about desire and disappointment (as its title suggests), it argues that such feelings are gregarious. Indeed, individual depth and social breadth, held in balance, account for much of the work's appeal. No other series in contemporary American comics features a cast as large, or as complexly interrelated, and few focus so resolutely on the complications of life among family, friends, and community. The beauty of *Heartbreak Soup* (as of brother Jaime's *Locas*,

FIGURE 57. Deep focus evokes the variety of life in Palomar. *Love & Rockets* #20 (April 1987). Reproduced by permission of Gilbert Hernandez and Fantagraphics Books.

but to an even greater degree) lies not simply in its colorful individual characters, but also in the depth and unpredictability of their interaction.

Given this focus on social life, *Heartbreak Soup* demands a new approach to comics storytelling—and indeed, Gilbert synthesized such an approach from the raw materials of comic books, comic strips, folklore, and film. Spurred by, and in turn spurring, brother Jaime's efforts, Gilbert developed a distinctive repertoire of techniques, perfectly suited to the kind of stories he tells. The formal challenge *Heartbreak Soup* presents is daunting: how to focus on subtle, often unspoken, emotions and relationships without sacrificing the energy of social interaction or freighting the comics page with too much verbiage. Emotional clarity is essential, but brisk movement is a must, too. Gilbert's approach tackles this problem in three main ways: first, through his drawings of characters, which while often broadly stylized nonetheless capture subtle nuances of expression and body language; second, through compositions that place his characters in a dynamic social context; and third, through sudden panel-to-panel transitions that allow him to cover long distances (spatially and temporally) between subjects without losing coherence. None of these strategies, of course, can be said to originate with Gilbert Hernandez, but his combination of them is radical in degree and intensity, born out of the complex narrative problems he has to solve.

The first point, Hernandez's drawings of characters, boils down to a matter of both style (i.e., the degree of abstraction) and technique (i.e., the finesse of the rendering).[7] The latter, technique, does not lend itself easily to criticism, though it influences meaning as surely as handwriting influences our

FIGURE 58. A vis-à-vis shot gives equal emphasis to both parties. *Love & Rockets* #22 (August 1987). Reproduced by permission of Gilbert Hernandez and Fantagraphics Books.

sense of a written message. The former, style, offers more room for analysis. At the very least, we should observe that Hernandez's style, though superficially plain, is complex insofar as it reconciles naturalism with caricatural abstraction.[8] In fact, Hernandez employs a sliding scale of realism, drawing some characters, such as children or comical stock characters, broadly and wildly, but other characters, such as many of the prominent adults in Palomar, in a restrained, naturalistic way. Such inconsistency is native to the art of cartooning, but Hernandez goes further, at times drawing even his most realistic characters with cartoony abandon, especially when they are in the grip of strong feelings like fear or rage (a technique widely practiced among Japanese comics artists but less common in the U.S.).[9]

But it is the second and third points, Hernandez's compositions and panel-to-panel transitions, that most demand study. Composition, as Harvey reminds us, refers to the arrangement of pictorial elements within a single comic book image, or panel.[10] Inasmuch as such arrangement determines the relative importance of elements within the panel, composition can define the relationships between characters, props, and settings and thus cue our emotional involvement. Here, as Harvey argues, the critical argot of cinema may prove useful, for despite the inescapable and profound differences between comics and film, the logic of the filmic "shot" can often be used to describe precisely the placement of elements within the panel.[11] Though film theory is not an inevitable (nor indeed always a useful) tool for comics criticism, in the case of Hernandez it proves helpful, since he has acknowledged film as a major influence on his work—and indeed, his stories invoke the movie camera's capacity for intimacy, naturalism, and movement.[12] In *Heartbreak Soup*, the relationships among characters and between each character and Palomar itself must be established and upheld with absolute clarity; hence, Hernandez's compositions favor cinematic devices that position his characters in close relation both to the reader and to each other: extreme close-ups, close two-shots, foreground framing, and deep focus.[13]

Individual close-ups and two-shots enable Hernandez to capture his characters' most intense emotions, whether openly displayed or barely concealed behind carefully-composed facades. The individual close-up allows such recurrent devices as direct asides to the reader (used sparingly in the early tales and later abandoned) and blank, silent panels revealing lone characters in unguarded moments of reaction or contemplation—still moments that, in a strip whose principals are usually shown in brisk motion, serve as dramatic punctuation, offering revealing snapshots of individual characters.[14] Similarly, the two-shot captures intimate exchanges, whether fierce, gentle, humorous, or erotic. In particular, what I call the *vis-à-vis shot* (that is, a close-up of two characters in profile) stresses the mutuality of the exchange by giving equal emphasis to both parties.

Foreground framing reinforces this sense of intimacy and serves the added purpose of strengthening our sense of continuity during exchanges that extend over several panels. The effect resembles a cinematic shot/reverse shot exchange (i.e., a tête-à-tête in which shots alternate from one character's viewpoint to another's). In each panel, the "framing" of one figure by another (or part of another) in the near foreground reminds us of the physical relationship between the figures and implies a larger space or world "outside" the panels. In such exchanges, Hernandez frequently uses silhouetting, filling the outline of the foreground character with black to simplify the composition and direct the reader's eye to the main figure. Like the close two-shot, foreground framing insists on the relationship, at once spatial and emotional, between the characters and lends visual variety to what could otherwise become repetitive, numbing sequences full of talking heads.

Hernandez's use of deep focus emphasizes the complexity of the larger social milieu of Palomar. Deep focus (here used in a metaphorical sense) refers to compositions in which elements in the near foreground and in the far background are equally clear, specific, and significant, so that the viewer can apprehend both at once without any loss of clarity or information. In deep focus, the spatial relationships between two or more pictorial elements are heightened, even insisted on, and interactions can take place across wide distances. The "space" between foreground and background characters can establish the complexity of a setting or underscore the emotions of an interchange (e.g., characters shouting angrily across a distance or keeping their distance from each other). *Heartbreak Soup* is in fact filled with panels in which elements on different planes are unobtrusively combined—sometimes to a specific narrative purpose, often simply to evoke the variety and unpredictability of Palomar as a place. Hernandez's deployment of deep focus creates not only a spatial but also a social background. If Palomar does come to life as a place, as a thoroughly imagined and imaginable world, it is partly because Hernandez's multi-plane compositions provide the perfect graphic setting for his emphasis, as writer, on the community itself.

Thus Hernandez's compositions respond to the thematic thrust of his stories. Yet the influence of his interest in community goes further, touching on that aspect of comics that Scott McCloud has highlighted as definitive: the manipulation of *closure* (i.e., our inference of logical connections, whether spatial, temporal, functional, or thematic, between disjointed parts—in this case, between successive images in a comic).[15] In comics, to achieve closure is to figure out the most logical link between one panel and the next; to manipulate closure is to influence that process of figuring out, whether through verbal cues, the graphic design of the page, or the content and composition of the images themselves (or some combination of these). Properly speaking, closure refers to the inferential work a reader does to turn a series of panels into a sequence, while Harvey's term *narrative breakdown* more aptly describes how a cartoonist divides a narrative sequence into panels in the first place.[16] *Closure* and *breakdown,* then, are complementary terms—closure describing the process of reading, breakdown describing the process of constructing. It is on the issue of panel-to-panel breakdown, thus defined, that Hernandez's narrative technique seems most radical.

Again, an analogy to cinema may prove helpful—but in this case it is the failure of the analogy that helps. As practiced by Hernandez, breakdown is roughly comparable to cinematic "cutting," or montage, but with the proviso that comics create meaning through static images laid out contiguously, in the form of a strip or page, unlike the successive frames of a film. The comics page gathers images into an overall graphic unit through which the reader may move at will, his or her pace of acquisition determined not by technological means but, as Will Eisner points out, by his or her own needs and interests.[17] *Heartbreak Soup* takes advantage of this, increasingly, as the series progresses. Though deeply influenced by cinema, Hernandez begins to exceed the limits of film with abrupt "cuts" between images that, in film, would jeopardize narrative momentum and coherence—but which make perfect sense in the printed medium of the comics page (where, as McCloud points out, "past" and "future" remain ever-visible, ever-present, elements).[18] The static nature of comics permits a self-paced reading, slow or fast according to the reader's desires, even recursive if need be, which allows Hernandez to make jump cuts between panels without sacrificing the continuity or prevailing naturalism of his narrative. This technique, what Joseph Witek has termed (after McCloud) *uncued closure,* responds to, and grows more and more audacious with, the growing complexity of Hernandez's story cycle.[19] Combined with the compositional techniques of close-up, two-shot, foreground framing, and deep focus, such abrupt, uncued breakdowns enable Hernandez to keep track of the overlapping relationships of his ever-expanding repertory company of characters.

Heartbreak Soup's emphasis on these relationships is evident from the very first. The inaugural story in the cycle, "Sopa de Gran Pena" (*Love & Rockets* 3–4, 1983), hinges on a tragic love triangle between Manuel, Soledad, and Pipo. It also introduces the mysterious *bañadora,* Luba, and, especially, highlights the friendship among "the guys," a group of adolescent boys composed of Vicente, Satch, Israel, Jesus, and the newcomer Heraclio. The adult lives of these men, covered in such later tales as "The Laughing Sun" and "Bullnecks and Bracelets," will account for much of *Heartbreak Soup*'s continuity, but in "Sopa" the relationships that bind the five together, and bind the reader to them, are only part of a larger network that includes not only the love triangle but many other relationships (e.g., Carmen and Pipo, Luba and Chelo) that will figure prominently in the cycle.

The complexity of such interlocking relationships becomes clear in the story "Ecce Homo" (*Love & Rockets* 10, 1984), which takes place at a town picnic or similar gathering and shows how secure Hernandez's grasp of Palomar really is. Here Borro, the ex-sheriff of Palomar, reappears, virtually reinvented since his early appearance in "Sopa," and Tonantzin Villaseñor, only briefly glimpsed before, is reintroduced and her promiscuity and desperate need for self-affirmation revealed. The relationship between Pipo and her abusive husband Gato, an ironic reversal of his unrequited longings in "Sopa," brings added tension and complexity. The coterie of male friends established in "Sopa" remains more or less intact, apart from the convict Jesus, but their

FIGURE 59. Social choreography in "Ecce Homo," *Love & Rockets* #10 (March 1985). Reproduced by permission of Gilbert Hernandez and Fantagraphics Books.

relationships have grown and changed, and in particular Heraclio's role has become more central. "Ecce Homo" is in fact a pageant of Palomar's citizenry, driven not by any particular plot or crisis but rather by the various relationships that Hernandez wants to establish, re-establish, or underline. As such, the story exploits Hernandez's arsenal of narrative techniques to the fullest.

Reading "Ecce Homo," one has the feeling of roving through a large party, encountering and later re-encountering various characters whose relationships are only beginning to come to light. Blending the disparate elements of *Heartbreak Soup*'s continuity into an organic whole, "Ecce" gives the town an aggregate identity of its own. The story allows us to stroll, as it were, through the scene, taking in relationships that connect the various characters to each other. Indeed, "Ecce" contains playful elements that suggest that Hernandez is not only taking roll but taking stock of all that has happened in *Love & Rockets* thus far. Besides the cast of *Heartbreak Soup*, various characters drawn by brothers Jaime and Mario make cameos. In fact, most of Jaime's major characters appear, as do a number of non-*Love & Rockets* "characters" (e.g., Frida Kahlo; R. Crumb; Hernandez and his wife, Carol; and several skeletons inspired by José Guadalupe Posada). Thus as we "stroll" through the Palomar scene, eavesdropping on its featured players, we also glimpse other visitors to this fictive world, fanciful visitors who remind us that we too are merely peeking into something larger and more complex. At once we are swept into the life of Palomar yet reminded of our visitor status.

"Ecce Homo" tells us much that we must know if we are to understand the relationships and issues at stake in later stories. Here for the first time, for instance, Luba's eldest daughter, Maricela, emerges as a distinct character, and we learn, albeit indirectly, of Luba's abuse. Here we witness Tonantzin falling prey to male flattery and in effect prostituting herself to shore up her uncertain sense of self-worth.[20] Here, too, we see Borro's crude advances on Luba, and his willingness to strike out violently when his desires are thwarted. Beneath the apparent frivolity of the cameos, and the drunken good humor of characters like Heraclio, there are undercurrents of tension, dark and disturbing aspects that will emerge most fully in later tales.

"Ecce Homo" represents a stretch for Hernandez the cartoonist, as it packs an entire town into sixteen pages. Here Hernandez's compositional and breakdown techniques are in constant practice, choreographing the interplay between at least two dozen established characters. Two-shots, foreground framing, silhouetting, shot/reverse shot exchanges and deep-focus compositions depict the complex social workings of Palomar, with its mingled friendships, loves, lusts, antagonisms, and misunderstandings. Throughout "Ecce Homo," Hernandez manages continuity of action, visual variety, and emotional nuance, while positioning foreground and background details to suggest an impinging social context.

If "Ecce Homo" romps through Hernandez's imaginary world, then the two-part story "Duck Feet" (*Love & Rockets* 17–18, 1986) captures this world in crisis. Struck by an epidemic brought on by the wrath of a disgruntled

FIGURE 60. Visitors to Palomar remind us of our own status as tourists and outsiders. "Ecce Homo," *Love & Rockets* #10 (March 1985). Reproduced by permission of Gilbert Hernandez and Fantagraphics Books.

bruja (witch), the Palomar of "Duck Feet" reveals a heretofore unknown potential for violence: Sheriff Chelo inadvertently kills the fugitive Roberto, and Tonantzin, acting as Chelo's deputy, is later assaulted by Roberto's gun-wielding cousin Geraldo. Meanwhile, Luba remains stuck in the bottom of a hole, despite her daughter Guadalupe's anxious efforts to free her. As the epidemic sweeps the town, many characters are physically transformed, their features grotesquely mottled, even distorted, by the symptoms of the disease. Several scenes take on a frankly nightmarish quality, as Guadalupe stumbles through the streets, retching and hallucinating. Here Hernandez's breakdowns seamlessly blend reality, memory, and vision, as when Guadalupe's fond memories of her mother give way to a frightening vision of Luba, which in turn gives way to the reality of Tonantzin shaking the bleary, vomiting child. Again, Hernandez's deployment of form echoes, in fact responds to, the dramatic demands of his narrative. As the scattered members of his cast all converge on the same moment of confrontation, his breakdowns grow more ambitious and the transitions more abrupt, juxtaposing subject to subject and action to action without warning. Narrow panels crowd together, creating a staccato rhythm that climaxes with discovery, violence, deliverance, and relief.

The final page of "Duck Feet," a quiet dénouement after a frantic tale, is in its way as radical a formal move as anything that has come before. A simple grid of nine wordless panels, each one showing a different subject, suggests the apparent calm that has settled over Palomar in the wake of the epidemic and tells us what has become of all of the featured characters in the story. Disconnected as the images are, they reveal what we need to know about each character and the town as a whole. In the first panel, for instance, we see the outside of Luba's house, where, we know, Luba and Guadalupe are convalescing while, in the second and third panels, we see the rest of her family at work. Panels four and seven show the sisters, Tonantzin and Diana, respectively: Tonantzin, who has been changed most by recent events, seems abstracted in thought, unconcerned with the masculine brawl going on (no doubt for her benefit) behind her; Diana, for her part, seems to be running for the sake of escaping from her own thoughts. In the penultimate panel we see Geraldo, confined to prison, his bandaged arm a reminder of the violence that has gone before. The last panel, showing the retreat of the mysterious *bruja*, ends the tale on a question mark. Here closure is a matter of divining a pattern from a series of apparent non sequiturs, silent and open to interpretation.

Thematically and formally, the novel-length *Human Diastrophism* (*Love & Rockets* 21–26, 1987–1988) trumps "Duck Feet" by placing the town in the grips of an even greater crisis.[21] *Human Diastrophism* echoes the first Palomar story, "Sopa de Gran Pena," in many ways, recalling or reworking some of its basic themes and motifs. Unlike the bucolic setting of "Sopa," the Palomar of *Diastrophism* seethes with anxiety, its fragile community jeopardized by violence, political terror, and disintegrating relationships. Here Hernandez creates his most complex network of interactions, pushing his techniques to the utmost to capture the way individual behavior affects the social dynamic. Indeed the crux of *Diastrophism* is the question of personal responsibility for the social good. Ironically, much of its dramatic tension stems from characters who remain unaware of, or unmoved by, the needs of the community as a whole.[22]

Broadly speaking, *Diastrophism* depicts traumatic changes that overtake Palomar and its citizens, alterations triggered by the intrusion of the outside world into the previously cloistered village. The most obvious public crisis in the novel is the search for a serial killer whose random attacks strike up a panic in Palomar's intimate population. As the search for the killer gathers momentum and the panic escalates, a horde of mischievous monkeys appears out of nowhere and sweeps the town like an epidemic, attacking people and

FIGURE 61. Transitions without signals, capturing Palomar in the wake of crisis. The final page of "Duck Feet," *Love & Rockets* #18 (September 1986). Reproduced by permission of Gilbert Hernandez and Fantagraphics Books.

FIGURES 62–64. Smooth transitions show the links between social relationships in Palomar. A crucial scene from *Human Diastrophism* (*Blood of Palomar*, 17–19). Reproduced by permission of Gilbert Hernandez and Fantagraphics Books.

IT WOULD MEAN THE END OF OUR INNOCENCE, SHERIFF CHELO...

THE ONLY INNOCENT PERSON IN THIS WORLD IS A SUCKLING BABE, ALCALDE.

IT WOULD HELP US OUT A LOT IN EMERGENCIES AND SUCH, CHUY. WHY YOU ACT LIKE THIS, HUH?? INSTANT EQUALITY WITH THE REST OF THE WORLD AT THE TWIRL OF A DIAL...

AN INSTANT END TO OUR PRIVACY, CHELO. I KNOW OF STRONGER CULTURES THAT WERE CRUSHED BY THE INVASION OF FASHION AND CONSUMERISM AND ROCK N' ROLL...

YOU'VE SAID YOURSELF THAT YOU WANT TO PRESERVE THE DIGNITY OF OUR PEOPLE THROUGH THE EDUCATION OF THE CHILDREN! FINE. WELL, I WANT TO KEEP OUR CULTURE AND HERITAGE INTACT.

THE OUTSIDE WORLD IS A STINKING DYING ELEPHANT AND TO BECOME DIRECTLY LINKED WITH IT WOULD MEAN OUR END AS WELL...

FEH...

YOU TALK AS IF COMMUNICATION ITSELF WERE EVIL. YOU AND I WON'T LOSE ANY CONTROL OVER WHAT COMES IN AND OUT OF HERE, I PROMISE YOU THAT. WELL...AT LEAST THINK ABOUT THAT PHONE, HUH ?

AWP. THERE SHE GOES, HUMBERTO. I HOPE YOU WERE THROUGH...

SEÑOR CALDERÓN! I--DIDN'T SEE YOU STANDING THERE...

WELL, I FIGURED YOU PROBABLY WOULDN'T HAVE LET ME WATCH IF YOU KNEW I WAS HERE. LET'S HAVE A LOOK, CHAGALL.

OH, BUT--BUT IT'S NOT VERY GOOD, UH...IT'S ONLY, UH, PRACTICE...I CAN'T DRAW PEOPLE LIKE REAL...UH, HEH...

NOW HOLD ON...HUMBERTO, I KNEW YOU DREW A LITTLE, BUT THIS IS SOMETHING! WHERE DID YOU LEARN ABOUT... WELL, REAL ART?

UH...WHEN I WAS LITTLE...I USED TO WATCH THESE PEOPLE COME TO, LIKE, DRAW AND PAINT THE OCEAN OR THE STATUE'S OUTSIDE TOWN, OR UH...WELL, I JUST LIKED WHAT THEY WERE DOING...

SO YOU DON'T KNOW ABOUT ARTISTS LIKE RIVERA, SIQUEIROS, UH, PICASSO, VAN GOGH, VAN GOGH MIGHT BE MY FAVORITE; MUNCH, TOULOUSE-LAUTREC, CHEEZ, THERE MUST BE DOZENS...VERMEER, MATISSE, REMBRANDT--

WELL, SHIT, YOU'RE IN FOR A TREAT, HUMBERTO! I'M GOING TO LEND YOU SOME PICTURE BOOKS OF MINE...

UH...NO, I DON'T THINK...ALL THOSE PEOPLE DRAW?

HEY HUMBERTO!

LET ME SEE YOUR PRETTY DRAWING, HUMBERCITO...

TSK NAW NAW--! IT'S JUST PRACTICE, IT'S NOT READY...! NO...!

AUGUSTIN...!

vandalizing houses. As omens of the encroachment of the modern world, the monkeys provide the population of Palomar with a cathartic outlet for, and welcome distraction from, its fears, hence the town's concerted effort to kill and cremate them. The resulting mayhem, at once risibly comic and brutally graphic, underscores the novel's prevailing tone of violence and hysteria.

Within this climate of terror, many of Palomar's individual citizens undergo diastrophic (literally, "earth-shaking") changes in their own lives. Most notably, Luba (by now familiar as a single mother of four and the proprietor of the local bathhouse) pursues her own fleeting youth in the person of Khamo, an old lover and the father of two of her children, who has returned to town unexpectedly as a worker in an archaeological dig (the same dig, incidentally, which has brought the killer to town). Luba's family, already strained by her neglect, begins to come apart at the seams as her affair with Khamo revives, then falters, shattering her self-confidence and driving her into a series of aimless sexual encounters. In particular, Luba's daughter Maricela, driven by her mother's violent abuse, plots to leave Palomar with Riri, with whom she has been pursuing a clandestine lesbian affair. Luba, oblivious to all but her own need for affirmation, remains aloof to Palomar's social crisis, unaware of the very complexities on which Hernandez's narrative technique insists.[23]

Meanwhile, Tonantzin worries her family and friends with prophetic talk of an impending holocaust. Set off by the paranoiac writings of the convict Geraldo (who assaulted her in "Duck Feet"), Tonantzin sees Palomar as a fragile pawn in a struggle between global superpowers, and her mind is filled with images of the apocalypse. Despite the well-meaning interference of friends and family, Tonantzin adopts the traditional garb of her Indian ancestors in a vain effort to make a "political statement." Inadvertently, she too provides the townspeople with much-needed distraction, a bitter irony given her lone commitment to meaningful social action.

In contrast to Tonantzin, Humberto (a character newly introduced in this novel) implicitly rejects direct social action, seeking instead to take part in the life of the town obliquely, through the medium of his art. An aspiring young artist, Humberto struggles to educate himself, and indeed redefine himself, by mastering the craft of drawing.[24] It is Humberto and Luba, both emotionally isolated characters, who serve as the focal points for Hernandez's exploration of social responsibility. Neither seems aware of the ripples of consequence spreading from his/her actions. As Luba, regardless of the town's disintegration, struggles to salvage her confidence after losing her hold on Khamo, so Humberto tries desperately to improve his art and to define its social place and value, heedless of the chaos erupting around him. As Luba puts herself and her family at risk through her random sexual liaisons, so Humberto puts himself and others at risk through his single-minded dedication to his art.

Through Humberto, Hernandez questions the power of art to intervene in social and political crises and probes the issue of the artist's social liability. As artist, Humberto becomes an unwitting accomplice to the murderer stalking the town. While eavesdropping with his drawing tablet in hand, he witnesses the killer Tomaso's attempted murder of the young woman Chancla. Rather than coming forward to testify as to what he has seen, he withdraws into a world of his own, compelled to replay the event over and over in his drawings. Humberto's art becomes his world. It is an ugly world indeed, as we see when Luba, stood up by Khamo, ducks into Humberto's house to escape from the drizzling rain. When Luba remarks that his art is "ugly as hell," Humberto replies curtly, "How else to you expect someone to draw hell." Goaded by Luba's intrusion, he declares, "I don't care about anyone—!," thus rejecting any form of human connection, any personal responsibility to the townspeople, the very subjects of his art.[25] By this point he has completely withdrawn from social contact.

His rejection of human contact has a dire effect on himself and the community. Though Humberto alone possesses the secret of the killer's identity, he cannot or at least does not divulge it, choosing instead to paper the town with drawings of the killer in hopes that his work will testify for him. When confronted with his drawings, he refuses to explicitly identify the culprit, claiming, "My work speaks for itself."[26] Obsessed with being a great artist, Humberto cannot intervene directly in the public crisis but tries to influence events through his drawings alone, guided by his belief that "great art reveals the deepest truths."[27] Unfortunately, his refusal to testify verbally allows Tomaso to go free—and to kill others. Thus, Humberto's art is inadequate to stem the chaos and social collapse taking place around him. Ultimately, Humberto becomes a pariah, cast out of Hernandez's carefully-constructed society for his refusal to act. Through Humberto, then, Hernandez attacks the artist's traditional presumptive role as a marginal or elevated social observer and questions the social efficacy of art itself.

If *Human Diastrophism*, ultimately, is a meditation on the power or impotence of art as a social instrument, it is also a supremely rigorous test of comics' ability to represent the complexities of social interaction—not to mention a bravura exercise of Hernandez's narrative skills. In fact, its very form insists on the social connectedness that Humberto tries to deny. Thus, as the novel progresses, its formal rhythms become more intense, its breakdowns bolder and more elaborate, in response to the town's mounting hysteria. In the novel's last third, having established the overlapping relationships among the characters, Hernandez shifts gears rapidly, jumping from one relationship or plotline to the next. Again, the community of Palomar becomes a character in its own right, a complex organism in which all sorts of reactions are taking place.

Early in the novel, Hernandez uses subtle, relatively easy transitions from panel to panel, subject to subject, in order to show the essential connectedness of all the goings-on in Palomar. Narrative economy is the byword here. For instance, in a twenty-panel sequence early in the novel (spanning pages 17 to 19), Hernandez reintroduces a number of significant characters, establishes several relationships and plotlines that will propel the novel, and underlines some of the essential themes that will give it its peculiar resonance. He does all this without once making a sudden shift from scene to scene. Instead, he follows several characters through the streets of Palomar, easing the reader from one encounter to the next by varying depth and perspective, and by repositioning key characters with respect to each other.

The sequence in question begins, significantly, with Tonantzin silhouetted in the top of a tree, watching a train go by in the distance (middle, page 17). Her sister Diana's pleas prompt Tonantzin to drop to the ground with this enigmatic warning: "We must try to maintain what's left of our dignity amidst the holocaust to come, Diana. Even if we wind up on our knees!" Thus, Palomar's relationship to the outside world is thrown into question and Tonantzin's paranoia decisively established.

After dismissing Diana to do her chores, Tonantzin passes by a building (page 18, panel one) in front of which stands Sheriff Chelo, who is debating with the mayor (seen through the window) the advantages and disadvantages of connecting Palomar to the outer world via telephone. Symbolically boxed inside the window frame, the mayor represents willful isolation: "The outside world is a stinking dying elephant and to become directly linked with it would mean our end as well. . . ." (panel three). As Chelo closes the conversation (panel four), deep focus reveals the tiny figures of Humberto and Heraclio in the distance—the former sitting and sketching the sheriff, the latter peeking over his shoulder. In the following panel, seen from behind Humberto, the artist realizes he is being watched and balks. Yet despite Humberto's protests, Heraclio praises his drawing, reassuring him that what he's doing is "real art." (Note the fluid shot/reverse shot exchanges and critical use of foreground framing in panels five through seven.) Then (panel eight) Heraclio begins to educate Humberto about great artists—a step that will of course have profound consequences for Palomar—as the two walk down the street. In the final panel on this page (panel nine), Augustin, Humberto's occasional companion and foil, interrupts Heraclio's pep talk by ridiculing Humberto's "pretty drawing." Humberto, not up to hearing his work criticized, bolts, provoking Augustin's scorn and Heraclio's dismay (top, page 19). Thus, Heraclio's protector/patron relationship vis-à-vis Humberto is clearly established, as is Humberto's sensitivity, talent, and ambition.

As Heraclio leaves Augustin behind (page 19, panel two), he comes upon Luba's daughter Guadalupe, who is being taunted by Boots and Concha, two girls who seem to be insinuating that Guadalupe's mother is a whore (thus the girl's tortured reply, "She is not, you stupid heads!!"). To spare Guadalupe further teasing, Heraclio steps in and scares the two offending girls away by claiming to be her father (ironically, he is indeed her father but does not know it). Then he rescues Guadalupe and carries her home, bringing an end to the sequence. Here we see the young girl's desperate need to defend her mother from criticism and a hidden but undeniable father/daughter bond that eventually comes out into the open.

The whole sequence is remarkably smooth, knit together by shot/reverse shot exchanges, shifts from foreground to background figures, varied distances (long, medium and close-up shots), and even spoken cues from off-panel characters. In the course of this relatively uneventful scene, Hernandez sets up crucial issues that underlie the novel: Palomar's isolation and vulnerability, highlighted by Tonantzin's fears; Humberto's artistic drive, encouraged by Heraclio's intellectual vanity; Luba's reputation, implied by Guadalupe's protectiveness; and, finally, the question of Guadalupe's paternity. The sequence is at once complicated and seemingly effortless.

In contrast, key sequences later in the novel shift from subject to subject with daring abruptness, reflecting the town's growing panic and the story's surging momentum. In particular, an extraordinary sequence two-thirds into the novel (pages 76 through 78 in *Blood of Palomar*) captures the growing frenzy of activity in the town and thus epitomizes Hernandez's control of rhythm and detail. Beginning with an aerial view of the town, labeled "ground zero," Hernandez moves the reader rapidly through a three-page, twenty-four panel sequence in which several plotlines come to fruition. As Khamo carries the wounded Chancla back to town, the population steps up its war with the invading monkeys, clubbing and killing, bagging and burning them en masse. At the same time, Luba's cousin Ofelia searches the crowd for Luba's daughter Doralis, lost among the monkeys (note the deployment of deep focus), and Maricela and Riri agree to leave town that evening. Meanwhile, Heraclio's wife Carmen and her friends try to break Tonantzin's hunger strike by forcing her to watch them eat, and Sheriff Chelo's deputies begin to round up suspects in the killings—summoning first Khamo, then Tomaso, then Humberto.

FIGURES 65–67. Abrupt transitions reflect the growing chaos in Palomar. A key sequence from *Human Diastrophism* (*Blood of Palomar*, 76–78). Reproduced by permission of Gilbert Hernandez and Fantagraphics Books.

While all of this is going on, the detective Borro achieves his long-held desire of having sex with Luba, and the panels of their energetic, almost feral, coupling punctuate the scene. As the sound of the monkeys' never-ending chittering, "chit chit," violates the borders between these panels, linking them formally and symbolically, Borro and Luba are equated quite clearly with the monkeys, especially Borro (compare page 76's close-up of his agitated face, eyes limned with raw, bestial passion). Indeed, the violence surrounding the monkeys serves to connect all of the different plotlines, bringing graphic and thematic continuity to the rapid-fire breakdowns. For example, on the second page, panel five, a happy-go-lucky monkey killer cavorts in the background, waving a bleeding, headless monkey corpse in an image as giddy and comical as it is insane. The image stands smack dab in the middle of the page, of course. Also, throughout the sequence, the monkeys' frantic chittering mingles with the noises of Palomar: the shouting of Chancla's sisters, Ofelia's calling for Doralis, Doralis's own monkey-like "chit"-ing, and, finally, the overwhelming chomping and gobbling of Carmen's friends as they try to break Tonantzin's fast. (Luba and Borro's sexual ferocity, though depicted wordlessly, likewise suggests noise and energy.)

The sequence closes with the monkeys as well. As the townspeople hurl bags of dead monkeys into a mass burning pit (bottom, page 78), the smoke of the cremation rises, leading to a final panel that breaks the frenetic rhythm of the scene: the image of a statue, still and inscrutable, smiling as smoke fills the sky. Here, at last, we can catch our breath, as the next scene restores a calmer, more even rhythm.

Such sequences are not simply grandstanding displays of technique. Rather, they arise from Hernandez's abiding interest in the complexity and simultaneity of communal life, whether in peace (as in the final page of "Duck Feet") or in crisis (as here). Conversely, his technique has evidently influenced his thematic interests. Over time the stories in the *Heartbreak Soup* cycle seem to have responded to new opportunities opened up by his increasing fluency in the comics form. As the above-discussed techniques enabled characters to interact on a vast scale without sacrificing the vivid singularity of each, they prompted ever larger and more complex narrative structures, culminating in the demanding multigenerational epic *Poison River* (*Love & Rockets* #29–40, 1989–1993) and subsequent stories, where nonchronological and nonlinear passages are common. These later stories, not coincidentally, have exceeded the limits of Palomar, giving Hernandez a much wider geographical stage on which to play out his increasingly baroque narrative gambits. The influence of content and form has been reciprocal.

FIGURE 68. Panels crowd together as plotlines converge. The climax of "Duck Feet," *Love & Rockets* #18 (September 1986). Reproduced by permission of Gilbert Hernandez and Fantagraphics Books.

Describing an arsenal of storytelling techniques like Gilbert Hernandez's is rigorous work, but it can help our understanding insofar as the descriptions allow us to see content and form in a generative, mutually informing relationship. Working out descriptions of form is but the first step in understanding comics; it remains to study the ways in which content is embedded in form and vice versa. The reciprocal influence of content and form will of course demand different things of different cartoonists and different stories, so what is true of Gilbert Hernandez may not be true of cartoonists generally. As a heuristic prompt, however, the idea of a fundamental link between what the cartoonist wants to represent (content) and how he chooses to represent it (form) sheds much light, not only on the craft of comics but on its very logic. In this connection *Love & Rockets* offers a staggering wealth of example as well as an uncommon cultural and political relevance that encourages, even demands, further study.

ENDNOTES

1. Mario's involvement with the series has been minimal since issue #3 (1983), but it was his initial prodding, and access to a print shop, that made *Love & Rockets* a reality. See Robert Fiore, Gary Groth, and Thom Powers, "Pleased to Meet Them . . . The Hernandez Bros. Interview," *The Comics Journal* 126 (January 1989): 72–74.

2. On the influence of punk music and punk culture, see Fiore, Groth, and Powers, "Pleased to Meet Them," 66–72.

3. This juvenilia has been publicly excerpted in Los Bros Hernandez, *Love & Rockets Sketchbook*, vol. 1 (Westlake Village, CA: Fantagraphics Books, 1989).

4. For evidence of the loyalty inspired by Los Bros' fresh outlook, see the letters from readers in early issues of *Love & Rockets* (1983–1986). For example, in issue #12 (July 1985) a self-styled "hard-core" punk applauds the book for portraying punks "as human beings with gen-yoo-wine personalities rather than the switchblade-wielding Nazi vermin we were in the mainstream publications." Similarly, a correspondent in #14 (November 1985) praises Jaime's depiction of the hardcore scene, which, he says, contributes to the book's "almost realistic" view of young people, in contrast to the aseptic "Hardy boys-type" of characterization found in most comic books. In #13 (September 1985), one reader lauds the multicultural cast of *Love & Rockets,* calling the book "the first real 'All-American' comic, in which the viewers find themselves totally immersed in the lives of different racial groups," while in #18 (September 1986) a woman from El Salvador writes, "I am extremely proud of the way you're representing our idiosyncrasy to the rest of the world. . . . You are vindicating our culture and introducing it better than any 'fine' artist. . . ." In #13, a female reader praises Los Bros' positive treatment of women, saying, "I absolutely love the strength of the females you've created. . . . It's about time some comic-book women were strong and human at the same time"; in #14, likewise, a woman writes, "At last, women who aren't portrayed as meek mouses who hold their men in God-like regard . . . or radical men-haters." Letters from people writing to a comic book "for the first time" and from readers who had all but sworn off comics until *Love & Rockets* pepper the early issues, as do accolades for Los Bros' portrayals of "real life" and "real people." In the commemorative booklet *Ten Years of Love & Rockets* (September 1992), Jaime gently pokes fun at the readers' strong responses to the book, with a strip in which his principal characters, Maggie and Hopey, mouth dialogue taken from fan letters (e.g., "I think I have a crush on Maggie" and "I never thought I'd ever fall in love with a comic book character"). Such responses clearly point to a large and faithful following.

5. Neil Gaiman, interview with Gilbert and Jaime Hernandez, *The Comics Journal* 178 (July 1993): 96.

6. Harvey's *The Art of the Funnies* (Jackson: University Press of Mississippi, 1994) and *The Art of the Comic Book* (Jackson: University Press of Mississippi, 1996) represent the leading edge of formalist criticism within academic publishing, although neither book aspires to be strictly academic in tone. Harvey's definitions of *breakdown, layout, composition,* and *verbal-visual blending* underlie both studies and are enormously helpful for formal analysis. McCloud's *Understanding Comics* (Northampton, MA: Tundra Publishing, 1993), a 200-page critical treatise in comics form, has become easily the most influential study by a contemporary comics practitioner, offering ambitious discussions of word-and-image combinations, stylistic variation, and, perhaps most importantly, panel-to-panel movement (i.e., closure). Behind *Understanding Comics* lies cartoonist Eisner's groundbreaking textbook, *Comics and Sequential Art* (Tamarac, FL: Poorhouse Press, 1985), the first book-length aesthetic study by an American practitioner. Eisner's recently-released *Graphic Storytelling* (Tamarac, FL: Poorhouse Press, 1996) carries on his critical project, offering cogent analyses of narrative technique.

7. The style/technique distinction here employed has been extrapolated from Eisner, *Comics and Sequential Art,* 151, 157.

8. Los Bros' distinctive styles, at once naturalistic and broadly comic, have been synthesized from a wide range of graphic influences—notably, the fabulism of Steve Ditko and Jack Kirby, the coy sex appeal of Dan DeCarlo and Harry Lucey on *Archie*, the gentle humor of Charles Schulz and Hank Ketcham, and the ironic, angst-filled cartooning of R. Crumb. Jaime has achieved a startling degree of realism in his drawings and is known as a master of stark, chiaroscuro technique. Gilbert has developed a wilder, more expressionistic approach strongly influenced by the comic distortions of such artists as Ditko, Crumb, and Harvey Kurtzman. See Fiore, Groth, and Powers, "Pleased to Meet Them," 98–105.

9. For an overview of Japanese manga styles, see Frederick L. Schodt, *Manga! Manga! The World of Japanese Comics* (Tokyo: Kodansha International, 1983); Frederick L. Schodt, *Dreamland Japan: Writings on Modern Manga* (Berkeley, CA: Stone Bridge Press, 1996); McCloud, *Understanding Comics*, 44, 210.

10. Harvey, *Art of the Funnies*, 17; Harvey, *Art of the Comic Book*, 9–10.

11. For discussions of the differences between comics and film, and illuminating critiques of the popular film/comics analogy, see both Harvey, *Art of the Comic Book*, 173–91 passim, and Eisner, *Graphic Storytelling*, 72–73. If comics creators can be classified according to the various other media they invoke in their work, perhaps we can broadly distinguish between "cinematic" storytellers (e.g., Los Bros) and those who persistently call attention to the comic as a *paper* artifact, à la books or newspapers (e.g., Art Spiegelman). Yet even among "cinematic" cartoonists the comparison to film has its limits; the analogy takes us only as far as the border of what is unique and interesting about the comics form.

12. William Anthony Nericcio, "Artif[r]acture: Virulent Pictures, Graphic Narrative and the Ideology of the Visual," *Mosaic* 28, no. 4 (December 1995) points out that Hernandez "captures and deftly comments upon the dynamics of cinema" (95). Nericcio shows that these cinematic touches inform a larger critique of U.S. cultural imperialism. Hernandez's movie references reveal an overarching interest in the impact of "image technologies" on the culture of Palomar and of Latin America in general (94–95). Thus, movies become part not only of the technique but also of the content of Hernandez's stories. Note, for instance, that Palomar's movie theater (run by the character Luba) displays posters for various bygone American and European films, posters that playfully suggest both the range of Hernandez's cinematic inspirations and the cultural relationship between Palomar and the "outside world." For more on *Heartbreak Soup*'s debt to film, see Fiore, Groth, and Powers, "Pleased to Meet Them," 87–88; Gary Groth, preface to *The Complete Love & Rockets*, vol. 2, *Chelo's Burden*, 2nd ed., by Los Bros Hernandez (Seattle: Fantagraphics Books, 1989).

13. For definitions of the film terms used in the following discussion, see, for example, Joseph M. Boggs, *The Art of Watching Films*, 4th ed. (Mountain View, CA: Mayfield Publishing, 1996); David Bordwell and Kristin Thompson, *Film Art: An Introduction*, 5th ed. (New York: McGraw-Hill, 1997); Ira Konisberg, *The Complete Film Dictionary* (New York: NAL-Dutton, 1989).

14. Harvey Pekar, writer of the comic book series *American Splendor*, has observed that silent panels are one of the strengths of comics storytelling in that they can act as "punctuation," and thus influence the timing and impact of a story. See, for example, Gary Groth, interview with Harvey Pekar, *The Comics Journal* 94 (April 1985): 47, 64.

15. McCloud, *Understanding Comics*, 60–93 passim.

16. Harvey, *Art of the Funnies*, 8, 15; Harvey, *Art of the Comic Book*, 9–10.

17. Eisner, *Graphic Storytelling*, 70.

18. McCloud, *Understanding Comics*, 104.

19. Joseph Witek, "Uncued Closure in *Love & Rockets*" (paper presented for the Comic Art and Comics section of the Popular Culture Association, Las Vegas, NV, March 28, 1996).

20. Named for a pre-Columbian Aztec earth goddess, the beautiful Tonantzin ("Revered Mother") bears the onus of a scandalous past—including, ironically, a series of abortions

resulting from her prodigal sexuality. As vendor of the local dietary staple, fried *babosas* (slugs), Tonantzin provides for her people much like her mythic namesake, yet, as established in such later stories as "An American in Palomar" (*Love & Rockets* #13–14, 1985) and "Duck Feet," her character has a tragic dimension. Ill educated and lacking both confidence and purpose, she is credulous, rash, and easily manipulated.

21. *Human Diastrophism* has since been collected and revised in Gilbert Hernandez, *The Complete Love & Rockets*, vol. 8, *Blood of Palomar* (Seattle: Fantagraphics Books, 1989). Citations throughout the rest of this paper refer to *Blood of Palomar*, since it offers the story in its most complete and accessible form.

22. The following six paragraphs have been distilled from "Art and Social Responsibility in Gilbert Hernandez's *Human Diastrophism*" (paper presented for the Comic Art and Comics section of the Popular Culture Association, Las Vegas, NV, March 28, 1996).

23. Over the course of the series, Luba has emerged as *Heartbreak Soup*'s most complexly developed female character and thus the central character in Hernandez's oeuvre. *Human Diastrophism* captures a crucial moment in her development from disreputable *bañadora* (bath-giver) to mayor; later stories, such as *Poison River* (1989–1993) and "Luba Conquers the World" (*Love & Rockets* 48, 1995) both fill in her harrowing life story and establish her authority as matriarch of Palomar.

24. Nericcio, "Artif[r]acture," 99–100, sees the novel as partly "a Bildungsroman of a struggling neophyte artist—Goethe's *Wilhelm Meisler* re-imagined pen in hand south of the border." Nericcio suggests, and I have argued elsewhere, that Humberto's existential crisis stems from not only the violence of his surroundings but also the anxiety of influence brought on by his sudden immersion in the works of his artistic forebears (Picasso, Klee, Cassatt, et al.). Swipes from many such artists occur throughout the novel.

25. Hernandez, *Blood of Palomar*, 55.

26. Hernandez, *Blood of Palomar*, 79.

27. Hernandez, *Blood of Palomar*, 83.

EMANATA

Percival Chubb and the League for the Improvement of the Children's Comic Supplement

AMY KISTE NYBERG

ALTHOUGH THE YELLOW KID and those who followed in his footsteps were very popular with newspaper readers, the introduction of the Sunday comic supplement was not universally welcomed. These early comics, populated by working-class characters, were crudely executed and relied heavily on vulgar humor, offending the literary and artistic sensibilities of the middle class. In addition, the disrespect for authority and the cruelty of the pranks depicted in the strips concerned parents and educators, who worried about the impact of such role models.

In her analysis of the development of newspaper comic strips, Elsa Nystrom notes that the opposition to comics from the "genteel critic," whose main objection was to the vulgarity and poor taste of the strip, posed little danger to the existence of the comic strip because the criticism was "intermittent, unorganized and found mainly in elitist publications." Progressive critics, however, feared the influence of the supplement on children and organized a highly focused protest against the funnies, hoping to force newspapers to eliminate, or at least improve, the Sunday supplement.[1] One of the most influential of these critics was Percival Chubb, a well-known New York educator and leader in the Ethical Culture Society, a humanistic religious movement founded in New York in 1876.

Chubb's reputation as an educator was established through his work with the Ethical Culture Society and its schools. He is thought to be one of the first advocates of incorporating drama, plays and festivals into the school curriculum. He wrote several articles, published in education journals including *Elementary School Teacher* and *Childhood Education*, that argued that children learn from dramatizing work in literature, history, and science and should be encouraged to produce their own dramatic festivals. He also wrote two books, *The Teaching of English in the Elementary and the Secondary School* and *Festivals and Plays in Schools and Elsewhere*.[2]

The Ethical Culture Society had strong ties to the progressive movement because of its emphasis on social action and community service, and many of its leaders were at the forefront of various reform movements as founders of the American Civil Liberties Union, the NAACP, and the Child Study Association of America. The society founded the District Nursing Department in 1877, which became the Visiting Nurses Association, a leader in the establishment of settlement houses.[3]

A major focus of the Ethical Culture Society was education. One of its first actions was to establish a free kindergarten for poor children in 1878. That was expanded into the Workingman's School in 1880. After reorganization in 1890, it began to admit paying students and changed its name to the Ethical Culture School. Today, the Ethical Culture School operates two facilities, one in the Bronx and one in Manhattan.[4]

Chubb was frequently invited to be the guest speaker at various educational meetings, and he occasionally used these as a platform to speak out against comic supplements. As the principal speaker at a 1909 meeting of the International Kindergarten Union, he called upon his listeners to ban comic supplements from the house. He argued that the comic strips glorified "the 'smart kid' . . . the worst American type of forward child." He also stressed the importance of the role of the school in helping to "transform the environment" of children:

> More and more the function of the school and the teacher becomes that of providing a protective environment in which for a few hours every day the child shall be surrounded with influences of health and quiet, of order and simple beauty. The school has to save the child from the unhealthy and unlovely world outside. . . . We must begin with ourselves by working for a clean press, and above all, a dignified Sunday press.[5]

Speaking at the annual spring meeting of the New York Public School Kindergarten Association a few weeks later, Chubb again called for parents to ban

A SECRET SOCIETY INITIATION IN HOGAN'S ALLEY.

FIGURE 69. Richard F. Outcault, *Hogan's Alley,* September 13, 1896.

comics from the home, arguing that the "elevation of taste" must come from the parent.[6] At the Child Welfare Exhibit in January 1911, Chubb once again attacked comic strips' glorification of the "cheeky, disrespectful, irreverent child." He expressed concern about the fact children were being exposed too early to an adult environment, stating, "The city is not a child's world."[7]

Chubb objected to the characters and the humor in the strips where the slums of New York City and the lives of the working class and immigrants were featured. These comics served as a chronicle of everyday life, exaggerated for emphasis.[8] The character who started it all, the Yellow Kid, was a bald-headed street urchin who occupied Hogan's Alley. His companions "frequently smoked, drank, and on occasion, tumbled from the windows of their tenement homes."[9] His dialogue, printed on the front of his nightshirt, was ungrammatical, to say the least.

The humor in early comics, like much of the humor of the period, was very physical. Roy McCardell, writing in 1905 of the early comic art, noted:

> Its humor is strenuous, not to say brutal; the knock-about comedians of the old-time music-halls might easily have posed for most of the pictures the supplement has printed in its ten years of life. The characters are thrown out of windows, clubbed, kicked, knocked down and out, laid flat by trunks dropped upon them; but they turn up smilingly the next Sunday to go through the same operations in other forms.[10]

As Nystrom notes in her analysis, because these early strips were directed at the working class, the most popular strips were critical of middle-class values and manners. The emphasis in early strips on children and animals as characters "gave them the power to act in a counter-productive or anarchic manner not appropriate for adults." Such characters had great appeal to those who had little control over their lives.[11]

Chubb took matters into his own hands in 1911, organizing a meeting in the auditorium of the Ethical Culture Society. At that meeting, he read letters of support for his proposed League for the Improvement of the Children's Comic Supplement. The meeting also featured a number of speakers. Among them were Norman Hapgood, editor of *Collier's Weekly*, who suggested that supporting "the right kind of endeavor" rather than a more radical move to eliminate the supplement altogether was the appropriate action; Lillian Wald, of the Nurses' Settlement, who pointed out that children ages five through twelve were especially susceptible to "instruction" from the pictorial Sunday supplement; and William Maxwell, superintendent of the public schools, who agreed that the work of the schools was being neutralized by the Sunday supplement.[12]

The League received a letter from the *New York World*, offering to turn over the newspaper's entire supplement on some Sunday to be illustrated and filled by the staff under the direction of the League. While it was a good public relations move for the *World*, there is no evidence that the League ever followed up on the invitation.[13] The founding of the League was greeted with editorial enthusiasm by *The Outlook*, which praised Chubb's efforts by noting that he "has rendered great service to the public in this connection," and concluding: "The League, under the leadership of Mr. Chubb, ought to have branches in every large city in the United States."[14] Despite the fanfare that greeted the formation of the League, there is no evidence that the League had any impact on comic supplements, and there is no further documentation of the League's activities. In fact, the greatest impact of the anti-supplement movement was felt four years earlier, when the *Boston Herald* announced that it would drop its comic supplement. In a statement explaining the move, the *Herald* noted: "The comic supplement has had its day. We discard it as we would throw aside any mechanism that has reached the end of its usefulness, of any 'feature' that had ceased to fulfill the purpose of attraction." It concluded: "The colored comic supplement is the clown of the newspaper establishment. The Herald believes that a great newspaper no longer needs a clown."[15]

While some magazine editors announced that the newspaper's action marked the beginning of the end for the comics, the *Herald*'s announcement of the death of the comic strip was premature. A few prominent newspapers nationwide, including *the Milwaukee Journal, The Indianapolis Star,* and the *New-York Tribune,* did drop their supplements briefly, but all of them, including the *Boston Herald,* had reinstated comics by 1915.[16] Clearly, the reform efforts directed at the comic supplements were, by and large, a failure. That failure can be attributed to several factors.

First, the work of the League was no doubt affected by the fact that Chubb left New York in September 1911 to become leader of the Ethical Culture Society in St. Louis. Without his leadership, the League seems to have disbanded. Second, as Nystrom has pointed out, the overwhelming popularity and profitability of the comic supplement ensured its survival. Third, the growing concern about the involvement of the United States in world affairs and the country's entry into World War I put an end to the crusade and to the urban progressive movement itself. Fourth, the nature of the comic strips themselves changed, moving away from slap-stick humor to the narrative "continuity" strip. Finally, there was a shift to middle-class themes, encouraged by the rise of syndicates, which removed the responsibility for the content of comic strips from individual newspapers.[17]

While the controversy over the comic strip was short-lived, the arguments put forth by its critics would be resurrected again with the introduction of each new form of popular entertainment—radio, television, and the comic book.

ENDNOTES

1. Elsa Nystrom, "A Rejection of Order: The Development of the Newspaper Comic Strip in America, 1830–1920" (PhD. diss., Loyola University of Chicago, 1989), 163–67.

2. Percival Chubb, Box I, Archives of the Ethical Culture Society, New York, NY.

3. Howard B. Radest, *Toward a Common Ground: The Story of the Ethical Societies in the United States* (New York: Frederick Ungar Publishing Co., 1969), 37, 120–32.

4. Radest, *Toward a Common Ground,* 42–43; Ethical Culture Society Catalog, "Ethical Culture Fieldston Schools" (New York: Ethical Culture Society, no date).

5. "The Vulgar Supplement Again," *The Outlook* (June 5, 1909): 307.

6. "Comic Supplements a Menace, He Says," *New York Times,* June 10, 1909, 7.

7. "Comic Supplements a Source of Evil," *New York Times,* January 27, 1911, 5.

8. Amos Stote, "Some Figures in the New Humor," *Bookman* (May 1910): 286.

9. Brian Walker, *The Sunday Funnies* (Bridgeport, CT: The Barnum Museum, 1994).

10. Roy McCardell, "Opper, Outcault and Company: The Comic Supplement and the Men who Made It," with annotations by Robert C. Harvey, *INKS* 2 (May 1995): 3.

11. Nystrom, "A Rejection of Order," 110–12, 132.

12. "Comic Supplements Publicly Denounced," *New York Times,* April 7, 1911, 4.

13. "Make 'Comics' Educational," *Survey* (April 15, 1911): 103.

14. "The Comic Supplement," *The Outlook* (April 15, 1911): 802.

15. Reprinted in "Sounding the Doom of the 'Comics,'" *Current Literature* (December 1908): 630–33.

16. Nystrom, "A Rejection of Order," 23–24.

17. David Frederick McCord, "The Social Rise of the Comics," *The American Mercury* (July 1935): 363–64; Nystrom, "A Rejection of Order," 186–94, 201–2.

Women and Children First

TRINA ROBBINS

IF THE PREREQUISITE for a cartoon to be considered a comic strip is continuity and panels, Rose O'Neill was writing and drawing comics for *Truth* magazine as early as 1896, or a year after the advent of the Yellow Kid. This fact is, however, not widely known. Cartoonist Diane DiMassa told in a recent interview about attending a panel discussion called "Under the Influence: Comic Art," that was held at the Exit Art gallery in New York City. Among the panelists speaking about comics history was *Maus* cartoonist Art Spiegelman. DiMassa relates that the subject of women cartoonists, and the absence of any mention of them during the panel, was brought up by members of the audience. "Someone had asked him [Spiegelman] why there wasn't any cartoon work done by women in the early 1900s, and he actually said, 'Well, they just weren't *doing* it then.'"[1]

It is unfortunate that people who should know better still hold this erroneous belief.[2] Within five year of O'Neill's work for *Truth*, comic strips by women were appearing in newspapers. By 1901, *Bun's Pun*, a kind of protocomic by Louise Quarles, was running in the *New York Herald*. It had panels and puns but lacked the continuity that makes for a true comic strip. The same newspaper printed *Tin Tan Tales for Children* by Grace Kasson, and the *Philadelphia Press* ran *The PhilaBusters* by Agnes Repplier.

Each year more women entered the field. The comics pages of newspapers in 1902 introduced Jean Mohr, Kate Carew, and Grace Gebbie Weiderseim, who in three more years would create the characters that became the Campbell Soup Kids. (In 1911 Weiderseim remarried and took the name by which she is most often known, Grace Drayton.) Jean Mohr's strip told the rather startling adventures of a pretty girl named Sallie Slick and her remarkable Aunt Amelia, a little old lady practical joker and past master of the art of hatpin self-defense. The strip changed names according to the story. For instance, one is called *Aunt Amelia Brings Sallie a Present, But Sallie Didn't Know It,* and another is *Aunt Amelia Builds Some Snow Men for Sallie.* A more traditional strip by Mohr, *Easy Edgar,* ran above it. *Easy Edgar* and Kate Carew's *The Angel Child* both featured cute kids getting into trouble, as did the long series of comic strips that Grace Gebbie Weiderseim Drayton would draw throughout her life.

There have always been trends in comic strips, and the reigning fashion in the early part of the twentieth century was for cute kids who get into trouble. This type of strip was drawn not only by women but also by men like Jimmy Swinnerton and Richard Felton Outcault. By 1910, cute-kid strips filled the newspaper pages, and many were by women, including *Gretchen Gratz* and *Snooks and Snicks* by Inez Townsend Tribit; *Jennie and Jack* by Grace Drayton's sister, Margaret Gebbie Hays; and *Kate and Karl* by Margaret's daughter and Grace's niece, Mary A. Hays. Meanwhile, Grace Drayton was prolifically turning out strips about adorable children with names like Toodles, Toddles, Dolly Drake, Bobby Blake, Dolly Dingle, Dolly Dimples, and Dotty Darling—all of whom looked exactly like the Campbell Kids. Rose O'Neill, whose *Kewpie* strips had started running in women's magazines as early as 1909, briefly syndicated a *Kewpies* newspaper strip in 1917, but it only lasted for a year. O'Neill did not return to the newspaper comics page until the 1930s. Cute kids, of course, are still going strong today, as evidenced by the immense popularity of *Calvin and Hobbes.*

Women cartoonists eventually branched out into other genres of cartooning. By 1911 Kate Carew was writing and illustrating a page of satirical political and social commentary for the *New York Journal-American,* dealing with such diverse topic as graft at Tammany Hall and votes for women. By 1916 Edwina Dumm was working for the *Columbus Monitor* as the country's first female political cartoonist. Within a year, Dumm was supplying that newspaper with a full page of cartoons titled *Spot-Light Sketches,* which featured a comic strip called *The Meanderings of Minnie* at the bottom of the page. This strip about

FIGURE 70. Nell Brinkley, "Puzzle—Who's Coming?" 1913.

a little girl and her dog became *Cap Stubbs* in 1918 when Minnie changed her sex, and it eventually turned into the long-running comic strip *Cap Stubbs and Tippie.*

As early as 1902, sixteen-year-old Marjorie Organ was working as the only woman in the *New York Journal's* art department. She was supplying the paper with a number of regular strips, including *Strange What a Difference a Mere Man Makes!, Reggie and the Heavenly Twins,* and *The Wrangle Sisters,* all of which fit into the category of early pretty-girl comics. That same year, another sixteen year old, Nell Brinkley, was hired by *The Denver Post* for the salary of $7 per week.[3] She was to become the godmother of the next major fad in comics for and by women: pretty girls.

By 1907 Nell Brinkley was a star illustrator for William Randolph Hearst's newspapers, and her "Brinkley Girls" were featured regularly all over the country. Hearst newspapers ran photos of her with captions that described her as "the clever artist whose work for 'The Examiner' has attracted so much attention."[4] Brinkley's daily panels, which were not usually in the form of comic strips, usually consisted of a single "pin-up" style drawing that included one or more of the windblown and ruffled beauties for which she was famous, along with various dogs, cupids, and/or handsome men. Commentary by the artist, written in the highly romantic style that was popular then, ran under the panels. By the very early 'teens, Nell Brinkley had inspired a host of imitators. Soon many American newspapers could boast of at least one comic strip or single-panel cartoon filled with romantic beauties in hobble skirts and high-button shoes, drawn by the likes of Eleanor Schorer, Juanita Hamel, and Stella Flores. By the 1920s, Brinkley was producing full-page, multi-paneled stories with continuity that, although they lacked panel borders, must be considered comics, and so were dozens of other women cartoonists. Women were undeniably *doing* it back then.

ENDNOTES

1. Joan Hilty, "Guillotines, Late Nights and Norman Rockwell: A Conversation with Alison Bechel & Diane DiMassa," *Oh* #6 (February 1994): 35–36.

2. The fact that women cartoonists have been so under-chronicled is the reason I wrote *A Century of Women Cartoonists* and co-authored *Women and the Comics* with catherine yronwode.

3. Idelle Dvorak, "Nell Brinkley, A Biography," *American Illustrators Research Group 1980 Annual*, unpaginated.

4. Clipping from *Los Angeles Examiner*, ca. 1908.

Boy Can He Draw

MARK J. COHEN

FROM A 1992 TV INTERVIEW with Whoopi Goldberg:

WHOOPI: "You're pretty suave!"
GUEST: "I wish I were. I've always wanted to be suave. . . . I'm from Minnesota. . . . There are no suave people in Minnesota! It's too cold to be suave!"

This is a typically self-effacing comment by Charles M. Schulz, the seventy-three-year-old creator of the most widely syndicated comic strip in history, *Peanuts.* Known to his friends as "Sparky," Schulz believes that what goes into a comic strip must come from the cartoonist's own life experiences and be a product of its creator's unique character. Because of this philosophy and the success of his comic strip, he is the world's most analyzed and written about cartoonist. Schulz has had a lifetime of experiences that could happen to Charlie Brown if he grew up. For instance,

When Sparky sent out his high school graduation announcements, he signed each one "Sincerely yours, Charles Schulz," not realizing that he had misspelled "sincerely" on every one.

After graduating from high school, Sparky answered a classified ad for the position of "Jr. Artist" placed by the Gile Letter Service, a direct-mail advertising company in Minneapolis. He was given an application and a test: "Draw a radio tower." Sparky remembered his correspondence school instructions always to draw from life, so he actually found a tower to draw. Based on his drawing, he was hired. The company was located quite a distance from his house, so he had to get up before dawn and take a long streetcar ride in order to get to work by eight o'clock. Mr. Gile, who it seemed was always squinting from behind a cloud of cigarette smoke, introduced him to the production manager, a big, red-haired woman, who instructed him to sweep out the office, deliver packages, and perform other menial chores. Several weeks later, Sparky asked the production manager when he would get to do artwork; she looked at him, rolled her eyes, and said, "Oh no! He did it again. There is no junior artist position. All the boss wanted was a delivery boy."

When Schulz was discharged from the Army after World War II, he began to pursue a career as a cartoonist. His work had been rejected by every major syndicate before he dreamed up the concept of *Peanuts,* which he sold to United Feature Syndicate in 1950. He is one of the very few cartoonists to win two of the National Cartoonists Society's (NCS) Reuben Awards, the equivalent of the Oscar for motion pictures. The Reuben, named after its designer, Rube Goldberg, is, without a doubt, one of the most ridiculous looking trophies ever created. It stands more than two feet tall and features four nude acrobats balanced one atop the other in bizarre positions. The topmost figure has a bottle of india ink balanced on his buns. Marge Devine, the secretary of the NCS for many years, ruled the club with an iron fist. Each year, as the Reuben was presented, Marge would be at the side of the dais to congratulate the winner. At the 1955 awards banquet, Schulz was astounded when he was declared the winner. After he accepted the award, Marge shook his hand and took some of the joy out of the occasion by saying, "We really wanted Rube [Goldberg] to win this year." Once the ceremony and all of its hoopla was over, Sparky had to make his way to the train station to catch the red-eye to Boston for an early morning appointment the next day. Sitting alone in the train seat, holding the silly looking Reuben statuette in the middle of the night was, says Schulz, "one of the loneliest moments of my life."

After forty-five years, Schulz has reached a pinnacle of success unheard of in the cartoon business. His work appears in more newspapers worldwide than any other cartoonist's, past or present; he has inspired generations of new cartoonists; and he continues to produce high-quality work. Has success spoiled Charles Schulz? Recently he commented that, "I've had a one man exhibit in Rome and at the Louvre in Paris, been presented the highest civilian award, the Order of the Commander of Arts and Letters, by both the French and Italian Ministers of Culture. I felt like I'd really arrived until I got home from Rome and there was a letter from Dinah Shore waiting for me. It said that I wouldn't be invited to play in her golf tournament because I wasn't important enough." [1]

At seventy-three, Charles Schulz still goes to his studio every day and draws *Peanuts*. Each letter, word, and line that appears in his comic strip is personally created, lettered, and drawn by him. He has never used outside writers or assistants on the strip. "Every day I try to turn out the very best comic strip I can," he says. Nobody but Charles Schulz will ever draw *Peanuts*. When Sparky retires or is no longer alive, there will be no more new *Peanuts* strips in the newspaper. This is part of his contract with United Feature Syndicate.

"What were five of the best comic strips ever done?" asks Schulz. *Skippy* by Percy Crosby, *Popeye* by E. C. Segar, *Krazy Kat* by George Herriman, *Li'l Abner* by Al Capp, and *Wash Tubbs* by Roy Crane are suggested as possible contenders. "Each one," says Sparky, "could only have been done by the artist that created it. They are a personal product of that person's life experiences and imagination, and that's what made them great." Schulz mentions a name or two, pauses, and then pays a compliment he reserves only for cartoonists that he holds in high regard: "Boy, could they draw."

Schulz is a cartoonist because he has no choice in the matter. He is doing what he loves to do. He cares about the history and the art of cartooning, and he is saddened because so many of the younger cartoonists are not familiar with the work of the masters such as Milton Caniff, C. M. Payne, Chester Gould, and Hal Foster. Schulz feels that too many of the new comic strips are designed to fill a market niche. "It just doesn't work that way," he says. A comic strip, he feels, is not a marketing ploy. It is a unique blending of an artist's psyche, life experiences, artistic and writing skills. Rather than trying to get syndicated by trying to find a market, Schulz says, "Persons should concentrate on producing the very best work that they can. Develop characters and writing skills, and find your own market."

Over the past few years, several cartoonists, such as Gary Larson, cartoonist for *The Far Side*; Garry Trudeau, of *Doonesbury*; and Bill Watterson, the genius behind *Calvin and Hobbes,* took time off from drawing their strips because of the stress that comes from having to write, draw, and be

FIGURE 71. Self-caricature by Charles Schulz from the private collection of Mark J Cohen. Reprinted by permission of Jean Schulz.

entertaining 365 days a year. When the cartoonist is on sabbatical, reruns appear in the newspapers. Their syndicate, Universal Press Syndicate, recently began offering its long-time cartoonists one month's vacation each year, during which old material will appear on the funny pages. Schulz, when hearing of this, said, "Don't let them tell you that this is a business that has so much stress that you have to have time off. Cartooning is what we wanted to do all our lives." He knows what he is talking about. Several years ago he crammed three months of work into two weeks so that he could take ninety days off to have coronary bypass surgery. Once he gained his lead time, he had the surgery and was back to work in about forty-five days. "I gained a month," he says.

Occasionally an aspiring cartoonist will bring Sparky samples of his or her work for suggestions. The master's comments are exacting. Schulz recently perused the work of a would-be cartoonist and said, "Why put so much work into your central character and then do such sloppy backgrounds. Your whole strip should be excellent. Go back and look at *Bringing Up Father* by George McManus or *Wash Tubbs* by Roy Crane and pay attention to their background detail." Another aspiring cartoonist was told, "Your strips are all drawn backwards. You have the set-up at the end of the strip and the punch line at the beginning. You'll have to re-do them."

Sparky realized early in the development of his cast of characters the importance of the supporting roles, what vaudevillians used to call the "second banana." Every character either plays off of Charlie Brown or another character in the strip. Charlie Brown may not be the strongest character, but without his loveable loser qualities, his everyman personality, and his hopeful, trusting nature, the rest of the strip's chemistry would be off. It is interesting that Charlie Brown is a different person to each character in the comic strip, from, simply, "that round head kid," to Snoopy, to Lucy's foil, Sally's big brother, and Linus's friend and confidant. Woodstock is another very popular character in *Peanuts,* and his role is as Snoopy's second banana—he has a supporting role to a supporting cast member.

Schulz has had the restraint to keep the characters as an ensemble cast and to not let one character overshadow the others. It would have been self-defeating and limiting, for example, to let one strong character, such as Snoopy or Lucy, become the star attraction of the strip. Within the ensemble cast of *Peanuts,* many of the characters have their own recurrent gags, what used to be called *shtick.*

Schulz's running gags have become a part of the world's popular culture. Can you imagine Halloween without Linus and "The Great Pumpkin?" Football season without Lucy pulling the football away from Charlie Brown? Linus without his security blanket or scriptures? Peppermint Patty not cribbing answers from Lucy? Or Schroeder without his piano and sheet music? These are running gags that we can look forward to, laugh at, and remember from years ago. They have become old friends.

By developing his characters, giving each a well-defined personality, a place in the scheme of the comic strip, and by having a wonderful series of ongoing gags, Sparky's creation has been able to transcend the comic pages to become a success in children's books, the musical theatre (*You're a Good Man Charlie Brown,* the most often-produced play in history, and *Snoopy, The Musical*), TV specials, and the movies. Because of the success of *Peanuts,* books and articles have been written about the *Peanuts* philosophy, the

Peanuts view on religion, and the *Peanuts* view of politics. Sparky, in response, just shrugs and says, "Heck! I just draw funny pictures."

And boy, can he draw.

ENDNOTE

1. The anecdotes described were told to the author by Charles Schulz on various occasions from 1986 to 1994.

BOOK REVIEWS

Understanding Comics by Scott McCloud

REVIEWED BY JOSEPH WITEK

IN THE SUMMER OF 1993 I undertook to teach an upper-division English course on Comics and/as Literature. Like anyone else bringing comics to the classroom, I faced a serious problem finding appropriate books. Primary texts have become easier to come by since the boom in graphic novels and soft-bound reprint volumes; a good thing, too, since college bookstores are more adept at ordering *Maus* and *Watchmen* from conventional book publishers than in assembling issues of individual comics.

But with the passing of the heroic age of coursepack photocopying, secondary sources have become harder to use than ever. While several fine books on comics have appeared in recent years, the tradition of critical discourse on comics in this country is neither broad nor deep, and of the worthwhile work that exists, very little travels well into the classroom. For example, David Kunzle's two trenchant volumes of his comic strip history are too massive, expensive, and specialized for undergraduates, while most other histories of comics are aimed at comics hobbyists or nostalgia buffs. Scarcest of all are works dealing with my own central critical concern, the textual specificity of the comics medium itself. Before 1985 there were but a handful of scattered articles concerned with how comics make meanings; not until the eminent comic creator Will Eisner's *Comics and Sequential Art* appeared did a full-length discussion of the specific techniques of comics narrative become available in English.[1]

Comics and Sequential Art seemed the best, indeed only, choice as a basic text for my course. In that pioneering volume Eisner's long experience with making instructional comics stands him in good stead as he expounds his ideas on the theory and (mostly) practice of comic art. His extended treatments of the component parts of the comics medium such as the interaction of words and images, framing, timing, and the semiotics (what he calls "vocabulary") of word balloons and panel borders are clear and illuminating, and in the past students have responded well to Eisner's straightforward approach and well-chosen examples.

For all its strengths, though, *Comics and Sequential Art* is not the ideal classroom introduction to comics that it first appears to be. For one thing, as Eisner says, "This work was originally written as a series of essays that appeared randomly in *The Spirit* magazine,"[2] and its disparate organization betrays its roots. The topics chosen are a bit idiosyncratic, and the book finally is most effective as a consideration of Eisner's own practice (valuable though that is) than as a complete introductory text. For example, Eisner's extended and fascinating discussion of one of his recent interests, the "meta-panel," a page design of borderless panels, suggests a greater importance for that technique in comics as a whole than has thus far been the case. More significantly, all the illustrations in the book are Eisner's own (several full-length *Spirit* stories are included), and while unity of vision thus is maintained, a sense of the breadth and variety of practice in comics is missing entirely. Beyond doubt, *Comics and Sequential Art* has been a boon to scholars and critics of the comics form by commencing with acumen and gusto a critical conversation on the comics medium that has been too long getting started in this country. But as time passes the book seems more like a good beginning than the final word.

My problem in choosing books was solved when, a few days before textbook orders were due for the summer term, a copy of cartoonist Scott McCloud's long-rumored *Understanding Comics* arrived at the local comics shop. *Understanding Comics* is nothing less than a full-length treatise in comic book form on the history and aesthetics of the comics medium; a cartoon figure calling itself Scott McCloud leads readers through chapters on the definition of comics (itself a vexed issue in the previous literature), iconic representation, transitions between panels, time and movement in the comics, synesthesia and expressionism, visual/verbal interaction, a unified theory of artistic creation, and the effects of color in comics. As the penultimate item on that list suggests, the range of McCloud's ambition is almost humorously massive, a refreshing quality in comics criticism, a field much given to self-denigration and meek apologies for its subject matter. The book treats each of its subjects in detail, it includes a wide range of examples, and it discusses with insight the comics traditions of Europe and Japan as well as that of the United States.

Understanding Comics, then, became the basic text for the course; after two weeks (out of eight in the term) with McCloud's book, we read Alan Moore and Dave Gibbon's *Watchmen,* Art Spiegelman's *Maus,* a reprint volume of George Herriman's *Krazy Kat,* and Jay Cantor's novel *Krazy Kat.* The class mixed advanced English majors with graduate students and avid comics fans with people who never even read the funnies; one student needed the course hours for graduation, another was a practicing comic book artist. Even the experienced comics buffs were little used to thinking about the medium analytically, though, and the group turned out to be a nearly ideal practical testing ground for McCloud's arguments.

Together my students and I found that *Understanding Comics* works very well in the classroom, as McCloud exploits the didactic potential of the comics medium to the hilt. As might be expected of a person who attempts a *Poetics* of the comics medium, McCloud's approach is eminently Aristotelian. A short but passionate survey of comics prehistory soon gives way to categories and taxonomies, with plenty of illustrative examples, charts, graphs, and nomenclature, old, new, and borrowed. While he is no academic, McCloud sprinkles his arguments liberally with references to authorities such as Rodolphe Töpffer, Rene Magritte, Wassily Kandinsky, Marshall McLuhan, and Max Ernst. Such references helped to locate the intellectual contexts of McCloud's arguments for students with philosophy and humanities backgrounds, while McCloud's lists and charts enabled students who were unfamiliar with the history and conventions of comics narratives to sort through a mass of new information.

Few students realized, however, that, in addition to the helpful presences of artists and philosophers, the immediate figures behind McCloud's approach to the comics medium and its history are David Kunzle and Will Eisner. Kunzle's history of comic strips backdates the medium to the Renaissance, well before the traditional turn-of-the-century, Ally Sloper/Yellow Kid, newspaper publishing wars startup that has become the conventional wisdom among comics historians. McCloud follows suit by emphasizing the contributions of William Hogarth and Rodolphe Töpffer in the development of the comics medium. McCloud, in fact, goes Kunzle several millennia better by linking comics to hieroglyphics and narrative tapestries, in a move designed not to ennoble comics by association, as has been done before, but to place comics in the larger context of visual narratives in Western culture.

At this point Eisner contributes the phrase *sequential art,* and McCloud embraces this term for the medium of which comic strips and comic books are specific forms. *Sequential art* is the latest contender as an alternative to *the comics* and has actually been used recently by writers other than its inventor, unlike previous pretenders such as *graphic fiction, panelology,* and Art Spiegelman's offering, *commix.* The term has attracted some scorn as a pretentious attempt to escape what even some comics enthusiasts see as the essentially puerile and sordid nature of comics, and no doubt some legitimizing impulse is attached to it. But my students, most of whom had no stake in raising the cultural status of comics, seemed to think that "sequential art" made a useful distinction as a name for the whole of which comic strips and comic books are parts.

Much of the beginning of *Understanding Comics* is devoted to the careful crafting of McCloud's definition of comics, "Juxtaposed pictorial and other images in deliberate sequence." While the definition itself raises some conceptual difficulties (Is a linked series of ads in a magazine "comics"?), its production is itself a tour de force performance of comics criticism. Most writers on comics (David Kunzle is the main exception, as ever) have followed Coulton Waugh's heavily content-based definition, which emphasized matters such as word balloons and continuing characters as the essentials of comics. McCloud's definition has the advantage of locating the medium in its formal qualities, and as with much in this book, it will no doubt set the terms of the critical debate that McCloud explicitly hopes will result from *Understanding Comics.*

But historical background and conceptual definitions were of limited interest to my students. The course assignments emphasized textual analysis of specific comics examples, so the class was concerned with developing an interpretive procedure that would work for comics. For us, then, the central parts of *Understanding Comics* became McCloud's discussions of the "iconic triangle" and his chartings of panel-to-panel transitions and word/image interdependence. These three elements represent a major advance in comics criticism by supplying a clear explanation of and vocabulary for some of the distinctive techniques of the comics medium. They each also engendered a number of problems, and it eventually became clear to us that this book is valuable both for the answers it offers and the questions it raises.

A case in point is McCloud's theory of the icon. By *icon* McCloud means all figures of representation, including words, symbols, and images; for McCloud, icons vary along an axis of meaning and one of abstraction. The theory is diagrammed in a triangle, the horizontal base of which stretches from "reality" (actually photographic realism) on the left through increasingly simplified forms of representation to written language on the right; the left diagonal stretches from the "reality" point up to pure geometric design ("the picture plane") at the apex. The further right toward meaning one goes the more simplified the figures become (at the right border, a smiley face slips over into the alphabet); the higher up one travels the more figures break down into abstract forms. McCloud then proceeds to locate nearly all the familiar styles of comics artists on this triangle; as might be expected, the lower right corner is quite crowded, the triangle's apex nearly bare. As an introduction to the variety of visual styles in comics, the triangle is an unparalleled teaching aid, and few students had trouble placing new examples on the appropriate spots on the chart.

But students' questions about how to use the triangle revealed a major issue, if not difficulty, with McCloud's whole approach in *Understanding Comics*. His cornucopia of examples invites readers to provide their own, but dubious cases arise quickly to hover annoyingly at the edges of the argument. Is an X-ray even more "real" than a photograph and thus placed further to the left? Is photomicroscopy more abstract or more real than photo portraiture? And where does the right border of the chart really end? Though his spectrum of pictorial styles is inclusive, McCloud does not say much about how words become more or less abstract or representational, and we all ended up in some confusion as to where to put writing/printing styles. The iconic triangle has the indubitable advantage of allowing a detailed taxonomy of what until now have been lumped as "realistic" or "cartoony" visual styles, but the ambiguities at its extremities suggest that the big issues of realism, representation, and meaning raised by the comics medium are being pointed to rather than systematically confronted.

Of perhaps the greatest practical value to us was McCloud's analysis of the ways comics make shifts in time and space from panel to panel; his five categories of narrative transitions supply a way of talking precisely about a narrative element that until now has been only erratically articulated. Of nearly equal interest were his graphs showing how various comics creators use these transitions. For example, even inexperienced comics readers sense that Art Spiegelman's self-reflexive and cerebral experimental comics differ greatly from the spare and straightforward *Maus*, but McCloud's graphs demonstrate that a major difference is that Spiegelman's early works use a wide range of transition types while *Maus*, like most narrative comics in general, mostly sticks to sequences that switch from one action to another within a scene, from one part of a scene to another, and from one scene to the next. These categories supplied my students, most of whom were unused to talking about comics texts at all, with a tool for making precise and nuanced analytical judgments.

Still, special cases cropped up faster than we could dispose of them, mostly because McCloud's examples of transitions use minimal text and we soon found that distinguishing among the various transitions depended largely on verbal cues to show where and when the narrative was going.

The same problem cropped up, though to a lesser degree, in McCloud's similar discussion of word/image interaction in panels. His seven categories of word/image combinations rationalize an often bewildering array of narrative techniques and, as in so much of *Understanding Comics*, McCloud does a major service to comics criticism by supplying names for complex concepts. But in practice we had a hard time distinguishing "duo-specific" panels (those sometimes hilarious instances when the caption repeats the message of the picture) from "additive" ones (where the text amplifies or elaborates the image). Certainly the students thought such ambiguities were a greater problem than I did, since they were worried about making mistakes in their essays, while I was more concerned with figuring out if the categories worked and made sense; they mostly do. Despite our questions, we all agreed that together the iconic triangle, the panel transitions, and the word/image combinations gave us invaluable ways of analyzing the specificities of comics texts that none of us had before.

A written survey at the end of the course revealed that my students responded very well to McCloud and his arguments. Most felt that the comic book format not only presented its complex information very effectively, but that the form itself bolstered McCloud's argument that comics are worth studying. Several students were bothered by McCloud's occasional apologies for the medium and found them intrusive and irrelevant; seasoned comics scholars will recognize the impulse to preface serious treatments of comics with some version of the proviso "Most people think all comics are simple and stupid, but they're not." Many thought that the theory of artistic creation detailed in chapter 7 was overly schematic and of dubious utility ("hokey drawings, too," sniffed one person); a few were pleased to find out that "art" included every human activity except those connected with survival and sex. Several rightly complained that the book's binding was poor (viewing the complete iconic triangle requires breaking the book's spine); a mysterious blob of ink marring the middle of the iconic triangle came under fire as well. And in a volume that aspires to be a textbook, the lack of an index is inexcusable.

These minor issues aside, *Understanding Comics* is a success in the classroom and I recommend it to anyone teaching comics. As a work of comics criticism, the book is wonderfully brave and intellectually ambitious, qualities all the more welcome in a professional cartoonist; analysis and theoretical inquiry generally have been anathema to most of McCloud's colleagues. The categories McCloud describes are themselves an important contribution to thinking about comics, and his argument should have an immediate effect on comics discourse. The missteps and limitations of *Understanding Comics* likewise should help to clarify issues for further work in the comics field. First, McCloud takes over existing critical terms with little sense of their history. For example, two key terms of McCloud's argument, *icon* and *closure,* both come with complex sets of intellectual baggage; he uses them idiosyncratically if not incorrectly. A more fundamental problem is the implicit reader-response theory that underlies McCloud's aesthetic of comics. He makes the argument, for example, that the simplicity and lack of visual specificity of cartoons enable readers to "identify" with the figures with little sense that recent arguments suggest that the concept of "identification" is by no means the transparent and self-evident proposition that he takes it to be.[3] (One student parodied McCloud's assertion that an iconic figure is more persuasive than a realistic one by donning a smiley-face mask to present his class report.) In addition, McCloud's crucial argument that words need to be decoded while pictures transmit messages instantaneously is a very dubious proposition by any measure, as the many people who declare their inability to read comics probably will agree. *Understanding Comics* is a work of great practical use, but I suspect that its spotty theoretical underpinnings will doom its grander ambitions as a work of aesthetics.

Students of comics long have needed a book that presents clearly and methodically the basic grammar and syntax of the medium; Scott McCloud's *Understanding Comics* is that book. Many previous writers on comics have ignored the formal specificities of the texts they discuss, treating comics as if they were simply illustrated novels or static movies and applying concepts from painting, film, and literature to comics in an ad hoc manner. Such neglect can no longer be justified. But, as my students and I discovered, a McCloudian reading of panel transitions and word/image relations does not by itself produce complete formal analyses of comics texts; too much other information is needed to make sense of the narrative. The next logical move in comics criticism, a step made possible by McCloud's intelligent work, is to begin a thorough discussion of the relations among comics and other media. For example, comics and film clearly have much in common. But how much? When do analogies between the two obscure more than they reveal? *Understanding Comics* should itself generate a vigorous discussion about the range and applicability of McCloud's arguments; it will likewise help to clarify the wide range of questions still facing the nascent field of comics criticism. In McCloud's words, "Here's to the Great Debate!"

ENDNOTES

1. Will Eisner, *Comics and Sequential Art* (Tamarac, FL: Poorhouse Press), 1985. Of the previous articles, the most complete is Lawrence L. Abbott, "Comic Art: Characteristics and Potentialities of a Narrative Medium," *Journal of Popular Culture* 19 (Spring 1986): 155–73.

2. Eisner, *Comics and Sequential Art*, 5.

3. See, for example, Martin Barker, *Comics: Ideology, Power & the Critics* (Manchester: Manchester University Press. 1989), especially chapter 5, "The Vicissitudes of Identification."

Adult Comics: An Introduction by Roger Sabin

REVIEWED BY FRANK STACK

I PICKED UP ROGER SABIN'S *Adult Comics* with some feeling of anticipation that this effort might be the long-awaited intelligent appraisal of the whole class of serious work by artists and writers who do not seem to fit into any respectable art or literary category. This study is by the London arts journalist Roger Sabin, and it is an intelligent appraisal, more or less, without managing to enlighten us very much about the subject. The author tells us in his introduction that he approaches the subject from a British perspective and that he, with scholarly caution, limited his study to a broad overview of "comic books" intended for an audience over the age of sixteen. There is no attempt to deal with newspaper comic strips, except as background for the comic book. The text is presented in three parts, the first two sections dealing with a historic overview of the development of comic books, first in Britain and then in the United States. The last section includes chapters on "Worldcomics," "Adult Comics and Other Media," women (in comics), and "The Graphic Novel."

Adult Comics proceeds rather predictably, laboring over history, background, and definitions of terms, dutifully dealing with everything the author has ever heard of that seems to fit the definition of comics drawn by and intended for adults. For an American reader, this book seems awfully, how shall I put it, pedantic? stuffy? patronizing? English! I was puzzled to find a chapter on underground comics in the section titled "Britain." Since I had not been aware that there was a significant underground comics movement in Britain, I turned immediately to that chapter. Of course, it was not about British comics. Sabin notes that, "in Britain, the comix were very much an import." The chapter is about the American underground (*Zap,* Rip Off Press, *Berkeley Barb,* etc.) and its subsequent influence in England, stimulating a small imitative response in the United Kingdom. The "underground press" did not really take hold until the appearance of *Viz* in the 1980s. The best part of the book is the chapter Sabin devotes to this wonderfully funny satiric publication, which, in recent years, has been the best-selling of all "adult comics," even without the U.S. market. Curiously, Sabin never mentions *The National Lampoon.*

The book is illustrated liberally, as a study of comics should be, with an illustration on every third page; but the pictures are not helpful. I normally expect, with a picture book, to flip through the book, stop at an interesting picture, and browse in the text to find why the author included that example and what he had to say about it. Not with this book. The binding is heavy, stiff and awkward, causing the book to snap shut every time you loosen your grip. Except for a few sample pages, the tiny illustrations turn out not to be worth the trouble of manhandling a book that will not stay open. I saw a few familiar images: work by Hugo Pratt, Gilbert Shelton, Harvey Kurtzman, Chris Donald (from *Viz*), all produced unsatisfactorily. Most of the illustrations were of covers, promotional material, or cryptic panels taken out of context. I did not see a single image in the book that would have stimulated me to seek out the original work.

The awkward binding of the book also makes the text a chore to read, with left-hand pages falling away into a crevice-like gutter. The text is no more interesting than the choice of illustrational material. There is a distant, alienated feeling about the whole thing, as if the author viewed his subject as a bizarre sociological phenomenon. In taking such a broad overview, he neglects to tell us much very specific or interesting about the artists, writers, and editors: who they are, how they came to the profession, or anything of their special creative characters. In typical journeyman style he reels off names and dates like a grocery list, giving the readers no reason in particular why he should be interested in these people and their books.

As a reader who is already interested, I certainly would have liked to have some personal stories, anecdotes—something to bring some of this stuff to life. I know some of these people, and the ones I know give lively interviews. The fact that Sabin was viewing the phenomenon as an outsider need not have been a disadvantage because he might have provided some special individual insight. Unfortunately, his point of view seems to be that of a disinterested scholar, making a potential textbook for studying comics as a curious manifestation of low culture of the later twentieth century. He does not treat it as an art form or show any particular interest in or sensitivity to the special expressive qualities that distinguish the form ("*la bande dessinée,*" "the graphic novel," stories in comic form, or simply sequential picture narrative) from novels, illustration, cinema, or from various nonsequential visual art media. Though the territory Sabin deals with has been generally uncharted in book form, there is very little original material in this book, as contrasted, for example, with *The Comics,* Coulton Waugh's 1947 study of newspaper strips, or Judith O'Sullivan's *The Great American Comic Strip* from 1990, which includes biographies of an exhaustive list of contemporary comics creators.

Appendices include the Comics Code printed in full, a lengthy bibliography of books on comics, and a long list of "key British and American comics." Except for the names of a few titles that were new to me, I really did not learn anything new from this book. The text is dry and humorless, as we expect from lengthy studies on the subject of humor. *Adult Comics* seems to be a book written for an audience that's not particularly interested in its subject. It is hard for me to envision any reader's *becoming* interested as a result of reading this book.

The Art of the Funnies: An Aesthetic History by Robert C. Harvey

REVIEWED BY IAN GORDON

IN HIS 1979 ESSAY "The Aesthetics of the Comic Strips," published in *The Journal of Popular Culture*, Robert C. Harvey argued that serious critical discussion of comics required an articulated theory of comic aesthetics. This volume, which opens with a reworked version of that essay, offers a history of comic strip art that flows from Harvey's two main premises:

> Comics are unique in the way they "weave word and picture together to achieve narrative purpose."

> The criteria for evaluating comic strips can be found in the history of the form because artists gave different ingredients of the form their finest expression in the "great" strips.

Although *The Art of the Funnies* covers many of the same artists as Richard Marschall's *America's Great Comic-Strip Artists*—the usual suspects: McCay, Herriman, Segar, Raymond, Caniff, and the rest—Harvey explains why and how individual strips were great. For instance, Milton Caniff's *Terry and the Pirates* stands out as much for Caniff's witty counterpoising of images and text as it does for his use of chiaroscuro techniques. One of the strengths of Harvey's account is that he draws his explanation out of the comic strips he reproduces in the volume rather than expecting his audience to acknowledge intrinsically that his favorite artists are great.

Harvey's careful argumentation sets him apart from other comic strip commentators. Whereas other writers seem to engage in conjecture and flights of fancy, Harvey footnotes the sources for his opinions and explains his logic. I also find it refreshing to read a work on comic strips in which, as far as I can tell from my own research, every date is correct. Another of Harvey's accomplishments is to extend the social context in which comics developed beyond the usual accounts about the growth of newspaper chains and features syndicates. He cites the importance of copyright laws and the maturation of consumerism in the 1920s as crucial factors that shaped comic strips. Harvey's attention to these sorts of details make his book a convincing read.

The aesthetic sensibilities Harvey brings to his readings of comic strips made me wish he had tackled the issue of caricature and racial stereotypes in comic art. He briefly touches on this subject when discussing Mort Walker's introduction of an African American character to *Beetle Bailey*, but a fuller examination seems in order. In *Comics: Ideology, Power, & The Critics*, Martin Barker dismissed comic art stereotypes as a non-issue in a field where all representation is caricature, but a fuller discussion of this issue seems warranted. To return to Caniff: what can we make of the Chinese sidekick Connie's language and visual representation compared to the mysterious sexuality of the other major Chinese character, the Dragon Lady? Harvey's suggestion that the strip's readers wanted sexy oriental women and, by extension, Yellow Kid-like Chinese cooks, and that presenting these characters gave the strip greater verisimilitude deserves further exploration.

I have two minor quibbles with Harvey. First, I think a work of history should be written in the past tense and he slips into present tense for dramatic effect on too many occasions. Second, he suggests that the comic strip in America achieved a form and importance it did not attain elsewhere. While comics may have achieved such a status in America before they did in other countries, the French, British, Japanese, and Australians would have trouble with this statement.

The Art of the Funnies is an important work in comics history. It would be a shame if Harvey's book were overshadowed by Scott McCloud's *Understanding Comics*. Comparisons are probably inevitable, but the works have different goals: Harvey delineates the aesthetic development of the form whereas McCloud tackles the broader structure of comic visual communication. Although lacking the color reproductions of Marschall's work, Harvey's book is probably the single-best comic strip history currently available.

100 Years of American Newspaper Comics edited by Maurice Horn

REVIEWED BY ROBERT C. HARVEY

An abbreviated version of this review was prepared for publication in The Comics Journal.

THIS TIME, let there be no shilly-shallying: Maurice Horn's latest perpetration, *100 Years of American Newspaper Comics,* is a travesty of scholarship and a mockery of historicity. This book is so seriously flawed—its assertions so dubious, its facts so frequently wrong—as to be worthless as a resource. No field of academic inquiry or interest, no matter how impoverished its libraries, can be improved by the advent of a wholly unreliable reference work like this. Random House should be ashamed of itself.

Strong words, I agree. But the last times Horn came among us with his *World Encyclopedia of Comics* (Chelsea House, 1976) and his *World Encyclopedia of Cartoons* (Chelsea House, 1980) we were too gentle. We welcomed the attention that these compendious tomes bestowed on cartooning. And while we painstakingly pointed out the errors in fact and judgment that ran through the text like water through a sieve, we were polite. We said we hoped the next editions of the books would be corrected. Until that could happen, we said—patiently, hopefully—we would accept Horn's books and use them. And we would be everlastingly thankful.

But there has been no revised second edition of either book. And the first editions have been scattered hither and yon and now sit on the shelves in reference libraries throughout the land, where their errors incubate and infect new generations of unsuspecting scholars with a contagion of inaccuracy and delusion. Horn is now back among us with more of the same—more errors, more of the claptrap of his misapprehensions about the medium, its workings and its history, more wrong-headed appraisals masquerading as well-considered assessments. Had we been more forthright with him before, perhaps he would have learned his lesson and kept silent on subjects about which he knows only enough to be dangerous.

This time, let us not make that mistake again.

Before I rehearse the evidence upon which these fulminations rest, let me applaud the organization of the book and the work of Horn's helpers. The organization is entirely straight-forward: descriptive histories of scores of comic strips are arranged by titles in alphabetical order, encyclopedia-style. A neat touch is that the beginning and ending dates for each strip are given immediately below the strip name, which serves as the title for each entry. (But only the years are given, not month or day—a telltale omission.)

Although by far the majority of the material is written by Horn, he recruited several others to contribute individual entries, and these contributors all seem responsible reporters and informed students of the medium. I read several of the entries written by these assistants (every entry carries the initials of its author), and while I did not find them as rife with error as Horn's entries are, they were all subjected to his editorial ministrations: who can say how many errors he might have introduced while editing the work of others? Because we cannot say—and because so much of the editor's work (everything initialed "M. H.") is laden with mistakes—we cannot rely upon this book, even though we know that many of those who contributed to it have done reliable work in other contexts. Here, they have participated in a charade, no doubt hoping their conscientious work would rescue Horn's posturing; but in the end, their work is rendered as useless as his by reason of the company they keep.

So just how laced with error is this book?

Through and through. Errors abound. In the first fifteen minutes of browsing—without, in other words, looking very hard, just thumbing pages and stopping at a few familiar strip titles—I found errors everywhere I stopped. For instance, Don Flowers' *Oh, Diana!* began in 1933, not in 1940 as Horn has it. (*Oh, Diana!* may, in fact, be a retitling of a 1931 Flowers strip called *Diana Dane*.)

Because I have written a biography of Milton Caniff, I turned to the entries about his strips almost at once. I knew enough about his work to determine, without checking any other source, how accurate (or inaccurate) Horn was. Alas, the Caniff strip entries bubble with bias and error. Horn asserts that Caniff decided to locate *Terry and the Pirates* in China; every history of the medium (and Caniff himself) says it was Captain Joseph Patterson, head of the Tribune-News Syndicate, who dictated the locale for the strip. Horn believes that when Caniff left *Terry* at the end of 1946, he abandoned the strip in a state of "inconclusion" (meaning, I suppose, inconclusiveness). Hardly. Caniff worked very hard to end his tenure on the strip with a conclusive moment, one that also permitted his successor to take the strip in any direction he might choose. (And it was a moment that occurred in both the daily strip and the Sunday page. Considering that Sunday pages were prepared six weeks before dailies were, this meant Caniff planned it all very very carefully, a circumstance decidedly the opposite of the situation suggested by Horn's diagnosis.)

Horn says Caniff left *Terry* to create a new strip for Marshall Field because "negotiations for his new contract [with the Tribune-News Syndicate] broke down." Hardly. He left because Field offered him a better deal: more money, complete editorial control, and sole ownership of the feature. Since Field made the offer when Caniff had two years to go on his current two-year Tribune-News contract, he was scarcely negotiating a "new" contract at the time. He had, in fact, just signed a new contract.

In the *Steve Canyon* entry, Horn says the strip started 19 January 1947. Hardly. It was 13 January. He tells us that Happy Easter was a "mechanic type." Hardly. Happy was a fugitive from the U.S. Cavalry and wore the uniform of the historic 7th (Custer's bunch). Horn refers to the Duchess of Denver as "poisonous"—a doubtful description since she never poisoned anyone that I know of. She was, in fact, a curiously meek and submissive person. (Her relationship with her lover was a perfect psychic pairing: she was a masochist; he, a sadist. Neither was a poisoner.)

Horn says that Steve Canyon's Air Force adventures included "flying all kinds of hush-hush new aircraft" as if Canyon were a test pilot. Steve doubtless flew one or two of these, but not enough to justify Horn's implication. In a run-through of characters in the strip, Horn mentions such enlisted men as Sweet Joseph and Chigger: neither, to my knowledge, ever appeared in the strip, but both appeared in a *Pageant* magazine article about Caniff as examples of the kind of rough sketch Caniff did when devising new characters.

Later, Horn lists all the artists who, at one time or another, assisted Caniff on the strip, but he does so in a way that suggests that Caniff took on assistants after the circulation of *Steve Canyon* began to slip during the Vietnam War.

Not so. The people he lists all made their contributions to the strip before 1960.

To return for a moment to the *Terry* entry, Horn has further skewed the history of this strip by slandering George Wunder, Caniff's successor on the strip. Horn says Wunder's "drawings were stiff and graceless, his depiction of characters heavy-handed, and his compositions static." George Wunder was never Milton Caniff; and in his last years on the strip, his characters' physiognomy was certainly peculiar. But in his early years, Wunder was a marvel. His use of black was often stunning; his compositions were dramatic, often startlingly so; and his renderings of figures at least as fluid and graceful as anything in the Caniff canon. Horn's evaluation of Wunder's work, in other words, is entirely a matter of opinion—his own. And such a broadside of subjective criticism wholly unsupported by the opinions of others (or by specific analytical examination of the works in question) has no place in a reference work. Subjective critical evaluations of works of art in reference books ought to represent a consensus of scholarly and critical opinion. Here, they are simply Horn's personal appraisals.

Having uncovered as much warped information as this in the first fifteen minutes of looking into Horn, I settled back to comb the volume more carefully, looking up other favorite strips of mine. The results confirmed my first impression: this book is a fraud. As a reference work, it is a snare and a delusion. Let me list a few of the things I unearthed in about an hour: *Bobby Thatcher* was produced by George Storm, not Robert Storm as Horn alleges. Russell Patterson's *Mamie* strip began 16 July 1950, not 1951. In discussing the Lawrence Lariar-John Spranger strip, which started as *Bodyguard* then became *Ben Friday* and finished as *The Bantam Prince*, Horn describes the tubby young monarch who usurped the title as "a swarthy little prince," but the prince was fair-skinned in all the reproductions I have seen. In tracing the long and tangled lineage of those who produced *Blondie*, Horn finishes by saying the strip is now drawn by Dean Young and Stan Drake, but Young only writes the strip; it is drawn by Drake. In the entry on *The Lone Ranger*, Horn says Tonto called the Lone Ranger "Kemo Sabay"; the correct spelling of this expression is "kemo sabe." On another occasion, he refers to Dudley Fisher's Sunday family-neighborhood feature, *Right Around Home*, as "a talking bird strip."

Some of these errors are trivial, admittedly. I cite them here simply by way of demonstrating how freighted with mistakes the book is. Virtually every other entry I examined had some sort of outright error or fictitious factoid in it, as in the entry on Roy Crane's *Wash Tubbs*, for example. Horn says Crane was persuaded to produce this daily gag strip about a grocery store clerk instead of the "sophisticated slice of big-city life" strip he had wanted to create. Never heard that story before, and I just finished listening to a taped interview with Crane in which he discusses how *Wash* was discovered by the cartoon editor of NEA, Charles N. Landon.

According to Crane, he had not given the concept for the strip very much thought at all. He worked up the comic strip in his spare time in the art department of the *New York World*. When Landon realized that Crane had taken the Landon correspondence cartoon course, he bought Crane's strip so he could claim that another Landon graduate had achieved success as a syndicated cartoonist. We cannot expect Horn to have heard this taped interview, but the story about how Crane got *Wash Tubbs* syndicated is pretty well known among comic strip historians worthy of the name.

A couple of paragraphs later, Horn asserts that Wash "grew in years" as soon as he left grocery clerking and began wandering the seven seas in search of treasure. I am not aware that Wash ever grew any older than he was at the strip's beginning. But Horn is soon off on another fanciful flight: he says that what distinguishes *Wash Tubbs* from other strips of the time, such as *Oliver's Adventures,* is that Wash had "openly erotic overtones." Openly erotic? What does that mean? The women were depicted nude? Wash's romantic encounters included bedroom scenes? "Openly erotic," it turns out, means simply that Wash met one beautiful member of the curvaceous gender after another and fell in love with them as soon as he saw them. Seems more like episodes of innocent adolescent infatuation than open eroticism.

But Horn is not celebrated for his precision with language. He spends a paragraph trying to describe Crane's graphic specialty—the creation of an almost photographic quality in his drawings by liberal use of light- and dark-gray tones that can be chemically produced in a drawing paper called Craftint doubletone. But Horn's attempts at explanation are so lingo-laden as to be virtually devoid of meaning. For instance, he states that Crane ". . . allied a forceful penline that sometimes resembled brushwork to a complex of atmospheric effects achieved with the judicious application of Doubletone." "Complex of atmospheric effects" indeed. Since he never explains what "Doubletone" is, only those who already know what he is talking about can understand what he referring to. But Horn's vacuous vaporizings in the book are not confined to the Crane entry. From the entry on *Scorchy Smith,* we have his description of Noel Sickles' contribution to the appearance of Caniff's *Terry*: "the compositions were opened up by way of airy perspectives against which the characters took on added relief." "Airy perspectives?" Does he mean panels with blank space for background rather than detailed renderings of furniture or landscape? "Added relief?" Does he mean that against the stark white of the blank background, the characters stood out in bold relief? Further in the same entry, Horn describes Sickles' style as "more pictorial than graphic." In common parlance, "pictorial" and "graphic" are virtually synonymous. Does he mean that Sickles drew pictures that were more photographic than linear?

Despite his maladroitness at describing Roy Crane's pictorial achievements in *Wash Tubbs*, at least he recognizes that Crane did something unusual. Horn never even mentions the distinctive hachuring that distinguishes Frank Miller's *Barney Baxter*. But that is not surprising. Although Horn is proclaimed as "one of the foremost international authorities on the comics," he displays no particularly penetrating understanding of the visual character of the medium. Indeed, he seems to have no eye for pictures or graphic technique whatsoever. He expends a half page on Gus Arriola's *Gordo* without once mentioning the stunning design quality of the Sunday pages in the last decades of the strip's run—the virtuoso deployment of color, shape, and texture to achieve startling visual effects that often were integral to the strip's gag that day. His daily strips were also often designed for visual impact.

In fact (although you would not know it by reading Horn's entry on *Gordo*), Arriola's strip went through three sharply different stylistic phases. In the first early forties material, his artwork was strictly MGM cartoon (at which animation studio Arriola had worked before getting his strip syndicated). Next came a nearly realistic treatment that lasted into the 1950s. Then in the middle of the decade, Arriola severely simplified his drawing style: for a while, Gordo and his friends occupied environs that looked almost cubist. What emerged by the 1960s was a beautifully simple style with a bold fluid line and decorative use of solid black.

Horn does not mention any of this. But he does say Gordo has a big moustache (he does not) and is pursued romantically by two women at the same time, the harridan Widow Gonzales and his housekeeper, Tehuana Mama. True, the Widow Gonzales chased after Gordo in the early days of the strip, but Tehuana Mama is a character from the last decade of *Gordo*'s run and was not around when the ravenous Widow was working her worst. (And Juan Pablo is not a windbag raconteur either; he is a quiet, mousy sort of fellow— albeit with a large moustache.)

This is the sort of misinformation you find while wandering through Horn's book. But for a succinct example of the sort of damage his kind of slovenly scholarship can do, the entry on Pete Hoffman's *Jeff Cobb* takes the prize. The entry is only four paragraphs long, but Horn makes a serious mistake in each of three of them. Horn says Hoffman relinquished the drawing of the strip to Winslow Mortimer, who performed the art chores for the last three years of the strip's 1954–1975 run. Two errors here. Reading this assertion,

Hoffman wrote Horn with copies to *INKS* and colleagues: "No *Jeff Cobb* art-work was relinquished to Winslow Mortimer or to anyone else. All of the artwork during the 1954–1978 life of the strip (twenty-one years domestically; three additional years abroad) was done by myself until 1978 when the strip ended. The only exception was part-time assistance on lettering and back-grounds for several years."

Horn's fraudulent statements about who drew the strip are in the con-text of denigrating descriptions of the strip: Hoffman drew in "a rather bland style"; "the writing deteriorated into a collection of pulp-story cliches"; and the "downward path" that the strip followed to its demise. While Horn may be entitled to his opinions on such matters (however misplaced they are in a reference work), these valuative remarks when coupled to his false assertions about who drew the strip create the impression that Hoffman was a lumbering hack. And that is scarcely the case. But let me return to this in connection with Horn's other error.

For years Hoffman had ghosted *Steve Roper*, written by Allen Saunders. Horn says that to repay Hoffman, Saunders contributed "anonymously" a number of continuities to *Jeff Cobb*. Anyone who has any familiarity with Hoffman's strip knows immediately that this statement is false. One of the things that distinguished *Jeff Cobb* was Hoffman's preference for telling his sto-ries with a minimum of verbiage. Sometimes whole daily installments would carry the narrative forward without a word appearing in either caption or speech balloon: Hoffman deftly managed his panel compositions to let the pictures tell the story. It was a tour de force of visual storytelling. This kind of performance is clearly the work of an artist not a wordsmith. While Saunders could draw a little, his forte was plotting and dialoguing not storytelling with pictures alone. In his letter, Hoffman sets the record straight: "Allen Saun-ders . . . never contributed (anonymously or otherwise) any continuities to *Jeff Cobb* . . . for better or worse, all of the writing was done by me."

As an example of incompetent history and ignorant attitudinizing, the *Jeff Cobb* entry is a gem. It is so wrong that it verges on libel.

Given Horn's myopia with respect to graphic technique, it is predictable that the pictorial element in this book is as vacuous as his persiflage. In an extensive color section, the color itself is somewhat washed out and some-times muddy. Sometimes only fragments of strips are reprinted; so we have only the first two tiers of a *Moon Mullins* Sunday—with no Moon in sight. Other color samples are also missing any clear depiction of the title characters: *Happy Hooligan, Captain Easy* (almost invisible), *Terry* (ditto), *Steve Canyon, Jungle Jim, Pogo, On Stage*. Throughout the book, individual panels from daily strips are reprinted in black and white, but they are often enlarged to fit a page layout—with disastrous consequences for the appearance of the artwork.

One might suppose from this diatribe that my objection to Horn's book is rooted in my disagreement with his opinions. That is always the situation in such instances. We are all egocentric, after all. But in Horn's case, my aversion is grounded in something more than simple difference of opinion. Fact is, I have little faith in the soundness of Horn's judgment. To put it plainly, he frequently does not seem to know what he is talking about. In the introduction of the book, for instance, he defines a comic strip as follows: It is ". . . characterized by a narrative told in a sequence of pictures, a continuing cast of characters, the inclusion of dialogue and/or text within the picture frame, as well as by a dynamic method of storytelling that would compel the eye to travel forward from one panel to the next. This last distinction is very important in that it separates the comics proper from most of the pictorial narratives of centuries past in which compositions were static and mainly served as illustrations to the text or the captions" (15–16).

"A dynamic method of storytelling that would compel the eye to travel forward from one panel to the next." Balderdash. He is unable to present any examples of this "dynamic method." That is because there is no such thing. What compels the eye forward from panel to panel is simple sequence. But Horn does not understand this; so to him, the process is a mystery—a secret ingredient, an unspecifiable "dynamic."

It is quite true that it is necessary to make a distinction between comic strip narration and the pictorial narratives of previous centuries. But the difference is that in comic strips the action is depicted in as nearly a continuous way as possible. That is the secret "dynamic": continuity of action, scene, character. A piddling point, perhaps. But I tend not to trust the judgment of a self-proclaimed comics expert who cannot tell us (or show us, even) what the mysterious "dynamic" of comic strips is. If he cannot describe the essential nature of the medium to us, how can we be expected to take his word for it when he says George Wunder's drawings are "stiff and graceless" or Pete Hoffman's "bland"?

The book's introductory material is an absolute treasure, an ample if unintended demonstration of its author's fatuous critical stance as well as his shortcomings as a historical scholar. In the opening sections of the book we find a "chronology" of the first one hundred years that lists events by year (as it did in the Chelsea House book) but does not give month or day; so we learn that Roy Crane's *Wash Tubbs* and Harold Gray's *Little Orphan Annie* both started in 1924, but we do not know which came first. Not that sequence made any difference here, but why give a chronology without complete dates?

But dates do concern Horn in another context. In his introductory essay, he takes severe umbrage at the decision of "a small coterie of self-proclaimed experts (with not one of the recognized historians of the medium among them)" in proclaiming 1895 as the birth year of the comic strip. Horn favors 1896. He admits that the matter has caused considerable debate "among scholars." But he says the 1896 date has been "upheld by every historian from Coulton Waugh on, and it has been officially reaffirmed by an international panel of scholars meeting in Lucca, Italy, in 1989." The erroneous claim for the year 1895, Horn says, "met with some initial success," but in proclaiming 1996 the anniversary year, "good sense and good scholarship again prevailed." I wonder if his opinion would be at all different if Random House had been able to bring Horn's book out in 1995 instead of 1996.

In any case, he offers no substantial evidence in support of his contention beyond asserting that R. F. Outcault's Yellow Kid did not acquire that name until 1896. Perhaps Horn also favors '96 because that was the year the circulation war between Hearst and Pulitzer began. Hearst did not acquire his New York newspaper until late in 1895; and he did not launch his much-touted Sunday comics supplement until 18 October 1896. It was during this battle for readers that the Yellow Kid proved the commercial value of comics, and the centennial of the comic strip celebrates the dawn of the marketplace potency of comics more than anything else. Without that commercial value, comic strips would never have developed. But Horn says nothing of any of this. He does not cite much actual history, despite his oft-cited credentials as a historian.

To rehearse briefly the key moments in the Yellow Kid's history—the character that was eventually dubbed the Yellow Kid first appeared in a humor magazine called *Truth* with the issue dated 2 June 1894. A later cartoon from that magazine (also with the Yellow Kid character in it) was reprinted in Pulitzer's *New York World* on 17 February 1895. On 5 May of that year, the first "Yellow Kid" cartoon *drawn expressly* for newspaper publication appeared. And on 5 January 1896, the bald waif first appeared in a yellow gown—earning him his nickname. According to Bill Blackbeard (in R. F Outcault's *Yellow Kid*; Kitchen Sink Press, 1995), the first *Yellow Kid* comic strip (a narrative sequence of words and pictures in which the verbal and the visual blend to make sense) to appear in a newspaper was published in Hearst's *Journal American* 25 October 1896. Take your choice: Which of these milestones marks the beginning of newspaper comics?

But all this is somewhat beside the point. My point here is that Horn does not regale us with any of this history. No facts, no discussion. Just his simple oracular pronouncement that 1896 is the official birth year. If he is the critic-historian he claims to be, it would be the work of less than a quarter hour to muster the facts assembled here. His cavalier attitude about such matters dramatizes the reasons for my distrust of his evaluations of the work of cartoonists: since he does not take the trouble to marshal the facts to support his interpretation of history, we may assume that he is equally nonchalant about supporting evidence for his opinions.

Bad history. Bad scholarship. And, even, bad criticism (a field of endeavor that often supports the work of opinionated ignoramuses). But Horn's book is clearly not supposed to be a scholarly enterprise. Rather, it is a bald-faced attempt to cash in on the centennial: its commercial value was clearly more important to its editor and its publisher than any historical or referential worth. And that is too bad.

No, it is more than too bad. It is a monstrous hoax. Judging from the organization of the book, it appears to be a reference book. And the appearance breeds disaster for scholarship in comics: because this book has been published, it will be in hundreds of libraries, and many of its readers, those unversed in the finer points of cartoon artistry, will take Horn's word for gospel. And it isn't. It is bad news.

CONTRIBUTORS

JULIA F. ANDREWS, Distinguished University Professor in the History of Art Department at The Ohio State University, is the author of *Painters and Politics in the People's Republic of China, 1949–1979,* which received the Joseph Levenson Book Prize for modern China, and, more recently, *Art of Modern China,* coauthored with Kuiyi Shen, which was awarded the International Convention of Asia Scholars Humanities Book Award. She is currently a Guggenheim fellow writing on painting societies in twentieth-century China.

DAVID BERONÄ (1950–2015) was a curator, scholar, librarian, and the world's foremost expert on wordless books. His book, *Wordless Books: The Original Graphic Novels* (2008), is the definitive work on the subject.

LUCY SHELTON CASWELL is a professor emerita and the founding curator of The Ohio State University Billy Ireland Cartoon Library & Museum. She has curated more than seventy-five cartoon exhibits and is the author of several articles and books, the most recent being the revised edition of *Billy Ireland.* She edited *INKS: Cartoon and Comic Art Studies* from 1994 to 1997.

MARK J. COHEN (1942–1999) was a collector as well as a cartoonists' agent and dealer of original comics art. His exhibition *Humor in a Jugular Vein: The Art, Artists and Artifacts of MAD Magazine* toured the United States in the 1990s. A *Gallery of Rogues,* featuring approximately 100 cartoonists' self-caricatures from his unique collection, was published by The Ohio State University Libraries in 1998. He was a frequent, uncredited writer for *Gasoline Alley.*

CHRISTIAN DAVENPORT is the author of five books and dozens of academic articles on the topics of political violence/conflict, social movements, and popular culture. Christian's latest book is entitled *How Social Movements Die* and is published with Cambridge University Press. For more information about him and his work, see www.christiandavenport.com.

WILL EISNER (1917–2005) was a cartoonist, theorist, educator, and businessman whose career helped shape comics from the birth of the comic book industry in the 1930s to the birth of the graphic novel form in the latter decades of the twentieth century. The field of comics studies is forever in his debt for his foundational work, *Comics and Sequential Art* (1985). Each year the comics industry recognizes its annual achievements with the Eisner Awards, named in his honor.

ROGER A. FISCHER (1939–2012) was a professor of history at the University of Minnesota-Duluth, and the author of *Them Damned Pictures: Explorations in American Political Cartoon Art* and *Tippecanoe and Trinkets Too: The Material Culture of American Presidential Campaigns, 1828–1984.* He was also a nationally recognized authority on Abraham Lincoln's presidency.

ALAN FRIED (1950–2003) was a professor in the Department of Journalism and Mass Communication at the University of South Carolina and a professor of advertising at San José State University, which offers a memorial scholarship in his name.

JARED GARDNER is a professor of English at The Ohio State University and the author of three monographs, including *Projections: Comics and the History of 21st-Century Storytelling* (2012). He is editor of *Inks: The Journal of the Comics Studies Society.*

IAN GORDON teaches American History at the National University of Singapore. His latest book, *Superman: The Persistence of an American Icon,* is forthcoming from Rutgers University Press.

OLIVER HARRINGTON (1912–1995) was a pioneering African American cartoonist whose comics often focused on the everyday life of those living in racist America. During World War II, Harrington served as a war correspondent, and, after returning to the United States, he began work for the NAACP, speaking out on the vital issues of the day. His activities garnered the attention of the FBI and HUAC, eventually forcing him to leave for France, where he joined a vibrant community of African Americans in exile, including James Baldwin and Richard Wright. Following Wright's death, Harrington sought political asylum in East Germany in 1961, where he resided for the remainder of his life.

ROBERT C. HARVEY is author of thirteen books on cartooning, and he is a cartoonist and comics chronicler who produces a fortnightly online magazine, *Rants & Raves,* of news, reviews, history, and lore at RCHarvey.com. His latest book is *Insider Histories of Cartooning: Rediscovering Forgotten Famous Comics and Their Creators.*

CHARLES HATFIELD, a professor at California State University, Northridge, is the author of *Hand of Fire: The Comics Art of Jack Kirby* (2011) and *Alternative Comics* (2005), coeditor of *The Superhero Reader* (2013), and curator of *Comic Book Apocalypse* (2015), the largest U.S. exhibition of Jack Kirby art. He is the founding president of the Comics Studies Society.

M. THOMAS INGE is the Blackwell Professor of Humanities at Randolph-Macon College in Ashland, Virginia, where he teaches and writes about American humor, animation, Walt Disney, comic art, Southern culture, and William Faulkner. He helped introduce the serious study of comic art to the academy through his essays and his book, *Comics as Culture.* Dr. Inge is currently the series editor for two series of books published by the University Press of Mississippi: Great Comic Artists and Conversations with Comic Artists.

CHRISTOPHER LAMB is a journalism professor at Indiana University-Indianapolis. He is the author of eight books, including *Drawn to Extremes: The Use and Abuse of Editorial Cartoons* (Columbia University Press, 2004). He has twice served as a Pulitzer Prize judge in the category of editorial cartooning.

JOHN A. LENT is the founding publisher/editor-in-chief of the *International Journal of Comic Art* and chairs five international organizations, which he founded, devoted to comic art or popular culture. He is the author or editor of 79 books, one of the latest being *Asian Comics*.

AMY KISTE NYBERG is an associate professor of journalism in the College of Communication and the Arts at Seton Hall University. She is the author of an in-depth history of comics censorship, *Seal of Approval: The History of the Comics Code*, as well as numerous articles and book chapters on comics. Her current research focus is comics journalism.

TRINA ROBBINS was a founding member of the *Wimmen's Comix Collective* and is the preeminent historian of women in comics, having published and edited numerous books on the subject, including *A Century of Women Cartoonists, From Girls to Grrlz*, and *The Brinkley Girls*.

FRANK STACK is a professor emeritus at the University of Missouri, where he taught in the Art Department for many years. He is one of the most important figures of the underground comix movement, having published *The Adventures of Jesus* in 1962 under the pseudonym Foolbert Sturgeon. He also collaborated with Harvey Pekar and Joyce Brabner on *Our Cancer Year* in 1994.

RICHARD SAMUEL WEST is an independent scholar who is the author or coauthor of five books on nineteenth- and twentieth-century political cartooning. He was the founder and editor of *Target, the Political Cartoon Quarterly* (1981–1987) and political cartoon editor of *INKS* (1994–1997). His most recent book, written with Michael A. Kahn, is *What Fools These Mortals Be! The Story of Puck* (2014).

MARK D. WINCHESTER (1965–2013) was a theater historian whose specialty was late nineteenth-and early twentieth-century touring theatrical productions based on newspaper comic strips.

JOSEPH WITEK is the Kathleen A. Johnson Professor of Humanities at Stetson University in DeLand, Florida. The author of *Comic Books as History: The Narrative Art of Jack Jackson, Art Spiegelman, and Harvey Pekar* and editor of *Art Spiegelman: Conversations,* Witek has been teaching courses and publishing essays on comics since 1989.

INDEX

Wild Pilgrimage, 92–94, 96 (*see also*: Ward, Lynd)

Willard, Frank, 111, 115, 121

Williams, Gregory H., 49

Wilson, Woodrow, 69, 74, 77–80, 83, 86

Winchester, Mark, viii, 31, 60

Windsor Star (Ontario), 139

Winnie Winkle, 111 (*see also*: Branner, Martin)

Witek, Joseph, 211, 218, 259–66

women cartoonists, 247–50

women's suffrage, 248

Wonder Woman (comic book character), 152

woodcut novel. *See* wordless novel

wordless novel, 88–100

The World of Lily Wong, 149–50 (*see also*: Feign, Larry)

World War I, 69–70, 74, 86, 90, 104, 107, 147, 187, 245

World War II, 8, 113, 139, 147

Wragg, Arthur, 95

Wrangle Sisters, 249 (*see also*: Organ, Marjorie)

Wright, Don, 126, 141

Wunder, George, 275, 279

Xenophobia, 31, 179

Xiaochenbao, 148

X-Men, 200, 203

Xu Youwu, 179

Yardley, Richard Q., 136–37

Ye Qianyu, 148

Yellow Kid, 24, 27, 52–57, 59, 61, 243, 247, 261, 271, 280

Yokoyama, Ryuichi, 147

Yomiuri Sunday Manga, 146

Yorty v. Chandler, 189–90

Yorty, Sam, 189

You're a Good Man, Charles Brown, 255

Young, Art, 135

Young Blacky Gets Married (Xiao erhei jie-hun), 167–68 (see Mi Gu)

Young, Art, 187–88

Young, Christopher, 149

Young, Dean, 275

yronwode, Catherine, 42

Zabo, Daniel, 148

Zap, 268

Zhang Leping, 148

Zhao Hongben, 162, 169–73

Zhou Libo, 176

Zimmerman, Eugene ("Zim"), 29

Zola, Émile, 92

Zunzi (Wong Kee-kwan), 149

Zwanna (comic book character), 200, 203–4, 207

STUDIES IN COMICS AND CARTOONS

Lucy Shelton Caswell and Jared Gardner, Series Editors

Books published in Studies in Comics and Cartoons will focus exclusively on comics and graphic literature, highlighting their relation to literary studies. The series will include monographs and edited collections that cover the history of comics and cartoons from the editorial cartoon and early sequential comics of the nineteenth century through webcomics of the twenty-first. Studies that focus on international comics will also be considered.

Drawing the Line: Comics Studies and INKS, 1994–1997
EDITED BY LUCY SHELTON CASWELL AND JARED GARDNER

The Humours of Parliament: Harry Furniss's View of Late-Victorian Political Culture
EDITED AND WITH AN INTRODUCTION BY GARETH CORDERY AND JOSEPH S. MEISEL

Redrawing French Empire in Comics
MARK McKINNEY